W9-BWH-255

Komura Jutarō
and
His Time

Komura
Jutarō
and
His Time

Okazaki Hisahiko

Translated by Noda Makito

Japan Publishing Industry Foundation for Culture

TRANSLATION NOTE

All Japanese names appearing in this book are written with surname first and given name last. In addition, all Japanese words and names have been romanized in accordance with the Hepburn system, and macrons have been applied to indicate long vowels where deemed appropriate.

Komura Jutaro and His Time
Okazaki Hisahiko. Translated by Noda Makito.

Published by
Japan Publishing Industry Foundation for Culture (JPIC)
2-2-30 Kanda-Jinbocho, Chiyoda-ku, Tokyo 101-0051, Japan

First English edition: March 2020

This book is the result of a collaborative effort between The Japan Institute of International Affairs (JIIA) and Japan Publishing Industry Foundation for Culture (JPIC).

Originally published in Japanese by PHP Institute, Inc., in 2003 under the title of *Komura Jutarō to sono jidai.*

Jacket and cover design: Seno Hiroya

Printed in Japan
ISBN 978-4-86658-072-2
https://www.jpic.or.jp/

CONTENTS

CHAPTER
8

Eruption of the Russo-Japanese War
—The Anglo-Japanese Alliance Makes Up for Japan's Weakness— 133

CHAPTER
9

Rise of Japan
—Japanese Patriotism Amazes the Entire World— 151

CHAPTER
10

Bloody Battle
—The Bitter Epic of the Siege of Lüshun Port—   171

CHAPTER
11

Turning Point in World History
—Miraculous Victory at the Battle of Tsushima—   191

Komura Jutarō (Photo: Kyodo News)

Entertaining Poverty

*—Conviction of a Nationalist Immersed in
State Affairs Despite His Poverty—*

Kaisei Gakkō: Forerunner of the University of Tokyo

Although Mutsu Munemitsu had steered the diplomacy of the modern state of Japan from the Meiji Restoration through the revision of the unequal treaties with the Western powers and the First Sino-Japanese War, it was Komura Jutarō (小村寿太郎) who was at the helm of Japanese diplomacy during the period of the Russo-Japanese War, on which Japan staked the fate of its empire.

Komura was born in 1855, two years after the arrival of Commodore Perry's fleet at Uraga, making him eleven years junior to Mutsu. Because Japan was undergoing drastic changes in the 1850s and 1860s, this ten-year difference put Mutsu and Komura in two different generations.

Until he turned fifteen years old, Komura received the traditional education of the Tokugawa period. Komura excelled in all his courses at the highly esteemed school owned by Obi-*han* (飫肥藩), a small local domain in Kyushu of only 50,000 *koku*.[1] Despite the miniscule size of its *han*, the

---

1   *Koku* was a Japanese unit of volume, originally defined as the quantity of rice (about 150 kilograms, or 330 pounds) sufficient to feed one person for one year.

domain's school had produced great Confucian scholars such as Yasui Sokken (安井息軒), under whom Mutsu had once studied. Here, Komura received the traditional teachings on the Chinese classics. Komura looked more like a girl than a boy, with a slender physique and handsome features, and was not well endowed in terms of physical strength or health. Nevertheless, he was so full of perseverance and determination that he would not tire out, even after eight successive training bouts in swordsmanship, whereas a normal boy would be exhausted in just two bouts.

Mutsu Munemitsu

Thus, under the feudal system of the Tokugawa period Komura was already distinguished from early childhood as a future member of the elite.

But Komura came from a low-ranking samurai family. As such, even though he was trained as a samurai at school during the day, he also studied arithmetic at home, and he was known to walk around with his abacus. This interest in math was something that high-ranking samurai despised in those days because of its link to commerce, which was considered beneath the samurai class and a part of the lowest class, the merchants.

Komura even engaged in farming, tending to the farmland owned by his uncle during the busy farming season. Later, in the journal he kept in English, he wrote that his classmates' sneering at his manual labor did not bother him at all. Obviously, Komura was a confident young man who firmly believed that, as long as he excelled in study and conduct, he had nothing to be ashamed of.

A man named Ogura Shohei (小倉処平), who was nicknamed "Saigō of the Obi-*han*," looked after Komura and managed to send him to an English cram school in Nagasaki in 1869 and, subsequently, to the Daigaku Nankō (大学南校) in Tokyo in 1870. Daigaku Nankō, or "University South School," was an institution for Western education. It was called the South School relative to the Shohei-kō (昌平校), an institution devoted to traditional Chinese teachings that was called the East School (大学東校). The South School was later reorganized into the Kaisei Gakkō (開成学校) school, which was renamed as the University of Tokyo (東京大学) in

1877. In 1887, it became Tokyo Imperial University (東京帝国大学), the prestigious center for educating modern Japanese elites.

In the early days of the Meiji Restoration, the South School was filled with sons of dignitaries from the Satsuma-Chōshū oligarchy. Although Ogura was one of the few faculty members of the South School who had come from an insignificant local domain, he soon distinguished himself. Eventually, he became the dean of the school. Later, Ogura became an official in the Ministry of Education in the Meiji government and, among other achievements, authored a proposal on educational reform.

As a result of this proposal, a *kōshin-sei* (貢進生) system was adopted to recruit students who behaved honorably from 300 domains across Japan by the ratio of three from each large domain with over 100,000 *koku*, two from each medium-sized domain with over 50,000 *koku*, and one from each small domain with less than 50,000 *koku*. Under this system, Komura was chosen from the Obi-*han* at the recommendation of Ogura. When Kaisei Gakkō instituted a scholarship for the top fifty students, Komura was again chosen.

Although it had long been the aspiration of male youth throughout the Tokugawa period to make their way up in the world through studying, active participation in the political turmoil provided a better opportunity to get ahead than studies during the short transition period from the shogunate to the Meiji government—the time during which Mutsu spent his late boyhood. As the dust of the Restoration settled, however, studying once again became the major source for determining one's future success. Komura was among the first generation of graduates of this new system.

Komura's View of the Meiji Restoration

An American English teacher at Kaisei Gakkō, William Elliot Griffis, left a collection of documents about Japan in those days. Among the recently discovered documents was a lengthy English autobiography written by Komura. From the documents, it also became clear that Griffis was amazed by the accuracy of the spelling and grammar Komura used in the autobiography.

Komura's initial decision to set his mind toward studying English required courage. He had already been recognized under the traditional education system as a future scholar of the Chinese classics. Komura had a strong wish to "continue [his] studies of Oriental classics," as disclosed in the above autobiography, and he agonized over being sandwiched between his father, who encouraged him to study the Western sciences in Nagasaki, and a friend, who opposed the idea. In the end, he resolutely chose to go to Nagasaki, and wrote the following in his farewell letter to his friend: "I cannot defer, my dear friend, to your opinion, for I have made up my mind to know everything about foreigners and to judge them accordingly." It was this intense motivation that enabled Komura to attain a level of English proficiency in only five years that seems simply beyond the reach of Japanese today.

What astonished Griffis more than Komura's mastery of English was his profound thinking as a youth. Komura wrote this autobiography six years after the Meiji Restoration and three years after the abolition of the *han* system and the establishment of prefectures. He left the following descriptions on these and other rapid changes in his autobiography:

> In order to consolidate the nation's power and bring prosperity to the country, it was necessary to overthrow the feudal system and establish a new central government. This was accomplished through a bloodless revolution and, as the result, taxation, military, and jurisdiction are now in the hands of the emperor . . . Which country in the world has succeeded in overthrowing a feudal system without shedding blood? It was only after much warfare that the centralization of government began in Britain, while in France, . . . rulers who had controlled peasants with force were not overthrown until the French Revolution in 1789. In contrast, feudalistic rulers were toppled without any bloodshed in Japan. This success was attributable to efforts made by the Japanese people and the government. Before the revolution erupted, many of the feudal lords had voluntarily resigned and handed over their domains with patriotic motivation. Even the stubborn feudal lords did not resist to the end, recognizing their own fate . . . With the political changes, my mind underwent an entire revolution . . . I was still loyal to my Prince, but when he was removed from office I rejoiced at it more than lamented, for national patriotism was greater than loyalty to him. It is strange that few foreigners understand the reason behind the voluntary handover of various privileges by feudal lords without resorting to a single fight. Furthermore, many foreigners

failed to understand why today's government leaders, who used to be retainers of feudal lords, would harm their former masters. Perhaps, these foreigners would understand this conduct once they realize that the sense of patriotism of the Meiji government leaders was, like me, much stronger than their loyalty to their former masters.[2]

The above observation by a Japanese youth who was still under twenty years old should be regarded as an invaluable testimony to the common reactions toward the Meiji Restoration among Japanese intellectuals in those days. And these sentences were written at such a high standard that they provided irrefutable evidence that Komura was indeed the brightest student at Kaisei Gakkō and, therefore, in all of Japan under the new educational system.

Traditional Mentality of High-Ranking Samurai

All *kōshin-sei* students were required to live in dormitories, where everyone's morale, not only Komura's, was reported to be extremely high. Feeling responsible as the representatives of their respective *han* and proud to be chosen as future leaders of modern Japan, these youths gladly led a well-regulated life, refusing to be stained by the vices of Tokyo. They all studied diligently, debated rigorously, read Japanese, Chinese, and Western intellectual legacies until deep into the night, and worked hard together to become useful servants of the country.

This climate among fellow *kōshin-sei*, of pursuing the perfection of one's personal and intellectual development and defying the vulgar glamour of the city, finds an echo in the later tradition of the old high school education system in the Meiji, Taishō, and early Shōwa eras. And its remote roots can be traced to the tradition since the Edo period of high-ranking samurai families training their children in both the literary and military arts—paying no heed to any training in worldly affairs—for the sake of nurturing young adults who would devote themselves to state and societal affairs.

---

2   Translated back from the Japanese translation of the original autobiography.

Fukuzawa Yukichi left very detailed descriptions of samurai society under feudal rule in his *Kyū-han jijō* (旧藩事情). Fukuzawa writes, "Drinking and partying are seen frequently among low-ranking samurai, while high-ranking samurai prefer a modest and simple life. While it is rare for the latter to sing or dance at the height of banquet, many lower-ranking samurai love to contribute to the gaiety of the party by displaying their respective hidden talents." Fukuzawa characterizes high-ranking samurai as "graceful and correct but naïve" and low-ranking samurai as "vulgar and shallow but spirited." Because high-ranking samurai engaged in such lofty activities as reading Confucian teachings and history, discussing books on strategy, and mastering the martial arts, their conduct, according to Fukuzawa, naturally became lofty and honorable.

Individuals like Mutsu and his father, Date Munehiro, who were great intellectuals but also indulged in demimonde pleasures, must have been rare among high-ranking samurai. It is not hard to imagine that such conduct must have earned frowns of disapproval from the majority of the high-ranking samurai.

Although Komura grew up in an environment where he must have been exposed to the vulgar and shallow ways of low-ranking samurai, he chose to maintain the traditional samurai disciplines throughout his life. This was probably due to Komura's self-respect as an elite individual who had been singled out since early childhood as a bright student representing his *han*. Komura only sang and danced at a banquet once: During his send-off party to Beijing, he became drunk and overcome with emotion and stood up abruptly to dance and cited something like an English poem. Of course, this "dance" must have been nothing but a mere fluttering of his limbs.

This was also a typical attitude of the traditional Japanese. And this Spartan-like or ancient-Roman-aristocrat-like disposition remained a backbone of the Japanese Empire from the Meiji era to World War II.

More Time for Books and Thoughts than Socializing

As the teaching of Western learning at Daigaku Nankō advanced, students' desire for studying abroad intensified. Because they were all poor students from samurai clans, they could by no means finance their own overseas tuition and living expenses. It cost a fortune to study abroad in those days, and only a few promising sons of the Satsuma-Chōshū oligarchy could afford to study in the West using their own funds.

Against this backdrop, Komura and five classmates submitted a proposal for the establishment of a government-sponsored overseas study program. Moved by the zeal of these students, the government decided to select by examination ten students to be sent overseas with the first Ministry of Education scholarship. Selected from the Faculty of Law at that time were, aside from Komura: Hatoyama Kazuo (鳩山和夫), speaker of the House of Representatives from 1896 to 1897, vice-minister of foreign affairs and president of Waseda University, and father and great-grandfather of Prime Ministers Hatoyama Ichirō and Hatoyama Yukio; Kikuchi Takeo (菊池武夫) Japan's first doctor of law, professor at the University of Tokyo, and subsequently president of Chuo University; and Saitō Shūichirō (斎藤修一郎) vice-minister for agriculture and commerce.

Thus, in many senses, Komura should be regarded as a member of the first generation of Meiji bureaucrats. Under this scholarship program, Komura entered Harvard University in 1875 (eighth year of Meiji), while Hatoyama was sent to Columbia University. Although Harvard policy required foreign students to take one year of intensive language training, Komura was exempt from this requirement in recognition of his outstanding competence in English. Komura's command of English remained incomparable even at the Foreign Ministry, which he joined later.

While in Boston, Komura shared lodgings with Kaneko Kentarō (金子堅太郎), later the minister of agriculture and commerce and minister of justice, who came to Harvard one year later, in order to save on rent. One time, both of them suffered from eye troubles and were advised by an ophthalmologist to refrain from heavy reading at night. While Kaneko, who was determined to become a diplomat, decided to follow the doctor's advice and began socializing in the evening, Komura would not join Kaneko. When Kaneko came home from socializing one evening, he found Komura meditating alone and staring at the ceiling. Komura explained to a puzzled Kaneko that he was meditating on what he had read earlier in the day.

Kaneko Kentarō

From a memorial photograph of the first Ministry of Education scholarship members, Komura is sitting on the far-right in the front row.

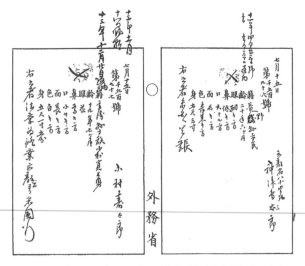

Komura's passport attachment sheets, dated July 15, 1875. His legal domicile and appearance are described in detail, along with the official purpose of his travels stating "This person is being sent to the United States for the establishment of a government-sponsored overseas study program."

This disposition remained unchanged until Komura's old age.

When he was later stationed in London in 1906 as the Japanese ambassador to Britain after the Russo-Japanese War, Komura devoted his time to reading and contemplation, paying no heed to the gaiety of Edwardian London. The city at the time was at the center of social events organized by the diplomatic corps, including days and nights of receptions, dances, and bridge parties. Komura once attempted to learn dancing by consulting a textbook, and he practiced the steps by himself. Naturally, this attempt, which relied solely on the textbook, was proven abortive, and Komura literally threw away the book.

In the memoir of Katsura Tarō (桂太郎; 1848–1913), the eleventh, thirteenth, and fifteenth prime minister of Japan, it is recorded that Valentine Tyrol, the foreign news editor of *The Times* at that time, complained directly to Katsura that Komura had evaded contact with the press. Knowing Komura's mindset, Katsura did not pay any attention to this complaint. In later years, hearing of Komura's death, Tyrol wrote, "Although I was quite close to Komura, his excessive secrecy was unbearable at times."

Komura indeed lacked an appreciation of the importance of public opinion and newspapers, a shortcoming Sergei Witte took advantage of to outmaneuver him in relations with the press during negotiations for the Treaty of Portsmouth in 1905.

Diplomacy without a Face

In many ways, Komura was typically Japanese, and totally different from Mutsu, who had transcended the framework of the Japanese.

Japanese samurai ethics set a high value on reticence, on action rather than speech, and on an absolute commitment to one's words. A man should pay no heed to appraisal and censure, and it would be dishonorable for a Japanese man to vindicate himself or make excuses.

The end product of this samurai ethic would be someone as uniquely Japanese as Komura. But this type of personality is bound to be unfit for a profession such as diplomacy, which involves frequent interactions with others. Particularly in the democratic system, a diplomat is expected to explain, persuade, and vindicate vis-à-vis public opinion and newspapers. "Actions speak louder than words" is as bad as no strategy at all. Diplomats who refused to socialize would be isolated from the diplomatic corps and the local community and shut off from information.

Credit for the birth of the Empire of Japan, as well as blame for its demise, should be at least partially attributed to the kind of Japanese diplomatic style represented by Komura.

Although Komura was a fine-looking man, he was short of stature; he is believed to have been about 150 cm tall. Li Hungchang once teased Komura at a reception attended by diplomats from various countries and said, "Are all Japanese as short as Your Excellency?" Komura replied, "No, some Japanese are as tall as Your Excellency, but they are all slow-witted and have to earn a living by becoming sumo wrestlers." This was a typical reaction expected of the Japanese in pre–World War II days. The Japanese in those days tended to overreact out of vengeance in order to protect the country's honor, even in reaction to such a small jest. The above episode was viewed in those days as a praiseworthy anecdote of the patriotic Komura.

Destitution Nurtures Boldness

Another fact that should not be forgotten about Komura is his poverty. Perhaps there has never been a statesman or diplomat in the history of the world who was as poor as Komura.

The only daily clothes he wore, winter or summer, was an old, worn-out frock coat. When asked whether it was too hot during the summer, Komura would reply that a poor man never felt the heat, even at the peak of summer. During lunchtime he was often seen clipping frays of thread from the sleeves of his frock coat. Often he only took tea for lunch, having no money for food.

The main cause of his destitution was the debt Komura had inherited from his parents, who had failed in a business venture. In debt to all the moneylenders in Tokyo, Komura lived in a house devoid of any valuables because everything had been thoroughly confiscated by bill collectors. He only owned two cushions, which he had to abandon when he had more than two guests. Having no umbrella, not to mention the money to hire a cab, he would simply walk in the rain, with raindrops dripping freely from his cap. And yet, Komura would enter the Foreign Ministry proudly from the main gate, even though the rear gate was much closer to his house.

At the send-off party held at Shinbashi Station as Komura was en route to Beijing, where he was assigned as deputy minister, one of his friends tried to present a watch to Komura, knowing he did not have one. He rejected the friend's offer, saying that loan sharks might be hidden among the well-wishers seeing him off at the station, and they would immediately jump on whatever valuables he might receive as his farewell gift. He asked this friend to give him the watch at the next station if he was really willing to give it to him.

Before being stationed in Beijing, Komura endured ten years of obscurity at the Foreign Ministry. He earned his position through the *kōshinsei* system and his Obi-*han* background and won his chance to study at Harvard thanks to the recognition and patronage of Ogura Shohei. But Ogura joined Saigō's forces in the Satsuma Rebellion while Komura was at Harvard and committed suicide after being defeated. Consequently, Komura became deprived of any supporter or patron in officialdom, which was dominated by the Satsuma-Chōshū oligarchy. Therefore, for ten long years, Komura had to watch his colleagues with powerful backing be promoted one after another while he was overlooked and remained assigned to the ministry's translation bureau.

While boldness might have been Komura's nature by birth, it must have been further enhanced by his living conditions—in other words, he was so poor that he had nothing to lose. No matter how heavily indebted he was, Komura said, "I am all right as long as I am not beaten by the debts."

Komura's contemporaries at the Foreign Ministry got together for dinner monthly. They split the cost, but Komura never contributed his due. Consequently, in time, it was decided that Komura should not be informed of the time and venue of the monthly banquet. Nevertheless, Komura somehow succeeded in pinpointing the time and place and never failed to show up in time to take the seat of honor, eat and drink more than the other members, and enjoy the occasion for freely discussing current affairs. Eventually, the other members agreed to exempt Komura from paying his portion of the cost.

Boldness must be accompanied by a supporting conviction. A devotion to state affairs allowed him to forget the misery of destitution.

Komura's Nationalism/Ultranationalism

Komura believed in nationalism/ultranationalism throughout his life.

One major origin of the nationalistic movement during the Meiji era was the antipathy toward the government's planned appointment of foreign judges as a concession to winning the revision of unequal treaties in the early days of the era.

In those days, Japan was still regarded as a semicivilized country, and Westerners worried that their own nationals might be treated unjustly by Japanese courts. This argument was used to justify consular jurisdiction over foreign nationals in Japan. In order to eliminate this humiliating practice and thereby become a genuine sovereign nation, the government of the time proposed allowing foreign judges to sit in on court proceedings when foreign nationals were tried. These foreign judges acted as watchdogs so to speak for a certain period of time in order to appease Westerners' apprehensions. This concession, which the Japanese people of the time looked upon as a national disgrace, provoked the heated backlash of public opinion.

It was this sort of nationalism that propelled the antigovernment movement around 1887 (twentieth year of Meiji), when the announcement of the date of the establishment of the Diet tamed the Freedom and People's Rights Movement.

In the summer of 1887, Komura abruptly announced to a gathering of his friends that he might rebel against the government soon. Referring to the treaty revisions planned by then the foreign minister Inoue Kaoru, Komura declared, "[These are] humiliating provisions for Japan. Being an official of the Foreign Ministry, what I intend to do might be considered treason against the government. But I nevertheless must do it for the state." After disclosing the details of Inoue's plan, Komura decided to team up with Sugiura Shigetake (杉浦重剛), a lifelong friend of Komura since his Daigaku Nankō days, to engage in activities to sabotage the negotiations.

This proposal on the revision of the treaties was aborted owing to, among other things, intracabinet resistance from Tani Tateki (谷干城). Another proposal was attempted by Foreign Minister Ōkuma Shigenobu, but this effort, too, was wrecked by the enraged public opinion against its content, which had been exposed by *The Times* of London. Both of these proposals contained the provision on the appointment of foreign judges.

It has been suspected that it was Komura who leaked the draft of the treaty to *The Times*. Judging from Komura's everyday words and conduct, this allegation does not seem to be totally groundless. It was indeed an act of fearlessness by a man who focused solely on state affairs and who had nothing to lose.

But Komura was not a slovenly person who could easily ignore official regulations. On the contrary, he observed the rules so rigorously that, in later years, foreign correspondents complained about his inflexibility. Depending on the time and occasion, however, Komura was capable of deciding that state affairs were much more important than compliance with the rules.

Skeptical of Party Politics

Komura once made the following comment on domestic politics in Japan: "There are too many political parties engaged in party affairs. We should have something more neutral and solid." "Neutral" in this comment refers to the standpoint that bases decisions on an objective assessment of national interest instead of party interest. Komura made the above comment in 1889, the year of the promulgation of the Meiji Constitution, in which every political party was running around in preparation for the first general election that was scheduled for the next year. It was against this backdrop that Komura revealed his skepticism of party politics. This political view remained unchanged throughout Komura's life.

Ten years later, the Ōkuma-Itagaki cabinet (隈板内閣), the first party administration in Japan, was formed in 1898. Highly appreciative of Komura's administrative capability, Ōkuma pleaded with Komura, who was vice-minister for foreign affairs by that time, to join his own Shimpotō (進歩党; Progressive Party). In those days, those who sought political power had no other choice than to ask for the protection of the *han* clique or to join a political party. For Komura, who had managed to become a vice-minister without any *han* clique's backing, joining the ranks of Shimpotō was definitely a natural course for him to take, but he had absolutely no interest in party politics. He had the following to say about political parties in Japan:

> I say so-called political parties in Japan are cliques of people with their own self-interest and political agenda, and they have no ideol-

ogy or ideal of their own. Their members would not hesitate to sell their honor to advance their self-interests or even to sacrifice their own party in order to accede to power. Although I have no intention of clinging to my position as vice-minister for foreign affairs for my own self-interest, I will not leave my position lest these party-related people should become in charge of Japan's diplomacy.

The *han* clique is already a shadow which no longer has any substance, while the political party is a fiction, so to speak, that was born from the idea of constitutional government. Neither has root or substance. I am afraid that a day will come to Japan in the future when these two empty forces will damage Japan beyond salvation.

Anyone that is concerned about the future of this country should be prepared to rescue Japan from this peril starting today. In order to do so, one has no other choice than to become nonpartisan, departing from any clan or political party, and to cultivate oneself.

Political history throughout the Meiji and Taishō eras was a history of the struggle between the *han*-clique camp and the parliamentarian camp. This struggle first resulted in the Taishō Democracy, or the establishment of party politics to overtake the autocracy of the *han* clique, thanks to the painstaking labor of Mutsu and his disciples, including Hoshi Tōru and Hara Takashi. While this was undoubtedly a great achievement, it was, in Komura's view, nothing but the victory of a fictitious parliamentary democracy over the *han* clique, which had long lost its substance.

Subsequent history shows the demise of the short-lived party politics, which were overtaken by autocracy—this time by the militarists and bureaucrats in the turmoil during the Shōwa era following the Great Depression. The ideological source of this shift can be found in the above-quoted comment by Komura, which testifies that, even in the infancy of democracy in Japan, there were some Japanese leaders who harbored skepticism about party politics.

In this sense, Komura was again an archetype of the right wingers who occupied a substantial portion of the pre–World War II Japanese population. In fact, most arguments that appeared in newspapers on the eve of the Pacific War condemned the corruption of party politics. The days of right-wing autocracy that Komura dreamed of had indeed come—and eventually ruined Japan.

A Taciturn and Stoic Nationalist

Mutsu and Komura were two extreme types of Japanese, but they were on different ends of the spectrum. While Mutsu belonged to an exceptional minority in Japan who understood the orthodoxy of parliamentary democracy and aspired to realize it, Komura advocated for autocracy, defending the objective national interest from the nonpartisan standpoint of a bureaucrat. While Mutsu was an advocate of Westernization, Komura was a nationalist. In contrast to Mutsu, who was loquacious and open minded, Komura remained taciturn and stoic.

These personal differences notwithstanding, Mutsu promoted Komura to the top position in the Foreign Ministry. At a time when Japanese diplomatic missions were almost exclusively staffed with officials who had the personal backing of the *han* clique, Mutsu appointed Komura to this important position against opposition within and outside the ministry, including from Prime Minister Itō. This indicates that, when promoting his subordinates, Mutsu chose people for their personalities rather than any other attributes.

Although Komura gave the impression of being an eccentric, and his words and conduct tended to be excessive, it was obvious to anyone that his only concern was the survival and prosperity of the Japanese Empire. Everyone could see that Komura was totally devoid of any self-interest.

Although Komura could be a dangerous person who would not hesitate to revolt against the government when he considered the fate of the state and nation was at stake, Mutsu himself had once conspired to assassinate Ōkubo and Itō at the time of the Satsuma Rebellion, giving him no right to call Komura dangerous. In fact, Mutsu might have felt empathy for Komura's boldness despite their ideological differences.

Komura in His Element

—Crazy and Pigheaded: As the Times Called for—

Crazy and Pigheaded

Once he was transferred to the forefront of Japan's diplomacy from the inconspicuous translation bureau of the Foreign Ministry, Komura immediately distinguished himself, becoming a central figure in Japanese diplomacy in a short period of time.

After being appointed to chargé d'affaires at the Japanese legation in Qing in 1893 (twenty-sixth year of Meiji), Komura successively assumed important posts as: the civilian administrator for territories Japan had captured in Manchuria in 1894 during the First Sino-Japanese War; director general of policy affairs of the Foreign Ministry, also in 1894; Japanese minister to Korea in 1895; vice-minister for foreign affairs in 1896; Japanese minister[1] to the United States in 1898; Japanese minister to Russia in 1900 and Japanese minister to Qing in the same year; and eventually, minister for foreign affairs in 1901. As foreign minister, the post he kept until

---

1   Present-day ambassador. Until Japan ranked among the major world powers after victory in the Russo-Japanese War, Japanese delegates were received as ministers, not as ambassadors, by host countries.

1906, Komura engaged in all affairs related to the Russo-Japanese War. Compared with his ten years of obscurity prior to 1893, it was almost as if Komura had become a totally different person in these years.

Komura's rapid promotion was undoubtedly due to his capabilities and courage, which made him stand out among fellow bureaucrats. In fact, he had always been competent. At the translation bureau, for instance, Komura's written English was reputed to be unparalleled in its refinement. He was also so audacious that people around him would often cringe. But nobody in those days put the two elements together to appreciate Komura's entire personality. Instead, he was regarded as a poorly balanced man who was inept at getting on in the world.

In pre–World War II Japan, there was no such expression as "a well-balanced man." Instead, such virtues as courage and boldness were mainly emphasized as manly virtues. In postwar Japan, however, "a well-balanced person" has become both a household term and one of the highest forms of praise for an adult.

The Sung dynasty statesman and poet Su Shi (also known as Su Dongpo) (蘇軾 or 蘇東坡; 1037–1101) once wrote:

> When peace has not yet been attained, people would compete with one another to demonstrate their own abilities. Once peace is attained, however, those in power would disfavor the brave and the ambitious and, instead, promote those who were spineless and punctilious. Within a few decades, those with abilities are deprived of opportunities to distinguish themselves with their talents, while those without abilities become even more inertial.
>
> When this happens, when the emperor looks around for a capable retainer to help him accomplish his own policy, he will find none. High-ranking vassals would be preoccupied with posing as unfathomable great men, while lowly retainers would repeatedly preach the virtue of the "middle course" (more properly "being well-balanced") . . . only to manifest how incompetent they really are.

Su Shi went on to deliberate about the deviation of the interpretation of the "middle road" from the original Confucian concept. According to Su Shi, Confucius and Mencius denounced those who used the "middle road," as in the above quote, as "enemies of virtue." They would rather be with the crazy (the *kyōsha* or 狂者; those who have great aspirations but are unable to translate it into reality) or, if not with them, with the pigheaded (*kenja* or 狷者; those who may be short in capabilities but are determined to defend specific values). The former is someone who will do things others will not, while the latter is someone who has faith in not necessarily doing what everyone else is doing. Thus, Su Shi insists that there is nothing better than promoting someone who is at once crazy and pigheaded, and also wise, in order to wake the world from its lazy dream.

It was fashionable among people in the Meiji era to call themselves *kyō* (crazy). Yamagata Aritomo, for instance, named himself "Kyō-suke," while Mutsu Munemitsu used "Rokuseki Kyōfu" as an appellation, calling himself the crazy man whose ambition was far too big for him.

In this sense, Komura was indeed both crazy and pigheaded. Whatever he might have been, he could never be classified as a well-balanced person. When the Japanese bureaucracy began to show signs of sclerosis thirty years after the Meiji Restoration, Japan must have been in such a crisis—due to the First Sino-Japanese War followed by the Russo-Japanese War—that the nation found the poorly balanced Komura irreplaceable. It was in fact only after the Russo-Japanese War that the historical evaluation of Komura's achievements became divided. At every moment of crisis prior to that time, his judgment had always proven to be accurate, backing up the appropriateness of his promotion. Japan at that time needed the crazy and the pigheaded, a calling of the time to which Komura responded splendidly.

In this chapter, I intend to briefly review Komura's accomplishments prior to the climax of his career during the Anglo-Japanese Alliance and Russo-Japanese War days.

Fighting It out with Qing is the Best Plan

The appointment to chargé d'affaires at the Japanese legation in Qing was more a continuation of the Foreign Ministry's cold treatment of Komura than a promotion. It so happened that when his post as the director general of the translation bureau had to be eliminated as a part of an administrative reform, Komura's friends suggested it was time he be given an overseas post. Thus, the Foreign Ministry decided to post Komura to Qing.

Japan's interest in Qing in those days was unimaginably lower than it is today. To begin with, the largest concern for Foreign Minister Mutsu was the revision of the unequal treaties with the Western powers. Furthermore, the main arena for Japan's own diplomacy was the Korean Peninsula. While it was customary for the minister to Korea to serve concurrently as minister to Qing, he hardly ever visited Beijing because he was swamped with Korean affairs. It was against this background that Komura became de facto in charge of the negotiations with Qing as the acting minister despite his official position as the Japanese legation's chargé d'affaires.

Also, in those days, the elite in the Foreign Ministry were stationed in Europe and the United States; appointments to Asian countries were considered demotions. It is amazing that this attitude remained in the Japanese Foreign Ministry even until very recently, when Asian countries began to show remarkable growth.

Nevertheless, Komura declared that the post in Qing was just what he had hoped for. It would be a great opportunity for him to study China, he claimed, because in contrast to his knowledge of the Western powers, he was ignorant about China. This kind of comment could come only from someone who was genuinely concerned about the future of Japanese diplomacy and paid no heed to his bureaucratic career. In fact, as soon as Komura was stationed in Beijing, he became painfully aware of the inadequacy of China studies in Japan and began to avidly read books on China by Western experts. He also sought meetings with a wide range of Japanese and non-Japanese residents in Beijing in order to hear their advice.

Komura was particularly interested in the prospect of a possible war between Japan and Qing. After careful observation of the discipline and morale of Qing soldiers, Komura concluded that Qing would not pose a serious threat to Japan. He became convinced that "Korea will inevitably become the source of turmoil in Asia, and this fundamental issue will decide the fate of Japan. As long as Qing continues to insist on ruling Korea, despite its ailing power, the best plan for Japan is to fight a decisive battle with Qing." This conviction remained at the base of Komura's subsequent policies toward Qing and Korea.

Eruption of the First Sino-Japanese War

The opportunity for a decisive war came sooner than he had expected. Six months after Komura assumed his post in Beijing, the Donghak Peasant Revolution erupted in Korea. This marked the beginning of the rapid march of events toward the war between Japan and Qing.

As is apparent in Mutsu's memoir, *Kenkenroku*, it was Mutsu Munemitsu who played a central role in the Japanese government and manipulated the course toward the First Sino-Japanese War. Komura, however, despite his lowly position as mere acting minister to Qing, also steered Japan toward a war with Qing at every juncture of his official duty by making it difficult to reverse course—ahead of Mutsu's own planning.

During the exchange between the Japanese and Qing governments over Korea, Komura received the Japanese government's ultimatum, which he was instructed to hand-deliver to the Qing side. The ultimatum read: "The Qing side merely demands the unilateral withdrawal of Japanese troops from Korea and refuses to sit at the negotiation table with Japan. This is a clear indication that the Qing government deliberately looks for trouble." Reading this ultimatum, Komura decided to add, at his discretion, "with the intention of starting a conflict" to provoke the Qing side.

When the war appeared imminent and unavoidable, Komura handed the declaration of the severance of diplomatic relations to the Qing government before the official instruction to do so had arrived from Tokyo, lowered the national flag at the Japanese embassy, and pulled the diplomatic mission out of Beijing.

The official instruction to sever diplomatic relations had actually been dispatched, but its arrival was delayed due to the poor communications infrastructure. Nevertheless, Komura was heard to say, "If we waste any more time, we might lose the chance to start the war. All right, I will be the one to start the war." Also, onboard the homebound ship, Komura freely revealed his thoughts to foreign journalists, which stirred up some controversy. To do all of these things, it takes a resolute man like Komura, who was only concerned about state affairs and paid no heed to whatever reprimand or demotion he might have to incur as a consequence.

When Komura arrived in Tokyo, Mutsu was at Shimbashi Station to meet him. Komura said he had come back resolved to be reprimanded, but Mutsu cut him off saying, "What you did was just fine. The situation has evolved exactly as you had predicted." It may have been at this moment that Mutsu strongly felt he had found an able person whom he could rely on as his successor. In fact, it was after this incident that Mutsu started to promote Komura to important positions at every occasion.

Firm Hand in the Management of Manchuria

After returning from Beijing, Komura was appointed to civilian administrator for the territories that Japan's First Army had captured in Manchuria in 1894.

Komura's occupation policy was based on his "five-point law," which reflected the three-point law (法三章) decreed by Liu Bang (劉邦), the builder of the Han Empire. Liu declared the three-point law to the former citizens of the Qin Empire (秦) when he conquered its capital city, Guanzhong (関中). To the citizens of Guanzhong, who had suffered under centralized tyranny and had been oppressed by harsh laws, Liu declared: "You all suffered for a long time under the tyranny of Qin. Now I am to rule Guanzhong. I now decree a three-point law: Those who kill shall be executed; those who cause injury shall be punished; and those who steal and rob shall be convicted. All other laws of Qin are abolished." This declaration was enthusiastically welcomed by the people of Guanzhong. Komura's five-point law included, aside from the death penalty for thieves and arsonists, three additional points that were deemed essential for the wartime administration, including a nighttime curfew and a ban on the transportation of goods outside the city. Citizens of the occupied areas welcomed the impartial implementation of these rules by Komura's administration, and people who had evacuated the area started returning to their houses one by one to resume their daily lives.

Dugald Christie (author of *Thirty Years in Mukuden*), who worked for the Red Cross in Manchuria in those days, left the following observation on the Japanese wartime administration in Manchuria: "For the first few months, the arrival of the Japanese troops was seen with horror. But by the spring of 1895, people accepted their rules with equanimity. This change of attitude on the part of the Chinese was attributable to the unexpectedly well-disciplined soldiers of the Japanese troops and their benevolent rules. While there were cases of unruly conduct by some of these soldiers in the beginning, their conduct gradually became strictly controlled, and the local people began to benefit from the orderly administration." This should be regarded as a fair description of how things were under the Japanese occupation in general, including cases of self-indulgence among Japanese soldiers during battle and the early days of the occupation, which was followed by strict but tolerant rule. While it is believed that a massacre took place during the battle of Lüshun, it is not hard to imagine that the Japanese troops were nevertheless welcomed by the people of the occupied areas, as the discipline of the Japanese troops in those days was much better than that of Qing's local military.

When Komura returned from his duty as civilian administrator in the area occupied by the Japanese troops, Emperor Meiji summoned him to the Imperial Palace and personally questioned him in detail about the situation in Manchuria.

Mutsu had already predicted that by this time it would be difficult to keep the Liaodong Peninsula even if Japan won the First Sino-Japanese War, and he planned the occupation of Taiwan instead. Mutsu had instructed Komura beforehand not to overemphasize the importance of Manchuria to the emperor. This is another indication of Mutsu's foresight and shrewdness.

Against Mutsu's instructions, however, Komura eloquently emphasized how promising a land Manchuria was for the future of Japan and how important the Liaodong Peninsula was for Japan's defense. Komura continued even when Mutsu tugged the hem of Komura's frock coat to stop him. After they retired from the imperial audience, Komura defended his conduct by saying, "I was so tense in front of His Imperial Majesty that I completely forgot your instructions." In response to this, the only thing Mutsu could do was smile wryly, as if to say, "You are hopeless." To Mutsu, Komura was at once crazy and pigheaded, just as Mutsu liked.

It appears that by this time Komura, as an imperialist, already harbored an unshakable political conviction about the importance of Manchuria, which he consistently maintained during and after the Russo-Japanese War.

As soon as the general policy was set for the administration of the occupied region in Manchuria, Komura was called back to the heart of the Foreign Ministry in Tokyo to steer Japanese diplomacy as a whole as the ministry's director general of political affairs. However, succumbing to the strain of overwork since his days in Manchuria, Komura developed a high fever and was hospitalized immediately prior to the official announcement of the Triple Intervention.

After being discharged from the hospital, Komura stayed in Ōiso, a seaside resort near Tokyo, to recuperate. Meanwhile, the international situation after the First Sino-Japanese War was undergoing great change, which did not allow Komura to rest.

The Assassination of Empress Myeongseong

After the conclusion of the First Sino-Japanese War, the faction in the Korean court headed by Empress Myeongseong (閔妃), the first official wife of King Gojong (高宗), advocated stronger ties with Russia in order to block Japanese influence in Korea. In response, the Japanese collaborated with the anti-empress faction within the court and eventually dispatched assassins to Gyeongbok Palace to assassinate the empress on October 8, 1895. This assassination was suspected to have been masterminded by Miura Gorō (三浦梧楼), the Japanese minister to Korea at that time, and became a serious international issue. Since nobody but Komura could handle the situation, he accepted an appointment as the new Japanese minister to Korea and rushed to Seoul despite the adamant objections of his doctor.

Komura immediately sent members of the Japanese diplomatic mission to Korea, as well as firebrands suspected of being involved in this incident, back to Japan. In an attempt to get things under control, he tried to convince the Korean court and the Western powers' diplomatic missions stationed in Seoul of Japan's good intentions. Despite these efforts, however, the Korean court, in consultation with the Russian government, evacuated to the Russian embassy in Seoul, from which it issued an imperial ordinance, under Russian protection, to execute all the pro-Japanese cabinet members of the Korean government. Accordingly, ministers identified as such were brutally slaughtered.

Coming home from Korea, Komura paid a visit to Katsu Kaishū. When Katsu asked Komura about the situation in Korea, the latter replied, "I encountered the same difficulty as Your Excellency did toward the end of the Tokugawa shogunate." To the puzzled Katsu, Komura added, "Like you, I was also in a hopeless situation because the opposing side seized the king"—to which both had a hearty laugh.

Thus, with all the pro-Japanese forces annihilated, this assassination caused Japan to lose the entire foothold it had won in Korea through the First Sino-Japanese War.

Among the firebrands sent back to Japan by Komura was Yosano Tekkan, a nationalist poet and later husband to the poet Yosano Akiko. Among the many poems that Yosano composed in those days was the following *waka*:[2]

> How could I die in Korea
> Before witnessing an interesting war
> Ten years later.

In the minds of nationalist agitators, there already existed a vision of the Russo-Japanese War that would erupt ten years hence. Komura himself was, in a sense, a firebrand himself, and must have shared the same view. His conviction that Japan would sooner or later have to confront Russia, one of the most powerful nations in the world in those days, must have formed around this time. Given the subsequent conduct of Russia, Komura's conviction that there was no other way than war with Russia proved to be highly accurate.

"Although Japan might be weak now, wait and see in ten years" was an attitude commonly seen among the Japanese in those days, revealing the self-confidence Meiji Japanese had about their own future.

If Only It Had Happened Ten Years Later

After Komura returned from Korea in 1896, he was appointed to vice-minister for foreign affairs. It was during Komura's tenure as vice-minister that the United States annexed Hawaii. When this happened, Komura cried out, "Oh, dear, if only it had happened ten years later!"

King Kalakaua of the Kingdom of Hawaii visited Japan as a state guest during his trip around the world in 1881. During his stay in Japan, King Kalakaua pleaded for Japan's help, lamenting that "The influence

---

2   *Waka* is a form of Japanese classical poetry, commonly known by its 5-7-5-7-7 meter.

of the Westerners is becoming overwhelming in Hawaii and, if unre stricted, it will threaten the future of my kingdom." As a countermeasure to the growing influence of the Westerners, King Kalakaua suggested that "Although I do not have a prince, I have a highly gifted niece. I happened to know that Prince Yamashina Sadamaro is an outstanding member of the Japanese Imperial family. I would be truly grateful if a marriage between His Highness and my niece is permitted." Although the majority of those present at the imperial family conference and the cabinet meeting held in the imperial presence were in favor of this proposition, Emperor Meiji appealed for prudence, and it was eventually decided that King Kalakaua's proposal should be declined. Judging from the wording used in the reply to the Hawaiian royal house, this decision was obviously reached to avoid competition with the United States for influence in Hawaii.

Emperor Meiji's concern was justified. In the instructions given to the American minister to Hawaii in December 1881, US Secretary of State James Blaine emphasized the strategic importance of Hawaii for the United States, revealing its intention to make the archipelago a de facto annexed territory.

Subsequently, the group centered around American residents in Hawaii rallied to abolish the Hawaiian monarchy, accusing it of being tyrannical, and declared the establishment of a revolutionary government in 1893. Although the royalist faction tried to resist this coup, Queen Liliuokalani was forced to declare "temporary abdication" when faced with the landing of more than 160 sailors and US Marines and a few cannons from the US battleship, although she protested the conduct of the US government in vain. This became the de facto end of the Kamehameha Dynasty.

It is not difficult to imagine that those American "revolutionary forces" did not by any means represent the will of the majority of Hawaiians. An 1896 survey conducted by the Japanese legation revealed, of the total Hawaiian population of 110,000 people, native Hawaiians and British, German, and French nationals were adamantly against the annexation of Hawaii. The majority of the 1,900 Americans there, some of whom were royalists, also opposed annexation. It was only 500 to 600 Americans who were enthusiastically in favor of the annexation.

The Japanese government also issued an official protest in which it pointed out that "only a small portion of Hawaiian nationals support the annexation." Upset by this statement, the US government flatly refuted it, declaring that only the government could judge the will of its own people, and therefore, the Japanese government's reference, as an outsider, to the will of Hawaiian nationals was simply beyond comprehension.

It was of course meaningless to speak of the people's will in that era of imperialism. And subsequent history witnessed Japan taking actions similar to this American conduct. At the time of Japan's annexation of Korea, the key members behind the movement—Iljinhoe (一進会; or Isshinkai in Japanese, meaning Progress Party)—were local Koreans, not foreign nationals as was the case in Hawaii. But the forces the movement succeeded in mustering were, similar to the Hawaiian incident, far less than the 1 million that the advocate claimed. In both cases, the American revolutionary forces and Iljinhoe were able to achieve the annexation of Hawaii and Korea only because they had the protection of American and Japanese military might respectively.

It all depended on the will of the United States. During President Benjamin Harrison's Republican administration (1889–93), the United States was on the brink of annexing Hawaii, while the succeeding Democratic administration under President Grover Cleveland (1893–97) adopted a noninterference policy, claiming that the Hawaiian people should decide their own governing body. The annexation of Hawaii was temporarily shelved as a result, but when the Republican William McKinley was elected as president in 1896, the argument for annexation was rekindled. The annexation of Hawaii was finally decided by both the Upper and Lower Houses in 1898 after the Spanish-American War stoked imperialistic ambitions in the United States.

Meanwhile, Hoshi Tōru, minister to the United States, advised the Itō government that Japan should block the annexation even if it required the dispatch of Japanese battleships. Foreign Minister Ōkuma also instructed that an official protest be issued. This protest was far more belligerent than the US government had anticipated, as it was a gesture to the Japanese Diet, which had been criticizing Ōkuma's weak-kneed diplomacy.

Prime Minister Itō was traveling abroad when this incident took place, but he was so apprehensive of Ōkuma's hard-line stance that he found it necessary to send his foreign minister a letter saying, "Since Britain and other Western powers seem to have no intention of obstructing American annexation of Hawaii, a hard-line protest would make the Japanese position difficult. Wouldn't it be more prudent to leave it to the natural course of events?" Actually, it was habitual for Ōkuma to use high-flown language and pose as a hardliner, but in actuality, he rarely delivered on what he bragged about. In this particular incident too, Ōkuma in the end de-escalated his bragging and started saying that the sole purpose of the dispatch of naval vessels was to protect the Japanese residents in Hawaii.

It would make no sense for Japan to loudly complain when it had no power or determination to confront the United States, as Itō rightly pointed out. If it had happened ten years later, as Komura said, there could have been a crisis in the Pacific between the Japanese navy, which had emerged as a new hegemon in East Asia by annihilating the Russian fleet, and the Mahan-inspired American fleet of Theodore Roosevelt.

Expectations from Ultranationalists

After serving as vice foreign minister, Komura was appointed Japanese minister to the United States, and he was given a rare opportunity to closely observe the United States during the era of American imperialism, a highly unusual period in the history of that country.

Subsequently, Komura was transferred to Russia as the Japanese minister. En route to Saint Petersburg, Komura visited London to observe the situation in Britain. The main concern for the British people in those days was the decline of their country, as the nation was militarily bogged down in the Boer War and diplomatically isolated. But Komura judged that this experience must have taught Britain a good lesson, making it more resilient in the future. To Komura, Britain remained a reliable superpower, and the scheme to team up with Britain to confront Russia must have already entered Komura's mind by this time.

Once in Saint Petersburg, Komura, with his insight on Asia, immediately became an influential figure in the diplomatic community. He was one of only a few people who knew what was going on in Asia, which was in a state of constant flux. Nevertheless, his tenure in Russia had to be cut short once again. An international conference to address the aftermath of the Boxer Rebellion (義和団事件; 1898–1901) had been organized, and it was unanimously decided that nobody but Komura could represent Japan at this conference. He therefore headed for Beijing via Tokyo.

During his one-week stopover in Tokyo, Komura was asked by ultranationalists such as Konoe Atsumaro (近衛篤麿) and Sugiura Shigetake to give a public lecture. Konoe was from the noblest of the noble families, the grandson of Shimazu Hisamitsu (島津久光) of the Satsuma-*han* and father of the future prime minister Konoe Fumimaro (近衛文麿). He was the hope of the court nobles and was deemed as a future candidate for prime minister, along with Saionji Kimmochi (西園寺公望), but unfortunately, he met a premature death. During his short life, however, Konoe established a Pan-Asian political movement called Tōa Dōbunkai (東亜同文会; East Asia Common Literary Culture Society), which promoted mutual understanding and the improvement of relations between Japan and Qing after the First Sino-Japanese War, as well as Tairo Dōshikai (対露同志会; Anti-Russia Society), which pushed for a hardline foreign policy toward the Russian Empire.

Although Komura put high value on secretive bureaucratic discipline when conducting his official duties, he opened up to these ultranationalists. He started his public lecture on current international affairs with the following announcement: "It goes without saying that the secrets of foreign policies should never be exposed. It is because I trust the nobility of your character that I will disclose a part of the current state of affairs. I therefore expect that you will not betray my trust." Komura concluded that, while the best foreign policy the authorities could adopt was to apply short-term symptomatic treatments to various current issues, raising the Japanese people's awareness of foreign affairs was indispensable. For this, he hoped, education and enlightenment would be effective.

Perhaps inspired by this public lecture, Konoe and his comrades devoted their time and energy to enlightening the Japanese people on foreign affairs, and established Tōa Dōbun Shoin (東亜同文書院; East Asia Common Literary Cultural College) in 1900, which trained a number of China specialists who later contributed to Sino-Japanese relations in the pre-World War II days.

While Mutsu had been backed up by the Tosa faction's freedom and people's rights activists, who enabled him to manage the Imperial Diet effectively in the early days of Japanese parliamentary democracy, Komura had always been supported and backed up by the nationalist and ultranationalist movement.

3

The Qing Empire Falls

—How Western Powers Easily Overpowered Asia's Last Empire—

Demise of the Great Asiatic Empires

During the 220 years that Japan had closed its doors to outsiders and lost interest in the outside world, the international situation on the Asian continent underwent tremendous changes.

In early seventeenth-century Asia, gigantic empires were still flourishing. In those days, the Ottoman Empire was a powerful factor in the European balance of power and presented occasional threats to Vienna, encompassing the Black Sea coast in the east, the Persian Gulf and the Red Sea in the south, all of North Africa in the west, and the Balkan Peninsula in the north. On the Indian subcontinent, the Mughal Empire had been expanding its territory and enjoying prosperity since the reign of Akbar the Great (1556–1605), as if to fulfill the prophecy that "He who rules Delhi rules the universe." In exchange for the export of its rich products, gold and silver poured into the empire, making India the most prosperous country in the world in those days. In China, the Qing Empire ruled the largest territory in the history of China, except during the time of the Mongol Empire. Under the reigns of Emperors Kangxi (康熙帝) and Qianlong (乾隆帝), Qing was known as the world's greatest empire and the most sophisticated civilization up until the eighteenth century.

The Mughal Empire in India was the first to be crippled by the invading Western powers. In a quest for India's wealth, Portugal was the first Western power to request a trading post in India, followed by the Netherlands, Britain, and France. In the eighteenth century, Britain gradually began to overwhelm the other Western powers, placing key locations in India under its control one after another. In 1805, the emperor came under the protection of Britain, marking the fall of the Mughal Empire.

If the eighteenth century was the history of the fall of the Mughal Empire, then the nineteenth century was the history of the collapse of the Ottoman Empire. In the one hundred years between the Napoleonic wars and the end of World War I, the Ottoman Empire lost all of its territory due to Russia's encroachment, the regaining of independence by the Balkan countries, the colonization of northern Africa by European powers, and, finally, the secession of the Arab countries.

Against this backdrop, the last empire remaining in Asia toward the end of the nineteenth century was the Qing Empire.

Qing had also suffered encroachment by Russia. As early as the late sixteenth century, Russian Cossacks invaded the Chinese territory beyond the Ural Mountains and repeatedly looted people from the strongholds

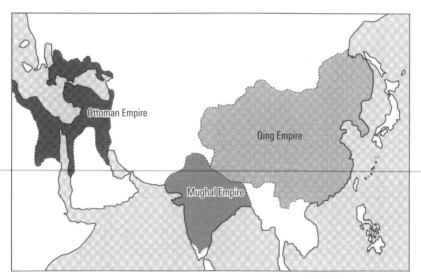

The territories of the three largest Asian empires.

they had set up in various locations in Siberia. Emperor Kangxi took an unbending stance against these activities. Although the Russians made various excuses to maintain the fait accompli, they were overwhelmed by Qing's massive number of troops who were armed with state-of-the-art cannons. Forced to sign the Treaty of Nerchinsk in 1689, the Russians withdrew from the area north of the Amur River. As a consequence, Russia changed the direction of its invasion. For the next seventy years, it concentrated on the conquest of Central Asia, situated in the south of the traffic route to the Far East. However, taking advantage of the Opium Wars, during which Qing could not afford to engage enemies in the north, Russia once again advanced to the Far East, this time all the way to Vladivostok, occupying the north bank of the Amur River as well as the east bank of the Ussuri River (1858–60).

Russia's defeat by Emperor Kangxi's mighty troops, however, long lingered in the memory of European countries, and Qing continued to be feared as a sleeping lion.

No Longer a Sleeping Lion

The First Sino-Japanese War turned out to be the most profound turning point in the modern history of East Asia. To begin with, it was fought in the heart of Qing instead of at its peripheries, which the Western powers had encroached upon. Watching the empire of the great Qing be easily beaten by the miniscule state of Japan, Western powers were initially shocked and dumbfounded. In no time, however, they realized Qing was no longer a sleeping lion to be feared; it was a spent force, just like the Mughal and Ottoman Empires had once been, that could be handled as they wished. The subsequent conduct of the Western powers was among the most shameless, even in the era of imperialism. As every history book on this issue describes, the Western powers were like vultures flocking over a carcass.

First, taking advantage of Qing's financial difficulties, which were caused by war-redemption payments to Japan, Western powers competed with one another to grant credit to Qing. In the context of present-day economic assistance to developing countries, granting credit may appear to benefit the recipient. In those days, however, it was a means frequently employed by Western powers to establish influence over the recipient. Once they succeeded in having the prey accept their loans, they were almost guaranteed to notch a decisive victory. This would allow the creditor country to confiscate the debtor's tariff revenues, obtain a variety of concessions, and dispatch "advisors" to control the finances of the debtor country, making it into a semi-colony. Although Persia in those days barely managed to remain independent, it was deeply in debt, resulting in the transfer of such concessions as mines and railroads to foreign hands, which divided its territory between the British and Russian spheres of influence.

In fact, Russia and France, two countries in the Triple Intervention vis-à-vis Japan, succeeded in lending 400 million francs to Qing on the pretext of aid for the war-redemption payments. Upon hearing this news, the British government reproached Qing for its insincerity in accepting loans from Russia and France, as Qing had been requesting the British government for a loan. Thus, Qing ended up with an additional loan of 32 million pounds from both the British government and the German government, who took advantage of the British action. To take a loan from a country in those days was tantamount to being part of its sphere of influence. Today, we would call it "debt diplomacy." Incidentally, after the collapse of the Soviet Union, when the Japanese government offered Central Asian countries low-interest, long-term yen loans, these countries were said to be frightened of any possible demands the Japanese government might make in the future.

The greatest concern for Russia at that time was to connect the Siberian Railway, which was under construction, directly to Vladivostok through Manchuria via Harbin, instead of running along the northern bank of the Amur River, as it does today. The railway would not only have been shorter but also much more advantageous for Russia, because it would have run through fertile Manchuria instead of barren Siberia, thereby offering better access to the heart of China.

When Nikolai II was crowned in 1896 (twenty-ninth year of the Meiji era), Li Hongzhang attended the coronation representing Qing. Since the Liaodong Peninsula had just been returned to Qing, thanks to the Triple Intervention by Russia, France, and Germany, the Qing court unanimously supported the policy to "ally with Russia to confront Japan . . . unaware of Russia's great ambition," according to Chinese journalist Wang Yunsheng (王芸生).

Buying over Li Hongzhang

When Li Hongzhang left for Saint Petersburg, the Russian court tried to block his visits to Britain and Germany en route to Russia. It dispatched members of the royal family, as well as the steamer *Russia*, to Suez to meet him and transport him directly to Odessa, giving him a red carpet welcome onboard.

Throughout the years before and after the Russo-Japanese War, the most influential individual on Russian foreign policies toward the Far East was Finance Minister Sergei Witte. According to Russian historian Boris Romanov's *Russia's Diplomatic History of Concessions in Manchuria*, "since the summer of 1900, it appeared as if Russia's foreign ministry had become a subsidiary of the finance ministry; it could not move even an inch in the Far East without reporting to the finance minister." It can be easily discerned, not only from his own memoir but also from the writings of Wang Yunsheng on the opposite side, that Witte was an outstanding diplomat, with keen insight into the international situation and excellent skills in diplomatic negotiation.

Convinced that negotiations with the Chinese should be conducted in a ceremonial, unhurried fashion, Witte welcomed Li with extreme courtesy, wearing the full dress worn for state ceremonies. After exchanging pleasantries, they moved to a different room where they exchanged news on their respective royal families and their own personal families over tea and refreshments, spending the entire first day of Li's visit without a single reference to his official business. According to Witte's memoir, this tactic was so effective that Li already appeared to be relaxed on the second day. On the third day, Witte visited Li to start the dialogue.

Fully utilizing his skills in rhetoric, Witte emphasized the importance of enabling the railway to reach Vladivostok via Manchuria, saying that "Russia has every intention of defending Qing's territory. At the time of the First Sino-Japanese War, however, we encountered difficulty in transporting our troops because we did not have the railway. By the time our troops reached Jilin, the war was practically over." Witte added that Japan would also agree to this railway because it would provide Japan with better access to European civilization—this reasoning was, of course, far from how Japan perceived the plan. The Japanese in those days were already fully aware of Russia's threat to Manchuria. Many were frightened by the proposed railway construction, viewing it as effectively opening the Far East to hordes of Cossacks on horseback.

When Li remained indecisive, Witte arranged a talk between Li and the Russian emperor. Receiving a direct request from the emperor, Li had to agree to the passage of the Siberian Railway through Manchuria. Witte then continued negotiations with Li to draft the outline of the Russo-Qing secret pact.

It has been rumored that in this process Li received a bribe from the Russian side. Although Witte's memoir denies this rumor, Romanov wrote that Witte promised to pay Li 3 million rubles in three installments. Judging from the situation surrounding the negotiation, as well as Li's subsequent conduct, it seems natural to believe that there was indeed a transfer of money between Li and Witte.

The secret pact agreed on the following three points: The first point was designed to save Li's face by emphasizing he had adamantly rejected the management of this railway by the Russian government. Instead, the Chinese Eastern Railway Company (東支鉄道会社), a nominally private company that would in actuality be run by the Russian government, was established to manage the railway. But the second point of the secret pact stipulated that the railway sites and land attached to the railway would be occupied by Russia, granting Russia the right to deploy its own police and garrison forces. As the third point, Russia and Qing agreed to form an offensive and defensive alliance in anticipation of a possible Japanese invasion.

Wang Yunsheng denounced this secret pact as a de facto concession of Qing's territory, administrative authority, and sovereignty to Russia, stating that "this is typical of a Qing diplomat, losing sovereignty, humiliating the country and its people, and, consequently, embellishing the surface in vain."

According to Witte's memoir, Li was recorded as making the following statement to Witte after signing the pact: "If you are truly eager to protect Russia's interests, you should under no circumstances consider advancing south of the Siberian railway, which ends at Vladivostok in the east. Dwellers in this region are averse to Caucasians, believing Caucasians would bring misfortunes on them. Should Russia harbor ambitions on this region, therefore, I must warn you that Russia's advance to the south of the railway would without fail invite political unrest and, moreover, unexpected disasters not only to Qing but also to Russia itself." This statement reveals that Li was well aware this secret pact would de facto put northern Manchuria under Russian control.

German and Russian Advances to China

Germany was not far behind Russia in terms of its demands on Qing for some kind of reward for its services during the Triple Intervention.

During the period of the unification of the empire, German leaders devoted themselves entirely to consolidating the foundations of the central European empire, showing no interest in the colonization race fought among the other Western powers. The German economy, as well as its

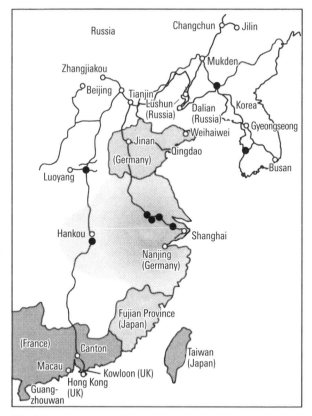

The Western powers advance to Qing.

population, showed remarkable growth after the unification; however, Germany had already started to launch its own quest for overseas territories toward the end of Bismarck's chancellorship (in the late 1880s). By that time, most of the better overseas territories had already been occupied by Britain. It was, therefore, only natural for the ambitious Kaiser Wilhelm II, who was eager to compete with Bismarck's achievements, to target Qing, the last empire left to be divided.

After the Triple Intervention, Germany promptly demanded settlements in Tianjin and Hankou and subsequently continued to demand a port from Qing. Qing's minister to Germany once lamented to the German foreign minister that "Once we make concessions to Germany, other Western powers are sure to follow suit and make more demands on us. If this happens, what would Germany do for us?" In response, the German foreign minister pointed out that Russia had already occupied Vladivostok, France had occupied Saigon, and Britain had occupied Hong Kong, and insisted that Germany, therefore, should also be given a port.

Germany aimed at gradually acquiring Jiaozhou Bay. When Kaiser Wilhelm II visited Russia in 1897, he conveyed the German intention to Nikolai II while onboard the carriage. Claiming that Nikolai's lack of vocal objection, which was more an act of diplomatic courtesy, represented the czar's silent approval, Germany readied itself to take whatever action necessary at any given time. It so happened that two German missionaries were murdered on Shandong, Peninsula at this particular moment. Although Qing authorities immediately arrested four suspects and attempted to close the case as soon as possible, Germany did not hesitate to take advantage of this incident by dispatching a landing party and occupying Jiaozhou Bay. Unable to do anything else, the Qing government was forced to approve the lease of the territory for the duration of ninety-nine years.

In response to Germany's conduct, other Western powers also pursued a policy of forcing similar concessions from Qing. Russia promptly took action to acquire the Liaodong Peninsula.

Possibly recalling Li's warning, Witte, according to his memoir, at first opposed the idea of advancing into southern Manchuria, but Russia's foreign minister and army minister persistently insisted on the occupation of Lüshun and Dalian, which Czar Nikolai II supported in the end. Convinced that it would be more prudent to obtain the peninsula through diplomatic means, Witte offered bribes of 500,000 rubles to Li and 250,000 rubles to the Qing diplomat Zhang Yinhuan to persuade Empress Dowager Cixi—who ended up agreeing to the lease of the Liaodong Peninsula, including Lüshun and Dalian. In his memoir, Witte predicted that, had Qing not agreed with the concession, Russian troops would have occupied Liaodong Peninsula anyway.

Moreover, now that Russia had occupied Dalian, Witte decided Russia had to expand its naval forces in the Far East and, as finance minister, approved an extrabudgetary disbursement of 90 million rubles for that purpose. This pleased the czar immensely.

At this point, expansion into the Far East and the occupation of Manchuria had become an established policy for Russia. And Qing's territory was completely at the mercy of the Western powers, with or without a pretext.

As another partner in the Triple Intervention, France obtained the lease of Guangzhouwan as well as the right to develop a railway and mines in southern China.

When Britain demanded the lease of Weihaiwei on the west of the Bohai Sea to counter Russia, which had obtained Lüshun and Dalian at the mouth of the Bohai Sea, the Qing court had no means to reject this demand. Britain also demanded and obtained the lease of the Kowloon Peninsula in southern China because France had expanded its concessions there.

At this point, Japan was internationally isolated due to the Triple Intervention and too exhausted by the First Sino-Japanese War to participate in the game of dividing China. The only concession Japan succeeded in obtaining from Qing was its promise not to cede Fujian Province to another country.

US Open Door Policy and Announcement on Territorial Integrity

The United States declared its Open Door Policy toward China in September 1899 (thirty-second year of Meiji), followed by its announcement of China's territorial integrity in July 1900. Today, these declarations, which proudly pursued American values on foreign soil, mark a milestone in the history of US diplomacy. However, in the history books of post–World War II Japan, which are heavily influenced by the Marxist historical view, they are explained as the capitalistic American quest to enter the Qing market as a latecomer.

Close scrutiny of the details reveals that historical facts were not necessarily as simple and clear cut as the above two views.

In his classic work, *American Diplomacy*, George Kennan objectively describes the process that culminated in these announcements. According to this book, in those days the United States initially pursued a policy of cooperating with Britain but subsequently started to base its diplomacy on domestic considerations.

The Open Door Policy had been originally advocated by Britain. British merchants, who monopolized about 80 percent of Qing's trade at that time, always wanted an open door policy. In fact, Arthur James Balfour, a senior member of the Conservative Party and later prime minister and foreign minister, stated in his remarks in the 1898 Parliament that "the open door policy . . . has been sickeningly repeated over and over."

In the same year (thirty-first year of Meiji), the British government sent a secret letter to the US government to sound out the possibility of whether the two countries could cooperate to block other Western powers from annexing or leasing Qing's territories to gain exclusive economic benefits from these territories.

According to Kennan, the then colonial secretary Joseph Chamberlain, an advocate of British-American cooperation and husband of an American wife, took the initiative for this secret letter. Although the British Foreign Ministry had been considering cooperation with Germany and Japan at that time, it pursued cooperation with the United States to save face for Chamberlain. But deep down, British leaders were inclined to take the pragmatic view that the Western powers would inevitably divide Qing and place it within their own spheres of influence.

Hearing of this secret letter, John Hay, US ambassador to Britain, advised the home government to support the British initiative. While his advice was not adopted at the time, the policy he later commissioned William Rockhill and Alfred Hippisley to draft when he was appointed secretary of state was approved by President McKinley. This policy would soon be called the Open Door Policy. Hippisley was a British customs officer stationed in Qing who also had an American wife. His professional experience made him a believer in equal opportunity in Qing's trade. In his view, the race for spheres of influence among the Western powers in China was already beyond control, but it should be contained to the areas of railways and mines. He judged that those spheres of influence must be prevented by all means from becoming the source of tariff barriers.

In December 1899, the US Department of State announced the Open Door Policy to the Western powers and requested their responses. Britain and Japan supported the policy in principle on the condition that other Western powers would also approve it. Russia, Germany, and France went only as far as to guarantee other countries the right of a most favored nation treatment in the areas that were de facto controlled by themselves. In comparison to what the United States had originally intended, this response was tantamount to outright rejection.

Politics in the Year of a Presidential Election

Despite the lukewarm responses from the Western powers, Hay decided to declare that the Open Door Policy had been satisfactorily received by these countries because the year 1900 happened to be the year of the United States' presidential election. He announced that the responses from the Western powers were "final and conclusive."

Japan's Foreign Ministry hesitated to accept Hay's announcement at face value and inquired about the US government's position in writing. It was answered as follows: "The United States, from the beginning, did not expect each of the Western powers to respond positively to the Open Door Policy. We just wished to ask for confirmation in writing of the policy that had been heretofore declared verbally. Nevertheless, all the responses gave a satisfactory guarantee to the world that those countries would maintain freedom of trade and equality of treatment. This is what the United States purported to obtain." This was the far-fetched explanation given by the US government to justify its endeavor as "a success."

When this happened, Komura had just been stationed in Washington, DC as the Japanese minister. He reported his own analysis to the home office as follows:

> The US government did not have a set view on its policy toward Qing. What happened was its Secretary of State adopted the advice submitted by bureaucrats who were knowledgeable of Qing's situa-

tion and made a recommendation to the president. The president initially hesitated to endorse it because Americans of German descent, particularly those in the state of Ohio where President McKinley is from, had always opposed a US-UK alliance. In order to prevent the Western powers from taking advantage of Britain's being tied up with the Boer War and advance to Qing, however, the US government decided to issue a notification on the Open Door Policy to the Western powers."

In the final analysis, the Open Door Policy benefited Britain the most, and its promotion was compatible with the argument in support of British-American cooperation.

How Japan Saved US Moral Diplomacy

In the meantime, the Boxer Rebellion (義和団の乱), a central theme of this chapter, erupted. The United States, in the middle of its presidential election, did not wish to be substantially involved in this incident; neither did it desire the revival of the imperialism debate fought in Congress since the annexation of the Philippines in the course of the Spanish-American War. It was against this background that Secretary of State Hay circulated a second message to the foreign powers involved in China, this time noting the importance of respecting the "territorial and administrative integrity" of China. The message was circulated on July 3, 1900, the eve of the Democratic National Convention.

It seems natural to believe that Secretary Hay was fully aware that the message was circulated solely for election campaign purposes and that its content was unrealistic in the face of reality, (i.e., the race being fought among Western powers for the expansion of their respective spheres of influence in China). As a matter of fact, in December after the presidential election, Hay instructed the US ambassador to Beijing to demand the concession of Sansha Bay in Fujian Province to utilize it as coal storage for the US Navy. However, since the Sino-Japanese treaty had banned the cession of Fujian Province, Hay sounded out the Japanese government's position. The Japanese government responded with a courteous and skillful reply—stating it had willingly accepted Secretary Hay's message on

China's territorial integrity, which could only be achieved through self-restriction on the part of all the countries concerned. Thus, Japan succeeded in nipping the US action in the bud.

As far as this conduct was concerned, the United States was no different from other imperialist nations. If the United States had really taken Sansha Bay, its announcement on territorial integrity would have been regarded as something obsolete due to a situational change in the East. Seen from this perspective, it could be argued the United States, unlike other imperialist nations, escaped the disgrace of tarnishing its history with imperialism thanks to Japan's implicit persuasion.

It may no longer be of any use to remember this kind of historical event in detail. In fact, the United States has been perceived by it own people, as well as by the rest of the world, as the nation that upheld the idealistic Open Door Policy and the territorial and administrative integrity of China all the way through to the era of decolonization after World War II, well ahead of the global trend, even daring to clash with Japan, which did not agree with these US ideals. Americans are immensely proud of this history. Since World War II, the United States has continued to demonstrate its idealism to the world by dispatching large numbers of troops again and again to Korea, Vietnam, and the Gulf region and then withdrawing them without demanding an inch of foreign territory.

But this has to be taken as one historical example of how we should refrain from trying to easily distinguish right from wrong by frivolously fitting a historical incident into a solitary image that is popular among contemporaries. After all, it should be recognized that history consists of all kinds of complicated backdrops.

The Boxer Rebellion

After being violated in this way by the Western powers, the Qing court finally felt the threat to its own survival.

Most of all, the need to modernize was keenly felt by some enlightened Chinese. Kang Youwei (康有為), an educator from a distinguished Guangdong family, stressed the urgent need for Qing to reform to Emperor Guangxu (光緒帝). He preached to the emperor that Qing lagged behind Japan because it had indulged in the refinement of technical trivia, such as the construction of railways and schools, instead of engaging in fundamental political reform like the Meiji Restoration. What was really called for was the thorough modernization of Qing.

Meanwhile, the argument for an alliance with Russia so as to counter Japan, which had once been prevalent in Qing, finally began to lose ground as more Chinese became aware of the true intentions of the Russians. Instead, the argument for an alliance with Japan began to gain strength. It so happened that Itō Hirobumi was scheduled to visit Qing in 1898. Some advisors recommended to the emperor that, during his stay, the Qing government should courteously ask for Itō's teachings on modernization; others went as far as suggesting that the Qing government request Itō to stay in Beijing as the prime minister of the new government.

The following statement was presented to the emperor as a rationale for partnership with Japan:

> Although all the other Western powers wish to weaken Qing so that they can divide up Qing among themselves, only Britain and Japan do not wish Qing to be weakened, even though they do not wish it to be stronger either. When Qing becomes weaker yet, Britain can no longer monopolize the benefit because Qing will be divided up by other Western powers. In the case of Japan, even when Qing becomes weaker, it cannot annex Qing because it will be divided up only by the Western powers . . . Siam has also relied on foreigners for its modernization. Japan, too, had mobilized foreign experts at first, but they have all been replaced by Japanese today. There are examples of European countries which have asked foreigners to stay on and become their ministers. There is nothing wrong with this.

The author of these statements was of the opinion that Japan and Britain were the only countries Qing could rely on at the time. And from this position, in order to protect China's territorial integrity and stability in East Asia, Qing had no other choice than to rely on the Britain-Japan alliance to block Russia's advance.

But this attempt at reform was crippled in 104 days with the rallying of the conservative faction in the Qing court, resulting in the house arrest of Emperor Guangxu and revival of rule by Empress Dowager Cixi. This abortive attempt was later called the Hundred Day's Reform.

While the modernization attempt mentioned above thus failed, it was only natural for the common people in Qing to harbor xenophobic sentiments in the face of such outrageous humiliations by the foreign powers.

The Righteous Harmony Society (義和団), known in English as the Boxers, was originally a cult-like martial arts group founded in a northern province that through its traditional Oriental superstitions became widespread among the Chinese. Members were convinced they could become invincible against swords, spears, or even bullets once they mastered the art. This thinking was analogous to Korea's Donghak (東学党) before the First Sino-Japanese War, whose members believed their religion would cure any disease. These two groups were also commonly linked to anti-Christian, xenophobic sentiment among the common people, causing a massive popular revolt. These are examples of what societies with prevailing premodern superstitions experience when they have been linked to emotional and fundamental nationalism.

Also behind the Boxer Rebellion was people's indignation at Qing tax officers, who filled their own pockets with tax revenues. These tax officers took advantage of the Qing government's order of imposing heavy taxes on the people, which were deemed necessary to finance the massive war-redemption payments to Japan. Naturally, therefore, people's resentment was also targeted at foreign powers.

Boxers became rampant even in Beijing around the spring of 1900, and they threatened the security of foreigners, chanting "destroy the foreign." Foreign residents in nearby Tianjin were completely isolated and surrounded by Boxers. In response, Western powers destroyed and occupied the Taku Forts, collectively mobilizing their battleships and landing their sailors to successfully reestablish communication with foreign residents in Tianjin. Beijing, in contrast, was completely beleaguered by the Boxers, and its foreign residents became isolated.

Meanwhile, a council meeting attended by Empress Dowager Cixi received an incorrect report that the foreign powers had issued an ultimatum. On June 20, the imperial proclamation of war against the foreign powers was issued.

After being defeated by tiny Japan in the First Sino-Japanese War and having succumbed to demands from foreign powers without resistance, the Qing court abruptly declared war against all Western powers.

War with No Chance of Winning

The imperial declaration of war proclaimed that Qing would conduct an all-out fight, relying on its 400 million people and a territory of twenty some provinces. The declaration stressed that "it would be far more honorable to fight it out than to prolong our lives and live on in shame."

In actuality, this was empty rhetoric that failed to inspire the Chinese people; the imperial family was evacuated from Beijing. To be sure, the Qing court had made countless misjudgments and had misgoverned; officials might have ruined the future of the country by indulging in power struggles and by pursuing personal gains. Viewed from a larger perspective, however, no matter how hopeless their cause may appear, any government or any people are likely to explode after being humiliated so freely by foreign countries.

When in 1941 Stanley Hornbeck, special advisor to the secretary of state on Far Eastern affairs, was warned on the eve of Japan's attack on Pearl Harbor that Japan would be cornered to start a war if the United States did not modify its policy, he shot back saying, "Tell me if you know of a single historic incident of a nation starting a war out of desperation." He meant to stress that it was unthinkable for any country to start a war that it had no chance of winning. History shows, however, that Japan did start a war immediately after this remark was made, an act that was like "jumping onto the deep precipice," according to a Zen aphorism quoted by Prime Minister Tōjō Hideki on that critical occasion. Confronted by Hornbeck, the other party had to back off and was unable to think of a historic example. But there actually had been such an example in the Far East less than half a century earlier.

The Strict Discipline of the Japanese Army

The Boxer Rebellion provided the first opportunity for Japan to be recognized as an equal to other world powers.

It was obvious to anyone that given the geographical proximity of Japan, the military forces that could be dispatched most promptly to rescue foreign residents in Beijing and Tianjin were Japanese troops. Although the Japanese side had maintained the readiness of its troops for dispatch at any time, it first sounded out the British intention in fear of a possible negative reaction from the Western powers. The British government had initially taken a wait-and-see attitude, but it recognized the need to dispatch Japanese troops as the situation grew intense. For its part, the British government then sounded out German and Russian intentions. While both Germany and Russia remained indecisive, the situation in Beijing and Tianjin became increasingly critical, prompting the British government to urge Japan to send its troops. Because neither Germany nor Russia opposed the British position on Japan, the Japanese government decided to dispatch an army division to Qing.

The Japanese played a central role in the Allied operations due to the large number of their troops and equipment, as well as their high morale. Troops from the other Allied countries, as well as foreign residents in Tianjin and Beijing, were deeply impressed by the valor and strict discipline of the Japanese soldiers.

After retaking Beijing from the Boxers, assaults and looting not only by mobs but also by members of the Allied forces became rampant in the city. In order to protect the Forbidden City from looting, Japanese troops were stationed at the north, east, and west gates of the city, while US troops defended the Meridian Gate in the south. Hearing how well disciplined the Japanese soldiers were, many Chinese citizens rushed to the area under the jurisdiction of the Japanese troops. Citizens also hoisted the Japanese Rising Sun flag on their houses and houseboats to discourage looters. So many people did this that the Japanese divisional commander had to ban this act in order to protect Japan's credibility.

About four decades later, when Japanese troops occupied Beijing in July 1937 as an overture to World War II, staff officer Ikeda Sumihisa strictly forbade vandalism and looting inside the walled city of Beijing. Some Beijing citizens, who remembered being looted by Caucasian soldiers during the Boxer Rebellion, were so appreciative of this noble decision that they proposed building a statue of Ikeda.

The Ideal Person to Represent Japan

In the meantime, Komura, who was serving as the Japanese minister to Russia, was busy sending telegrams to the home office in Tokyo with an analysis of Russia's response to the Boxer Rebellion. When Russia dispatched its troops to Manchuria upon the Qing's declaration of war, Komura sent this prediction: "Although Russia might formally withdraw its regulars from Manchuria after the settlement of the Rebellion, Manchuria will remain de facto under seizure by Russian troops." Komura's message was that in anticipation of this kind of development, Japan too should protect its own interests. Although at this stage Russia had repeatedly announced it harbored no territorial ambition over Manchuria, it gradually became obvious to everyone that Komura's prediction was accurate.

Inside the Qing court, the influence of the antiforeign faction ebbed rapidly after the defeat of the Boxers, and the emperor ordered Li to begin peace negotiations with the foreign powers. Suspicious of the remaining influence of the antiforeign faction within the Court, Western powers were doubtful even of the power bestowed on Li and refused to take him seriously. Faced with this situation, Li sent a personal note to Prime Minister Itō to request his friendly support. The Japanese government suggested Prince Qing, who was regarded as a moderate, should also be present at the negotiations along with Li, thus enabling a successful start to the peace negotiations. This episode reveals the high esteem in which Japan was held in Qing in those days.

During the peace negotiations between Qing and the foreign powers, nobody other than Komura Jutarō could represent Japan and compete with representatives of other countries in this negotiation.

Komura had been stationed in Russia for only ten months before he was transferred to Beijing. En route to Beijing, he spent a week in Tokyo, during which time Prime Minister Itō confided his utmost concern to Komura— whether Japan could really join the "concert of powers." Itō was genuinely worried Japan alone would be excluded from this concert of powers. Japan's national power, as well as its international reputation, in those days did not guarantee automatic membership in this group. It was only after Japan won the Russo-Japanese War a few years later that it was recognized as a world power. Prior to this, it was altogether uncertain whether Japan would be allowed to sit at the same table as the other powers.

During the peace negotiations, Komura more than met the expectations of the Japanese government. It goes without saying that his success was supported by the accomplishments of the Japanese army during the Boxer incident, particularly the comportment of its strictly disciplined soldiers, who earned praise as the army of a civilized country.

During the conference, members gave Komura equal footing with Western participants and listened closely to what he had to say. The succession of telegrams Komura received from the home office during the negotiations contained such messages as, "You are granted full authority to flexibly respond to the situation as far as these negotiations are concerned" and "Because the Japanese government is fully aware that you will do your utmost to defend our country's rights and interests, we entrust everything to your discretion with regard to these negotiations." These messages were an indication of the depth of trust the Japanese government had in Komura at the time.

Foreign Minister Komura Jutarō

When the Katsura Tarō cabinet was formed on June 2, 1901 (thirty-fourth year of Meiji), Komura was appointed foreign minister. Because Komura could not be spared from the ongoing conference in Beijing, the Katsura cabinet was initially without a foreign minister. As soon as the direction of the conference became predictable, Komura rushed back to Tokyo and assumed the post of minister for foreign affairs on September 21. Komura was then forty-seven years old.

It was only eight years since he had been stationed in Beijing after years of obscurity. In his speech at the reception celebrating his promotion, Komura said, "Now is not the time to evaluate my accomplishments or my character. It is simply premature to do so, and I will not allow it. Whatever I have accomplished so far has only been preparation for the difficult times to come."

To be sure, Komura's ability and character were at the time still known only by a few. There were those, however, who placed high hopes on him, and one of them was Konoe Atsumaro, the central figure of Kokumin Dōmei-kai (国民同盟会; National Alliance Society). Konoe, father of the future prime minister Konoe Fumimaro, was the leading advocate of conservative pan-Asianism, as opposed to the pro-Western liberalism of Saionji Kinmochi. Kokumin Dōmei-kai was a powerful organization that was supported by leading nationalists of the time. When Komura became foreign minister, Konoe announced that there was no need for his nationalist movement to exist any longer, as long as Komura held a top policy-making position. With the conclusion of the Anglo-Japanese Alliance, Konoe dissolved the Kokumin Dōmei-kai and held a party for Komura in recognition of his achievement.

This was a decision that could be made only by someone who fully appreciated the personality of Komura and what he had carried out with conviction. And, for his part, Komura proved to be worthy of his friends' expectations. He was an archetypal Japanese nationalist/ultranationalist who had the courage not only to hold on to his convictions but also to carry them out whenever he found a chance to do so. And this was the kind of character the era of dog-eat-dog imperialism called for. Komura's mettle enabled him to defend Japan's national interests.

CHAPTER

4

Unyielding Struggle for Parliamentary Democracy

*—The Life of Hoshi Tōru: The Man Who Kept the Fire of the Freedom
and People's Rights Movement Alive—*

Era of the Han-Clique/Political Party Coalition

Around the time Komura became a cabinet member, parliamentary politics was still far from being firmly rooted in Japan, even though it had been gradually embedded in the system over the ten years since the establishment of the Imperial Diet.

Before the First Sino-Japanese War, Itō Hirobumi and Mutsu Munemitsu faced a series of crises in parliamentary democracy, being caught between anti-*han*-clique parties fiercely resentful of years of government oppression on the one hand, and bigoted conservative *han*-clique politicians with absolutely no understanding of parliamentary politics on the other. The pair had managed to overcome these crises and avoid possible suspension of the constitution. They utilized all means at hand, hard and soft, which ranged from the dissolution of the Diet to reaching compromises with opposition parties and cashing in on the mutual trust between Mutsu and the Tosa faction within Jiyūtō.

Once the war erupted in 1894, the Diet became charged with patriotism and gave its full support to the war effort, thus allowing the survival of the first phase of Japanese parliamentary politics. When peace returned, however, the government again had to face the challenge of managing a Diet

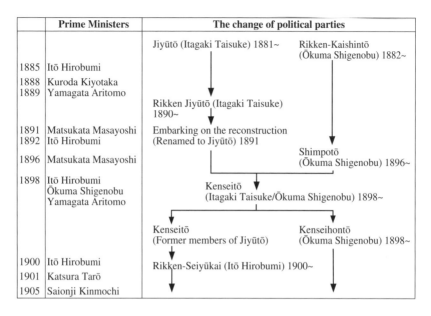

	Prime Ministers	The change of political parties
		Jiyūtō (Itagaki Taisuke) 1881~ · · · Rikken-Kaishintō (Ōkuma Shigenobu) 1882~
1885	Itō Hirobumi	
1888	Kuroda Kiyotaka	
1889	Yamagata Aritomo	
		Rikken Jiyūtō (Itagaki Taisuke) 1890~
1891	Matsukata Masayoshi	Embarking on the reconstruction
1892	Itō Hirobumi	(Renamed to Jiyūtō) 1891
1896	Matsukata Masayoshi	Shimpotō (Ōkuma Shigenobu) 1896~
1898	Itō Hirobumi / Ōkuma Shigenobu / Yamagata Aritomo	Kenseitō (Itagaki Taisuke/Ōkuma Shigenobu) 1898~
		Kenseitō (Former members of Jiyūtō) · · · Kenseihontō (Ōkuma Shigenobu) 1898~
1900	Itō Hirobumi	Rikken-Seiyūkai (Itō Hirobumi) 1900~
1901	Katsura Tarō	
1905	Saionji Kinmochi	

in which anti-*han*-clique parties always occupied the majority.

The cooperation between Itō and Jiyūtō that Mutsu had designed remained an important pillar in Japanese politics and repeatedly salvaged parliamentary politics in Japan. In particular, Jiyūtō's decision to work together with the government for the cause of *Gashin Shōtan* (臥薪嘗胆; persevering through hardship for the sake of revenge against Russia) after the forced return of the Liaodong Peninsula to Qing coincided well with the people's sentiment in those days. In 1896, Jiyūtō decided to cooperate in an effort to establish an Itō cabinet, and Itagaki Taisuke left the party to join the cabinet as home minister.

This was tantamount to the emergence of a government party in Japanese politics. This precedent was immediately adopted by the subsequent Matsukata cabinet in which Shimpotō collaborated with Prime Minister Matsukata Masayoshi this time, sending Ōkuma Shigenobu to the cabinet as foreign-minister-cum-deputy-prime-minister. This was what came to be called the era of the government-opposition party coalitions. Japanese politics had already entered an era in which a cabinet could not be sustained without the cooperation of at least one of the anti-*han*-clique parties.

Meanwhile, leaders of the anti-*han*-clique parties became convinced that it would be far more beneficial for them to "complete parliamentary politics"—to command the overwhelming majority in the House of Representatives by establishing an unified party called the Kenseitō party through the merger of Jiyūtō and Shimpotō—than to remain fragmented and continue hoping to form partnerships with each separate *han*-clique cabinet.

At this point, the *han*-clique government had no other choice than to accept the natural result of parliamentary democracy: the majority party in the parliament would form the government. This was just what Mutsu had once predicted as a natural result of introducing a parliamentary system.

Initially, Itō believed that by exercising his personal influence he could muster a sufficient number of people to form his own party. However, witnessing how powerful political parties had become in Japanese politics, even Itō had to admit his idea was unrealistic. Anti-*han*-clique parties that had been active since the days of the Freedom and People's Rights Movement had already established firm electoral bases in numerous districts. It was utterly improbable, even for Itō, to establish a new party that could compete with these parties. Thus, Itō stepped down, passing the government to Ōkuma and Itagaki.

This by no means meant that all the conservatives in the *han* clique had accepted the role of political parties. A particularly adamant voice within the anti-party forces was Yamagata Aritomo, who confronted Itō head-on, lamenting that "with a party cabinet, Japanese politics degenerates into democracy against Japan's national polity."

Second Peaceful Revolution

When the Ōkuma-Itagaki cabinet was formed, Yamagata went as far as to lament that "the Meiji government has fallen."

At this point, Itō's flexibility, which had prompted him to pass the government to Ōkuma and Itagaki, saved Japan's parliamentary politics. Had Itō followed Yamagata's advice instead, the government would have had no other option than to repeatedly exercise its right to dissolve the Lower House. If that had actually happened, no incremental budget would have been passed, which would have paralyzed all government functions. Facing the imminent threat from Russia, Japan would have had no other choice than

Yamagata Aritomo
(Photo: Kyodo News)

to return to the *han*-clique autocracy—which would have meant suspending the constitution—in order to prepare for war with Russia.

Being the very first party cabinet, the Ōkuma-Itagaki cabinet collapsed due to a schism within Kenseitō before it could make any major accomplishments. But it was extremely significant that a party cabinet was formed peacefully in Japan within ten years of the adoption of parliamentary politics, even though Meiji leaders had originally claimed Japan would pursue the system of a nonpartisan cabinet. A party cabinet never materialized in Germany, which had been the model for the Meiji Constitution, before World War I. Japan had accomplished, so to speak, a second peaceful revolution after the Meiji Restoration. This was possible only because of the mutual trust among the Japanese leaders. In Itō's mind, both Ōkuma and Itagaki had been his comrades, together carrying the revolution called the Meiji Restoration on their shoulders. Itō must have trusted that Ōkuma and Itagaki shared the same love for their country, despite their political differences, when he passed the government to them.

The second Yamagata cabinet that succeeded the Ōkuma-Itagaki cabinet returned to the old reliance on partnership with one of the anti-*han*-clique parties—former members of Jiyūtō this time—but it too was short-lived. Meanwhile, Itō once again explored a way to organize his own party. This time, though, instead of starting up a totally new party, he established Rikken-Seiyūkai, with former members of Jiyūtō as the nucleus, and became its president. One hundred and fifty-five of the 300 seats in the House of Representatives were occupied by members of this Rikken-Seiyūkai. This was the genesis of Seiyūkai, the party that would play a central role in accomplishing parliamentary democracy in Japan over the next three decades—(from 1912 through the 1930s) between the era of the *han*-clique government and the rise of militarism.

Parliamentary democracy in Japan was achieved by Itō from the *han*-clique side and Jiyūtō from the anti-*han*-clique parties. It was the partnership between these two that contributed to a successful termination of the *han*-clique regime. To counter Rikken-Seiyūkai, newer parties, including Kaishintō, Shimpotō, and Minseitō, were established. These newer parties and Rikken-Seiyūkai formed the two mainstreams that went on to support parliamentary democracy in Japan over the next three decades.

Because the Itō cabinet this time had to take over the government quite unprepared, just like the Ōkuma-Itagaki cabinet, it ended up being short-lived.

Katsura Tarō Cabinet

After the fall of the fourth Itō cabinet, there was no longer anyone among the Meiji Restoration's elder statesmens to volunteer to bear the responsibilities of the state. As a result, gencrational changes took place, which resulted in the formation of the Katsura Tarō cabinet. Komura joined this cabinet as its foreign minister.

Together with Saionji Kinmochi, who would alternately share the responsibility from that time onward, Katsura, born in Chōshū-*han* in 1847, belonged to the youngest generation among the Meiji Restoration leaders. He was a career soldier with a distinguished military service record, including service in northern Japan as a company commander during the Boshin War (戊辰戦争).

After Saigō Takamori left the government, Yamagata from Chōshū and Ōyama Iwao from Satsuma were symbolic elders in the Japanese Imperial Army, under whom Katsura from Chōshū and Kawakami Sōroku from Satsuma were the most influential generals.

Some say that the First Sino-Japanese War was Kawakami's war—in other words, that it was Kawakami who commanded all the operations throughout the war as vice-chief of the general staff. Because the chief of the general staff was the aging Prince Arisugawa Taruhito, who had led the Imperial Army during the Meiji Restoration wars, Kawakami was the de facto chief of the general staff.

According to the Meiji journalist Tokutomi Sohō, Ōyama, out of the conviction that future of the Imperial Army rested on the shoulders of Kawakami and Katsura, had deliberately assigned these two archrivals to separate areas of responsibility in order to prevent them from competing with each other. Thus, Kawakami was put in charge of military operations or military command, while Katsura was assigned to posts in charge of military government or military administration. Katsura was sent to Germany twice to study military systems, and on his return, he devoted himself to the consolidation of the Japanese military structure.

While both Kawakami and Katsura worked well together to support the Imperial Army, Kawakami met a premature death from overwork during the First Sino-Japanese War. Katsura survived and eventually became prime minister.

A Remote Cause of a Runaway Military

Incidentally, today it is generally believed the arbitrary actions of the military in Japan that culminated in World War II originated from the exclusive imperial right of military command under the Meiji Constitution. This issue will be discussed in more detail when we touch upon the London Naval Conference in 1930 and after. But it should be stressed here that in fact it was the law, which stipulated the need for generals and admirals on active duty to become war and naval ministers, that encouraged the arbitrary conduct of the military in the 1930s. The law had its origin in this period and the beginning of party politics.

In 1901 the Yamagata cabinet revised the administrative regulation so that ministers and vice-ministers of the navy and army had to be selected from among high-ranking admirals and generals on active duty. It is believed that this revision aimed to prevent such anti-Yamagata ex-military officers as Tani Tateki and Miura Gorō from becoming naval or war ministers. Whether this conjecture is justified or not, it seems undeniable that Yamagata, apprehensive of the imminent domination of Japan's politics by political parties, applied this revision in order to make the military a sanctuary that the party cabinet could not touch.

Prior to this revision, when the Ōkuma-Itagaki cabinet was formed in 1898, Yamagata expressed his wish that "at least war and navy ministers should transcend political parties." Kawakami Sōroku, who had earlier lamented that a "party cabinet is harmful to the nation's grand design," also attempted to obstruct the formation of the Ōkuma-Itagaki cabinet by preventing war and naval ministers from the military from joining the cabinet. This indicates that the idea of sabotaging a party cabinet by refusing to send military ministers into government, as practiced in the 1930s, existed from the very beginning. In the face of the deadlock, Emperor Meiji had to order War Minister Katsura and Naval Minister Saigō Tsugumichi from the former cabinet to stay in office in order to launch the Ōkuma-Itagaki cabinet.

It was during the second Yamagata cabinet, which succeeded the doomed Ōkuma-Itagaki cabinet, that Yamagata enacted the above regulation concerning war and naval ministers. As such, Yamagata's intention seems to be self-evident.

Because of this revision, it became virtually impossible to form a cabinet without the approval of the military. As political parties grew more powerful, they became highly critical of this law. In 1913 (second year of Taishō), the law was revised to allow admirals and generals on reserve duty to assume the ministerial posts. However, because the power of the military remained formidable, no one who was not on active duty ever became war or naval ministers. After the February 26 Incident (2.26事件) of 1936 was settled, the law was revised back to its original wording.

Any system can be abused if there is a will to do so. In particular, when such a powerful institution as the military is granted a privilege, there is nothing that can stop its abuse except for its own self-restraint.

Throughout the Meiji, Taishō, and early Shōwa eras, however, the Japanese military often failed to exercise such self-restraint. Particularly after the February 26 Incident in 1936, the military's conduct can be described as tyrannical—certainly far worse than simply failing to restrain itself.

By 1936, the minister of war, rather than the prime minister, had the real power to form a cabinet. Unless the Imperial Army appointed the war minister for the next cabinet, the cabinet itself could not be formed. And this gave the army unlimited power to meddle in politics. The army conditioned its participation in the cabinet by interfering in the general policy of the cabinet, and even in the selection of other cabinet members. If these requests from the military were not granted, the appointed war minister would refuse to join the cabinet, thereby blocking the formation of the cabinet. In short, by this time, the cabinet had no other choice but to accept all of the military's demands, even those having to do with policies and personnel.

In retrospect, this dominance by the military was completely attributable to Yamagata's stubborn determination to reject party politics. In this sense, Yamagata accomplished his original objective—the end result of which delivered fatal blows to Japan's parliamentary democracy thirty to forty years later and devastated the country as a consequence.

Civil Service Appointment Ordinance

Another measure that Yamagata took to restrict party politics was the enactment of the Civil Service Appointment Ordinance (文官任用令) of 1899 (thirty-second year of Meiji).

Before this ordinance was enacted, government offices could freely appoint anyone for the post of *Chokunin-kan* (勅任官; an official appointed by the emperor), the equivalent of today's high-ranking government official who has passed the national civil service examination. Consequently, the Satsuma- Chōshū oligarchy had been able to appoint whomever they wished to government posts.

From the perspective of party members who had long been out of the government, they suddenly became eligible to be appointed to assume various government posts, and this drove them to aggressively seek office.

Against this backdrop, the Civil Service Appointment Ordinance stipulated that all government officials must pass a national examination. A similar system is still in use in Japan today.

The merits and demerits of this system are still controversial. Had it not been for this ordinance, Japanese bureaucracy would have resembled that of the United States today. Internationally, however, the American bureaucratic system stands out alone as a peculiar system, while those of other Western countries are more or less similar to Japan's. While opposition parties were bitterly disappointed and reacted violently at the time, it is still premature to evaluate whether the Civil Service Appointment Ordinance was a bad one or not.

A Genius Nurtured by Mutsu Munemitsu

On the anti-*han*-clique parties' side, it was Hoshi Tōru who exercised the greatest influence on the political situation in this period.

Hoshi had once been offered the post of foreign minister in the Yamagata cabinet. Hoshi devoted his energies to the formation of the succeeding Itō-Rikken-Seiyūkai cabinet, in which he served as minister for communications and transportation. Hoshi was not from a samurai clan; in fact, he was the son of an impoverished family at the bottom of society. It was extremely rare in those days (and still is today) for such a person to be promoted that far.

Because Hoshi's life was in itself the history of Japanese parliamentary politics in its infancy, let me review some aspects of political development around that time by tracing the footsteps of Hoshi.

Hoshi Tōru was a genius who Mutsu Munemitsu cultivated. It is no exaggeration to say that there would have been no Hoshi if it had not been for Mutsu. Hoshi was Mutsu's protégé, and as someone once said, "Hoshi is normally a tiger, but in front of Mutsu he becomes a tamed cat."

Hoshi's biological father was a plasterer who failed at his job because of heavy drinking and eventually abandoned his family. Hoshi's older sisters were sold to a brothel in Shinagawa for payment of the family's debts. Hoshi's mother worked as a maidservant to support the family, with the still-nursing baby Tōru tied to her back. She became so tired and despondent that she once thought of throwing the baby into a pond. Being at a loss as to what to do, she consulted a fortuneteller by the name of Hoshi Taijun, who took pity on her and offered to marry her. Hence, baby Tōru became Hoshi Tōru.

Hoshi Taijun had been living a destitute life, earning his living by giving sailors moxa treatment or by fortunetelling in Uraga. Riding the boom caused by the opening of the port of Yokohama, he was able to open his own clinic in Yokohama, which somewhat helped to stabilize his living. At this point, Hoshi Taijun also adopted Tōru's two older sisters and moreover, he decided to support Tōru's decrepit father, the former husband of his wife. Hoshi Taijun was indeed a kindhearted man.

Hoshi Tōru remained a man of haughty arrogance throughout his life. It is not hard to imagine that his arrogance stemmed from the inferiority complex he had nursed throughout his upbringing. Also, having come from a non-samurai clan, he had no aversion to monetary affairs.[1] In later years, this allowed him to lavishly pour money he had obtained from vested interests into political maneuvering, thus earning himself a bad name as a politician who was contaminated by money scandals.

Yet Hoshi was able to stay away from the aristocratic vices of pretention and self-indulgence. On the contrary, he maintained a strong aversion to these bad habits throughout his life. Rare for a Meiji Restoration leader, Hoshi rarely sought pleasure in the demimonde.

He married the daughter of a tatami mat maker in order to ensure good relations between his

Hoshi Tōru

---

1   The samurai class was known for having an aversion towards handling money.

mother and wife, which was one of numerous considerations he showed to his family. This can be attributed to his experiences at the bottom of society and to his warm-hearted stepfather, who had taught Hoshi the value of human kindness and the importance of family.

Aspiring to follow in his stepfather's footsteps, Hoshi initially became a live-in student under a Western medicine practitioner. When he began his studies, he displayed prodigious talent in English. In no time, he became an expert in English, thanks to his perseverance, and took a job as an English teacher. It was around this time that Hoshi enrolled under the banner of Mutsu. He began to accompany Mutsu everywhere he went, including to Wakayama and Kanagawa. Hoshi was only twenty-four years old when he was appointed director of customs at the port of Yokohama, in part due to his English ability.

Subsequently, with the help of Mutsu, Hoshi was sent to Britain to study. He became the first Japanese to be certified as a barrister. Upon returning to Japan, Hoshi launched his own legal office, earning quite a fortune in no time.

In 1882, at the age of thirty-two, Hoshi joined Jiyūtō, a natural course for him to take. Because he had no *han*-clique backing and Mutsu, his only protector, was imprisoned at the time, Hoshi's prospects for success as a government official were extremely slim. Even if he had become a government official, he would not have served out his time given his ferocious antipathy toward lineage and the elite and the benefits accrued to them by birth.

Even after he joined Jiyūtō, Hoshi continued to be the most radical advocate of the annihilation of the "spurious party" Kaishintō.

The feud between Jiyūtō and Kaishintō dated back to the establishment of the latter. In terms of passing on the tradition of the Freedom and People's Rights Movement, the establishment of Kaishintō was tantamount to forming a new sect. *Jiyūtō-shi* (History of Jiyūtō), edited and supervised by Itagaki Taishuke, had the following to say about Kaishintō:

> In launching Kaishintō, its founders felt a little guilty about Jiyūtō. That was why Kōno Togama, a Kaishintō leader, had to justify the move to Itagaki by characterizing Kaishintō as a separate force within Jiyūtō. Because Jiyūtō was an incorruptible protector of justice and a friend of the poor, he argued, rich people did not feel comfortable with the party. And because it was mostly made up of the young and energetic, the elderly and pragmatists did not care much

for Jiyūtō. Kaishintō was established, according to Kōno, in order to prevent these potential supporters from abandoning Jiyūtō by pooling them in the separate force named Kaishintō. Kōno said that they intended to integrate this force with the main force in the future. In response, Itagaki reproved Kōno to his face, saying, "Kaishintō intends to hound us out, and snatch all of our games. There is nothing more cunning than that." Kōno was at a loss for words.

After this showdown, *Jiyūtō-shi* continued to criticize Kaishintō and stated that Kaishintō had started denouncing Jiyūtō as vulgar and radical. Consequently, the difference between the two, which had originally been only marginal, grew further apart.

Hoshi's Lonely Battle to Keep the Freedom and People's Rights Movement Alive

Although Kaishintō claimed to be moderate and decent, Hoshi found its former samurai-clan members, whom he thought to be smug and elitist, utterly incompatible with himself. But even Mutsu, whose aversion to Ōkuma was well known, grew somewhat weary of Hoshi's tireless attacks on Kaishintō and had to restrain Hoshi by saying, "Do you really think that we can do without collaborating with Kaishintō in the days to come?" In 1884, when Itagaki decided to dissolve Jiyūtō, which had been dormant for quite some time, Hoshi alone vigorously gave public lectures across Japan to revitalize the party. In May, he invested his own funds to publish the illustrated daily *Jiyū no tomoshibi* (自由燈; The Light of Liberty). It would not be an overstatement to say that the dissolution of Jiyūtō in October of the same year was timed to take advantage of Hoshi's detention for insulting government officials. Hoshi sent a telegram from his prison cell opposing Jiyūtō's dissolution and instructed *Jiyū no tomoshibi* staff to dispose of his estate in order to sustain the daily even after the dissolution of the party.

When Hoshi was released from prison in October 1885, he found the Jiyūtō faction in utter distress. Former members of the party even evaded seeing Hoshi when he visited them. Given this situation, Hoshi decided to resurrect the Freedom and People's Rights Movement by regrouping scattered former members who had fallen on hard times and withdrawn from society. So as to emphasize his resolution to ignore minor differences for the sake of the unity of the group, Hoshi renamed his daily *Tomoshibi Shimbun* (燈新聞), removing the word *Jiyū* from its name.

This turned out to be the starting point for the movement to unite parties under common interests. Triggered by the unequal treaty issue, the movement intensified after 1887. It was solely due to Hoshi's efforts that the fire of the Freedom and People's Rights Movement was kept burning. And it was the small stream of the movement that Hoshi had protected which later became the mainstream in Japanese politics, including Rikken-Jiyūtō, Kenseitō, Rikken-Seiyūkai, and eventually Jiyu-Minshutō (自由民主党; Liberal Democratic Party) after World War II.

Meanwhile, Hoshi was fighting a solitary and lonely battle, though some were watching closely over it. One day, Itō privately said to Mutsu, "There is nobody outside the government more bighearted and daring than Hoshi. I consider him a great man. Would you introduce me to him because I want him to work for me." In response, Mutsu advised Itō: "I could easily introduce you to Hoshi, but I am afraid that meeting him will not be beneficial to you. Hoshi cherishes people's rights as the supreme cause, and he shoulders the expectations of tens of thousands of people with whom he is committed to live and die. It would not be oblique for him if, for some reason, he should betray you, a new acquaintance with whom he does not share political conviction." Hearing this, Itō was strongly impressed by Mutsu's insight. Meanwhile, Hoshi marveled, "Mr. Mutsu is someone who really knows me."

This is another episode from which one can detect the scale of Itō as an individual. Compared to the standard of discourse among politicians and other leaders in Japan today, the level of intellectual dialogue between Itō and Mutsu is admirable.

Hoshi Tōru: Speaker of the House

Although Hoshi was once again arrested for violating the code of publication, he was released in 1889 on a general pardon at the occasion of the promulgation of the Meiji Constitution. He was also able to regain his lawyer's license.

Hoshi happened to be traveling abroad during the first general election, in which he had his proxy run instead, but he was elected to the House of Representatives in the second general election. Partly thanks to Mutsu's indirect maneuvering, Hoshi was elected to Speaker of House of Representatives. Taking advantage of this position, he remained thoroughly ruthless toward the cabinet of Matsukata, who had shamelessly interfered in the second general election. Hoshi's House of Representatives passed a cabinet impeachment bill, which, under normal conditions, would necessitate the dissolution of the House of Representatives, but nobody wished for another election. No new budget proposal by the Matsukata cabinet passed the House of Representatives, exposing the government to merciless abuse by opposition parties throughout the Diet's session. In the end, Matsukata resigned as prime minister.

To replace the Matsukata cabinet, a so-called Meiji Restoration Builders Cabinet was formed, with Itō Hirobumi as prime minister and Mutsu Munemitsu as foreign minister, to face Hoshi's House of Representatives. Hoshi conspired with Mutsu to pass the last military budget proposal in order to prepare for the imminent First Sino-Japanese War while still maintaining a tough face vis-à-vis the government on the surface.

While Hoshi was steadily making necessary arrangements within the House of Representatives for a revision of the unequal treaties—the next and ultimate concern of Mutsu—he was expelled from the house for a trifle that could hardly justify such treatment. Behind this affair was hostility against the arrogant and insolent Hoshi, particularly among members of Kaishintō, where he had countless enemies. Also, although this should be counted as one of Hoshi's virtues, Hoshi's open support of the government's military budget and his pursuit of a revision of the unequal treaties, based on his own convictions about national prosperity, defense, and independence, gave other anti-*han*-clique parties, which bigotedly believed they were there to oppose whatever the government had proposed, a convenient excuse to expel Hoshi.

Breakup of Kenseitō

During the First Sino-Japanese War, Hoshi was dispatched to Seoul as legal advisor to the Korean government. Then, starting in 1896, he was appointed Japanese minister to the United States in Washington, DC for two and a half years.

When Jiyūtō and Shimpotō merged to form Kenseitō, giving birth to the Ōkuma-Itagaki cabinet, Hoshi returned to Japan against instructions from the Foreign Ministry, believing that his time in Japanese politics had finally come. Members of the former Jiyūtō faction within Kenseitō negotiated with Ōkuma to appoint Hoshi to foreign minister. Ōkuma was apprehensive of Hoshi, however, and would not give in. Seeing that negotiations were deadlocked, Hoshi resorted to drastic actions.

Prior to the Kenseitō party convention scheduled for November 1, 1898 (thirty-first year of Meiji), Hoshi made his move. First, he had the former Jiyūtō faction within Kenseitō propose the dissolution of Kenseitō. Next, he convened an extraordinary party convention among only former Jiyūtō faction members on October 29, just three days before the scheduled party convention, at which participants decided on the dissolution of Kenseitō. Immediately after this, Hoshi held the inaugural convention of the new Kenseitō, which was established by former members of Jiyūtō. Since the party headquarters had belonged to Jiyūtō, the belongings of the former Shimpotō faction were removed from the building and piled up on the roadside. Members of the former Shimpotō faction were naturally furious and rushed to party headquarters, only to be driven off by dozens of defenders in kendo (Japanese fencing) protectors who were armed with wooden swords.

This was the incident that triggered the fall of the Ōkuma-Itagaki cabinet.

Rikken-Seiyūkai

Now Hoshi was again in sole command, and he set about working out a collaboration with the Yamagata cabinet that had replaced the Ōkuma-Itagaki one. Hoshi had no other choice but to side with the government this time because he had just high-handedly expelled former Shimpotō members from Kenseitō.

Given the international situation of the time, facing the southbound advance of Russia, it was only natural for Hoshi to render the government every cooperation he could muster. In retrospect, we can see that it was the military expansion plan drafted by Hoshi, in the course of which he made great compromises with the Yamagata cabinet, and the land tax increase plan to support it that finally made Japan financially ready for the Russo-Japanese War. In fact, it is believed that Hoshi decided to align with Yamagata because Itō had advised him to do so, saying: "At this point, it would be beneficial for you to gain the trust of both the government and people by cooperating with the government."

Given Yamagata's aversion to party politics, however, the Hoshi-Yamagata partnership was nothing more than a matter of convenience, utterly incomparable to the partnerships between Itō and Mutsu and between Mutsu and Hoshi. Therefore, it was only natural for the newly established Kenseitō to keep its distance from Yamagata and propose a partnership with Itō.

Kenseitō leaders had at first hoped to invite Itō to become party president. But Itō held fast to his wish to establish a completely new party. Consequently, on August 25, 1900, the founding of Rikken-Seiyūkai was declared.

In his declaration of this new party, Itō once again stressed the spirit of the Meiji Constitution, which he had drafted: cabinet members were to be appointed by the emperor, not by political parties. While some former members of Jiyūtō complained that a compromise of this magnitude was tantamount to total submission to Itō, Hoshi had the following to say in his August 27 speech: "Now that Lord Itō has decided to throw himself into our party, let us welcome him open-heartedly. This is the best way to conduct parliamentary politics in Japan. Certain words in Lord Itō's declaration are nothing but trifles."

It took someone of Hoshi's caliber to enable the foundation of Rikken-Seiyūkai. Hoshi also said in later days that "If a political party continues to expand its powers, it will be able to form a cabinet," which soon proved correct. Although both Mutsu and Hoshi had relied on the flexibility of Itō, they both chose to take concrete steps toward the remote goal of accomplishing a parliamentary democracy in Japan, which was far beyond the imagination of Itō. For his part, Itō kept on acquiescing to the progress made by Mutsu and Hoshi as each step unfolded. It was through this steady process that parliamentary democracy in Japan was eventually accomplished.

Hoshi's Legacy

Although Hoshi initially joined the Itō-Rikken-Seiyūkai cabinet, he was forced to resign on suspicion of bribery. In light of the political situation in those days, however, this was just part of transient political bargaining. Hoshi's political influence within Rikken-Seiyūkai had already become so enormous that nobody dared to challenge him. Had Hoshi survived, it would most certainly have been him, not Hara Takashi, who formed the first genuine party cabinet in Japan.

Conventional history books describe Hoshi as a master of bribery and corruption. Both in terms of their upbringings and their aggressive dispositions, Hoshi appeared to share a lot in common with Tanaka Kakuei, the plutocratic prime minister of postwar Japan. Both of them uninhibitedly and shamelessly manipulated Japanese politics with the power of money and the force of numbers they had bought with money—totally free from the diffidence or pretentiousness of upper-class gentlemen.

In contrast to Tanaka, who left a huge private fortune, all Hoshi left were heavy debts, but his words and deeds were unforgivable from the viewpoint of the Japanese people in those days, when the tradition of the code of the samurai still lingered.

Hoshi was stabbed to death in June 1901 (thirty-fourth year of Meiji) by Iba Sōtarō. Iba, son of an Edo swordmanship instructor, was a reputable gentleman with a good education and social status, someone who did not appear suspicious when he approached Hoshi. Iba had long loathed Hoshi, who was, in his judgment, "polluting Edo's samurai culture." But it was a speech by Hoshi that Iba had read five days earlier that made him decide to kill Hoshi.

In this fatal speech, Hoshi criticized traditional Confucian teaching and stressed the need for educational reform, stating that "It is inevitable for a person of promise to have a flaw or two. It is not wise to discard anybody with a flaw and enumerate in textbooks only the histories of those who might have been clean and spotless but totally idle." This was a naked confession of Hoshi's lifelong conviction, and in that sense, it can be regarded as Hoshi's verbal will. But it made Iba greatly indignant because, in his eyes, it was a prescription to "demoralize students all over Japan."

On June 2, 1901, the same month Hoshi was assassinated, the Katsura cabinet was formed. Komura would soon join the cabinet as its foreign minister. The Katsura cabinet was not a party cabinet.

After Hoshi's assassination, his obsession with parliamentary democracy was succeeded by Hara Takashi of Rikken-Seiyūkai. Hara, like Hoshi, was a disciple of Mutsu, and Hoshi had pinned his hopes on Hara.

Russia's Eastbound Advance

—Russian Method of Establishing Faits Accomplis through Violence and Smooth Talk—

The Farther Away the Border the Better

In 1853, the year Commodore Perry's fleet reached Uraga, the Russian admiral Yevfimy Putyatin arrived in Nagasaki. And in 1858 and 1860 Russia annexed the Amur River basin from which it had once withdrawn following the Treaty of Nerchinsk in 1689.

Seen from a long-term, historical perspective, these moves by Russia were part of the Western powers' eastbound advancement since the Age of Discovery, which had finally reached the eastern edge of the Eurasian continent in the mid-nineteenth century. And Russia, which had advanced eastward on the Eurasian continent, encountered the United States, which had reached the Pacific coast, the western end of the New World, in Japan, which was located at the eastern edge of East Asia.

The Russian eastbound advance, however, had a different historical background from the advances by other European powers. Its original objective was liberation from the yoke of Tatar, which Russia accomplished in 1552 when it conquered the Khanate of Kazan and reached the shore of the Volga River. Ferdinand Magellan had already landed on the Philippine archipelago thirty years earlier (1521), while Portuguese matchlock guns had reached Japan's Tanegashima Island (種子島) ten

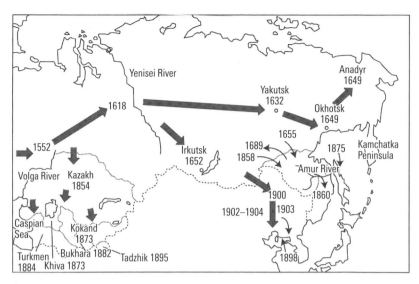

Yenisei River

Anadyr
1649

Yakutsk
1632

Okhotsk
1649

1618

1655

1552

Irkutsk
1652

1689
1858

1875

Kamchatka
Peninsula

Volga River Kazakh
1854

Amur River

Caspian
Sea

Kokand
1873

1900
1902–1904

1860
1903

Turkmen
1884

Bukhara 1882
Khiva 1873

Tadzhik 1895

1898

Russia's expansion

years earlier (1543). In other words, Russia was by a long way a latecomer to the region.

For the next half-century, the Russians continued to fight Tatars to further their eastbound movement. They conquered western Siberia, reaching the Yenisei River in 1618. After the Tatars ceased to resist, the Russians sped up their eastward advancement, as if marching into a no man's land, in search of the products of the Siberian woods, particularly furs that fetched a high price. Russian exploration parties reached Yakutsk in 1632, and in 1649 they reached Anadyr, the northeastern tip of Siberia, across from the North American continent via the Bering Sea. Around the time Japan closed its doors to the outside world in 1639, the world had already undergone remarkable geopolitical changes.

Russia's expansion was originally a defensive move to ensure its survival. In a situation in which the Russians were dwelling in a vast steppe region with no natural obstacles but under constant threat from the pillaging Tatars, it was vital for the Russians to establish a border as far away as possible. Furthermore, the farther away the border, the easier it was for them to defend their newly acquired territory. Russia was therefore forever expanding its territory for the sake of self-defense.

Tsar Nikolai I once declared, "In the land where the Russian flag is once raised, it should never come down." In 1858, seven years before the north bank of the Amur River became Russian territory, the Russian officer Newelskoi went up the river, landed on its north bank, raised the Russian flag, and named the river Nikolayevsk after the tsar. Because this act was a violation of the Treaty of Nerchinsk, the Russian government was compelled to court-martial Newelskoi in order to prevent a confrontation with Qing—a situation Russia could ill afford given the mounting tensions on its European front. The tsar made the above declaration when he intervened in the court-martial to grant amnesty to Newelskoi. The tsar's declaration is a well-known statement that, at the time, caused quite a stir throughout Europe.

While this statement clearly reflects the imperialistic climate of Europe at the time, behind it was Russia's traditional zeal to expand its territory as much as possible and whenever it could.

Discrepancy between Russia's Words and Deeds

One of the problems I encountered when analyzing Russia's policies for this chapter was the frequent discrepancy between its official statements and its actual conduct. Reading the Russian government's statements in chronological order, one gets the impression that Russia never had any intention of invading neighboring territories. On many occasions, however, Russia ended up expanding its territory. There was certainly a rivalry between the moderates and the hardliners within the Russian government, and a few of the government's decisions could actually be explained as the result of the influence of these hardliners due to situational developments or sheer coincidence. Looking at the entire flow of events, however, it is undeniable that Russia constantly invaded foreign territories, although it also employed peaceful expansion where possible.

As one possible approach to objectively reviewing the discrepancy between Russia's words and its actions, let me quote the portion on Russia's scheme in Central Asia from Henry Kissinger's *Diplomacy*:

> The same pattern was repeated again and again. Each year, Russian troops would penetrate deeper into the heart of Central Asia. Great Britain would ask for an explanation and receive all kinds of

assurances that the tsar did not intend to annex one square meter of land. At first, such soothing words were able to put matters to rest. But, inevitably, another Russian advance would reopen the issue. For instance, after the Russian army occupied Samarkand (in present-day Uzbekistan) in May 1868, Gorchakov told the British Ambassador, Sir Andrew Buchanan, "that the Russian Government not only did not wish, but that they deeply regretted, the occupation of that city, and he was assured that it would not be permanently retained." Samarkand, of course, remained under Russian sovereignty until the collapse of the Soviet Union in 1991, more than a century later.

In 1872, the same charade was repeated a few hundred miles to the southeast with respect to the principality of Khiva on the border of present-day Afghanistan. Count Shuvalov, the tsar's aide-de-camp, was sent to London to reassure the British that Russia had no intention of annexing additional territory in Central Asia:

> Not only was it far from the intention of the emperor to take possession of Khiva, but positive orders had been prepared to prevent it, and directions given that conditions imposed should be such as could not in any way lead to a prolonged occupation of Khiva.

These assurances had hardly been uttered when word arrived that Russian General Kaufmann had crushed Khiva and imposed a treaty, which was the dramatic opposite of Shuvalov's assertions.

In 1875, these methods were applied to Kokand, another principality on the border of Afghanistan. On this occasion, Chancellor Gorchakov felt some need to justify the gap between Russia's assurances and its actions. Ingeniously, he devised an unprecedented distinction between unilateral assurances (which, according to his definition, had no binding force) and formal, bilateral engagements. "The Cabinet in London," he wrote in a note, "appears to derive, from the fact of our having on several occasions spontaneously and amicably communicated to them our views with respect to Central Asia, and particularly our firm resolve not to pursue a policy of conquest or annexation, a conviction that we have contracted definite engagements toward them in regard to this matter." In other words, Russia would insist on a free hand in Central Asia, would set its own limits, and not be bound even by its own assurances.[1]

This is indeed an amazing passage. While admitting that he had sponta-neously and amicably communicated to the British government Russia's firm resolve not to pursue a policy of conquest or annexation with respect to Central Asia, on several occasions, Gorchakov claimed the British gov-ernment appeared to believe what he had told them even though no com-mitment had been made in the official document. If this sort of sophistry should be accepted, there would be no more trust in words, which are so fundamental to human society.

With respect to its commitment to withdraw its troops from Manchuria in 1902, Russia dared to continue the occupation while violating the for-mal treaty with Qing. In this case, it did not seem to matter to the Russians whether the pledge had been made by a verbal commitment or in the form of a formal treaty.

Now that we have a clearer picture of Russian's behavioral pattern, all we need to do to review Russia's policies and activities in the Far East is to accurately trace what actually happened. Russia might have acted upon the unintended consequences of rivalry with neighboring countries or due to the political domination by the hawks over the doves within Russia. As far as the analysis of Russia's Far Eastern policies in those days is con-cerned, I daresay textual verification of these "historical facts" would be a waste of time.

Russia's Approach to Japan's Northern Frontier

As previously mentioned, Russia's explorers had already reached the deep eastern region of Siberia by the mid-seventeenth century. It took them almost the entire eighteenth century to further advance and conquer the Kamchatka Peninsula. Natives on the peninsula were fierce and cun-ning, and they quickly mastered the use of firearms to stubbornly resist

---

1   Henry A. Kissinger, *Diplomacy* (New York: Simon & Schuster, 1994), 151–52.

the invaders. This was why it took Russia half a century just to set their hand to the management of the Kamchatka Peninsula, even though its whereabouts had long been known. It was Atlak, the cavalier leader of the Cossacks, who relentlessly pillaged the local people and accomplished the task of conquering the peninsula. Atlak succeeded in invading deep into the peninsula in 1698. Natives continued their resistance, however, oftentimes sinking the entire peninsula into a state of anarchy. It thus took another hundred years before Russian rule was firmly established there.

The first half of those one hundred years coincided with the reign of Peter the Great (1689–1725). Management of the North Pacific was the grand enterprise Peter the Great had envisioned late in his life after accomplishing the unification of Russia. Although the tsar passed away soon after he signed the imperial order for exploration of the North Pacific, his carefully planned enterprise was passed on to his successors after his death. It was through this endeavor that Vitus Bering discovered what became known as the Bering Sea and the North American continent, and Martin Spanberg was ordered to explore the Japanese archipelago. Peter the Great was also interested in the Kuril Islands (千島列島), to which an exploration party was dispatched.

Departing Kamchatka in 1739, Spanberg sailed southwestward toward Japan and cast anchor near the Oshika Peninsula (牡鹿半島) in northeast Japan and the Bōsō Peninsula (房総半島) near Edo. His travel documents match the record on the Japanese side: Spanberg never took provocative actions and presented vodka in exchange for drinking water and perishables wherever he visited. Needless to say, the purpose of his visit was to gather information and, ultimately, contribute to the expansion of Russian territory. In his trip report, he stated that Russia could annex the northern part of the Kuril Islands as its territory if the Russian fleet could act in concert without being dispersed.

Whenever Russia decided to expand its territory, it made thorough preparations. These preparations began with an exhaustive study of the situation on the targeted land. For this purpose, Russia trained explorers to be proficient in the language of the targeted land. The Japanese language school that Peter the Great founded in 1705 was, undoubtedly, the first school for Japanese language studies in the world.

This school searched for Japanese sailors who were cast ashore on the Kamchatka Peninsula and compelled them to become Japanese instructors. Its first instructor was Denbei (cast ashore in 1696) from Osaka, who was succeeded by Sanima (cast ashore in 1710) and then Gonza and Sōza (cast ashore in 1729).

Therefore, by the time Perry and Putyatin arrived in Japan in succession, Russia had far more knowledge about Japan than any other country. This tradition still lingers in the excellence of Japanese studies in today's Saint Petersburg.

Subsequently, throughout the eighteenth century, Russia continued to explore the Kuril Islands. Some exploration parties occasionally spent winters on Urup Island, but they failed to settle on the island because they were ejected by hostile natives.

The Japanese side, for its part, was concerned about the frequent appearance of Russians on the northern frontier even though it had absolutely no idea of the grand scheme of Peter the Great. In 1784, Kudō Heisuke, a physician affiliated with the Sendai-*han*, compiled a two-volume *Akaezo Fūsetsu-ko*, an account of the Russians' advance to Japan's northern frontier that was supplemented with what he had learned from those who had studied Western sciences. Kudō submitted his work to a cabinet member of the shogunate that same year.

In 1785, the Tokugawa government dispatched an expedition party to explore the northern frontier (Ezochi; 蝦夷地), including the Kuril and Sakhalin Islands. Although a variety of new discoveries were made on these islands by this expedition, the shogunate's scheme to put Ezochi under its control was derailed with the fall of Tanuma Okitsugu (田沼意次), *rōjū* (senior counselor) of the Tokugawa government.

The principle reason behind the shogunate's decision to give up on placing Ezochi under its management was the poor prospects for valuable local products or any benefit from trade. Russia, in contrast, regarded the furs from sea animals in the North Pacific as a vital source of income and further advanced its control of the Aleutian Islands. In 1799, Russia founded the Russian American Company, a state-sponsored trading company modeled after Britain's East India Company, and granted it full authority to establish colonies on the Kamchatka Peninsula and the Alaskan seashore across the Bering Sea. The company was also given partial military and judiciary authority.

Because the ultimate concern of the Russian American Company was to secure the sea route to Qing, which was a major market for furs, and to obtain a supply source for the resource-scant North Pacific region, it was imperative for the company to approach Japan.

Drastic Change: From Amity to Armed Assault

In 1803, Nikolai Petrovich Rezanov, advisor to the tsar and the de facto owner of the Russian American Company, was appointed by Tsar Alexander I as visiting ambassador extraordinary and plenipotentiary to Japan. Rezanov headed for Japan, armed with the tsar's personal letter and bountiful offerings, half a century ahead of Commodore Perry's arrival in Uraga. Even though Rezanov was only on an unofficial mission for the Russian American Company, this expensive trip was fully funded by the imperial coffers, and Rezanov's ships were allowed to hoist the flag of the Russian navy. The tsar himself visited Rezanov's fleet at the port, which stirred people's interest in joining the mission, so much so that officials were compelled to decline their offers. Volunteers included a number of scholars and physicians, including the German naturalists Wilhelm Gottlief Tilesius von Tilenau and Georg Heinrich von Langsdorff, as well as Johann Caspar Horner, a Swiss physicist and astronomer.

This was an indication of the zeal and eagerness to explore the unknown since the period of the Age of Discovery.

When the mission arrived in Nagasaki in southern Japan in 1804, Rezanov reported to the magistrate of Nagasaki that Russians had escorted Japanese seamen who had been shipwrecked and that they wished to establish friendly relations with Japan. But this mission proved futile. Members of the mission were prohibited from landing. After being confined to uncomfortable days onboard a ship for six long months, mission members were told that Japan would, after all, uphold its policy of seclusion and they were ordered to return to Russia. Thus, the mission left Japan empty-handed.

While, admittedly, there was nothing else Japan could do at that time, objectively speaking, it was a regrettable outcome for Rezanov. Shiba Kōkan (司馬江漢), master of Western learning and Western painting, denounced the shogunate's handling of the mission as "rude and arrogant" and lamented: "Rezanov was an envoy of the tsar of Russia. Is the tsar of Russia any different from the ruler of our country? Courtesy is the first lesson to be learned in human society. Failing to show courtesy to Rezanov, he and his fellow Russians must now regard us as vulgar as a beast. How deplorable it is." Indeed, it is not hard to imagine that Rezanov must have completely lost face in the eyes of the tsar.

When Rezanov returned to Kamchatka in 1805, he proposed to the tsar that, this time, Russia coerce Japan into opening trade with Russia by intimidating it with force. Rezanov instructed his subordinates to prepare for such action even though he knew the tsar would never give his permission. While documents do not reveal why Rezanov was so pessimistic about the tsar's response to his request, it was only natural that the tsar could not pay any attention to the Far East because Russia was in the midst of a war with Napoleon's France, and it was the eve of the Battle of Austerlitz in 1805.

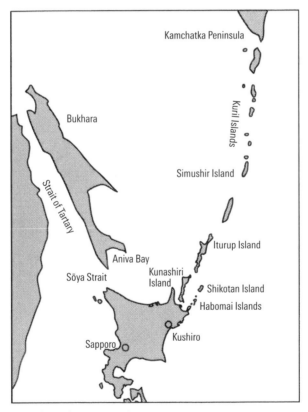

Japan's northern extremity

Lieutenant N. A. Khvostov, who Rezanov had ordered to attack Japan, went ahead with the assault on Japan while Rezanov remained undecided. In September 1806, Khvostov's party landed on Sakhalin Island at Aniva Bay and raided the outpost of the Matsumae-*han*. The party abducted keepers, who were watching the facility during the fishing off-season, looted food and furniture, and burned down all the buildings after announcing that Sakhalin Island was the territory of the Russian tsar. Then, in 1807, Khvostov landed on Iturup Island and there repeated the assault he had launched the previous year. In subsequent years, Khvostov raided Sakhalin Island again and repeatedly assaulted Japanese vessels off the island of Hokkaido, looting their cargoes.

Despite these attacks, the Tokugawa shogunate's policy of seclusion was upheld until Commodore Perry's gunboat diplomacy. Perry led his fleet deep into the Bay of Edo instead of to the northern frontier as Russia had done. It was, therefore, the Anglo-American world that seized the initiative in opening Japan's door to the outside world.

Russia's Full-Scale Eastbound Advance

One noteworthy event that took place during this Russian offensive was the demarcation of the Russian-Japanese border. Since the series of raids by Khvostov, Russo-Japanese relations had deteriorated. Japan became wary of Russia's conduct. Thus, when the vessel commanded by the Russian Navy Commander Vasily Golovnin visited Kunashir Island in 1811, he was taken prisoner by the Japanese. During his interrogation, Golovnin insisted the Russian government had nothing to do with Khvostov's conduct. This made the Japanese side decide to demand, as a condition Golovnin's release, an official announcement by the Russian government about Khvostov's rash acts. In response, the Russian government sent Petr Ivanovich Rikord, governor of Kamchatka, to Hakodate to hand-deliver an official document proclaiming that Khvostov had not acted on the Russian government's order and that Golovnin should be sent back to Russia.

Because of these incidents, cabinet members of the shogunate recognized the need to establish the border with Russia. The two governments agreed that the land south of Iturup Island was Japanese territory, the land north of Shimoshiri was Russian territory, and the zone around Urap and the surrounding islands would be considered neutral territory. There was no reference to Sakhalin Island. In his masterpiece *Kindai Nippon gaikoku kankeishi* (History of Modern Japan's Foreign Relations), the Taishō-Shōwa historian Tabohashi Kiyoshi (田歩橋潔) attributes the lack of reference to Sakhalin to the Japanese assumption in those days that the island was naturally a Japanese territory because a small Japanese colony had been established and no Russian colony had ever existed there. Already well aware of the importance of Sakhalin Island, the Russians decided to remain silent and took advantage of this oversight. Bringing up the topic of Sakhalin Island probably simply did not occur to the Japanese side.

It was the Japanese explorer Mamiya Rinzō (間宮林蔵) who had discovered that Sakhalin was an island and not connected to the Asian continent. Thus, it was indisputable even in those days that Sakhalin was a Japanese territory on all accounts, including its discovery, exploration, and settlement. Nevertheless, in later days, Russia was able to take advantage of the fact that there was no reference to this island in the bilateral agreement. For the subsequent half-century leading up to the Meiji Restoration, Russia launched a full-scale attempt to advance to the Far East via the Amur River.

Since the Treaty of Nerchinsk, the territories north of the Amur River and east of the mouth of the Argun River had belonged to Qing. Because the great river of Amur, which runs through eastern Siberia from west to east, was the perfect route for Russia to reach the Pacific, its basin was an object of avid desire for Russia. Under the administration of Governor-General Nikolai Muravyov-Amursky of Irkutsk and Yeniseysk, Lieutenant Colonel Gennadi Iwanowitch Newelskoi somewhat arbitrarily explored the Pacific coast of eastern Siberia and founded Nikolayevsk-on-Amur, the first Russian settlement in the region, in 1847. Realizing the strategic importance of Sakhalin Island at the mouth of the Amur River during this expedition, Newelskoi proposed to the czar that Russia should occupy the island. This proposal received imperial sanction.

When the Crimean War erupted in 1853, Muravyov-Amursky openly sent troops and immigrants to the northern bank of the Amur River, making the area a de facto Russian territory. Muravyov-Amursky claimed the action was necessary to defend the Far East from British and French attacks. Although Russia subsequently negotiated with Qing on the cession of this area to Russia "in order to defend the mouth of the Amur River from the invasion by third countries," Qing did not concur. However, taking advantage of the confusion caused by the Nian Rebellion and the Treaty of Tianjin in 1858, Russia expanded its occupied territory in one stretch, all the way to Primorsky Krai.

In the course of his forays, Muravyov-Amursky discovered what came to be called the Peter the Great Gulf. There, he constructed a town by the name of Vladivostok, which means to "possess the East." One reason why it took such a long time for Muravyov-Amursky's scheme to receive imperial sanction was that Russian Prime-Minister-cum-Foreign-Minister Karl Robert von Nesselrode prioritized control of the Near East, including the Dardanelles, as the central policy of Russia. Nesselrode's ambition was crippled, however, by the eruption of the Crimean War (1853–56). After constructing Vladivostok, Muravyov-Amursky proudly gave names to points inside the Peter the Great Gulf, such as Bosporus and Golden Horn in the east. This must have been the expression of his pride and fervor at having realized the Russian dream of advancing to the open sea in the east, which had failed in the west.

Thus, around the time of the Meiji Restoration, Russia was already well prepared to make further advances in the Far East.

Commodore Perry's Fleet and Russian Vessels

The US government's plan to dispatch Commodore Perry's fleet to Uraga in 1853 had been openly announced one year earlier. Although Rezanov's attempt to establish trade relations with Japan half a century earlier had been a complete failure, the Russian government hoped it could be successful this time when working with the United States. Thus, the Russian government immediately appointed Count Yevfimy Putyatin, vice admiral and chamberlain to Tsar Nikolai I, as commanding-admiral-of-the-East-Asian-fleet-cum-visiting-ambassador to Japan, hoping he would be a good match for Perry.

Believing that a Russian-American joint expedition could double the pressure on Japan, Russia proposed a concerted operation with the American fleets. The United States rejected the Russian proposal out of allegiance to its traditional policy that it could not take an offensive act vis-à-vis a third country in cooperation with European powers. Instead, the United States simply instructed Commodore Perry to maintain friendly relations with the Russian fleet.

In terms of knowledge about Japan, Russia was far more advanced than the United States. In contrast to Perry, who, out of his militaristic temperament, kept the participation of civilian experts in his expedition to a minimum, because he thought they might weaken onboard discipline, Putyatin welcomed the participation of Russian scholars of Oriental studies, scholars who were among the best Orientalists in the world at that time. The expedition even included the then minor finance ministry official Ivan Goncharov, who was a writer well known for numerous works, including the widely successful novel *Oblomov*. He had been recommended by the Education Ministry.

The Russian fleet that arrived in Japan a month after the American fleet dropped its anchors in Nagasaki instead of Edo Bay in order to emphasize its intention to comply with Japanese law. In any event, Russia was not yet a prominent naval power and could not dispatch warships comparable to the American fleet, making it impossible for it to conduct gunboat diplomacy even if it had wished to do so.

Every ship in the Russian fleet hung a white flag from its mast with the words *"Oroshia no Fune"* (a Russian ship) written in big letters in Japanese. After the fleet arrived in Nagasaki port, it deliberately took an attitude that contrasted sharply with that of Perry, who tried to intimidate the Japanese. The magistrate of Nagasaki had to admit that "[Russians remain] extremely calm and modest on board, . . . making no action against our law."

Based on the record of his subordinates' conversations with the Russian visitors, the magistrate compiled a proposal on how to deal with Russia, which reads:

Recently, the American fleet has made an uninvited call on Uraga and demonstrated its willingness to resort to war if necessary. Contingent upon our response to its demands, the American fleet seems ready to invade our country. This may be a sign that the United State is conspiring to colonize Japan. It appears that the mission of the current fleet from Russia is to shield Japan from the American troops if they start to attack Japan, purely for the benefit of Japan, and to conclude an eternal relationship of trust with Japan. If we give the

Russians the wrong response, however, they could become a formidable foe. Rich in gold, silver, and copper, the only thing Russia wants from us is grain. As long as we allow Russians to trade with us and sell them grain only in years of good harvest, we can maintain peaceful relations with this country for eternity.

While there is no knowing how much of the above observation was the result of Russian propaganda, the naiveté of the Nagasaki magistrate is simply appalling.

When Russia occupied the north bank of the Amur River, it did so under the pretext of defending itself against invasions by third countries (i.e., Britain and France). When it sought the concession of the Chinese Eastern Railway in Manchuria in later years, Russia also used the pretext of defense against Japan's invasion. This was tantamount to saying, "I will grab this because someone else will grab it otherwise." At the time of Putyatin's mission, too, Russians gave the reason for its presence as defending Japan from a US invasion. But it should be recalled that Russia had proposed a joint operation with the United States for this expedition, which the latter had turned down. Furthermore, to begin with, Russia's naval power at that time was no match whatsoever for the US Navy.

Firm Intention to Occupy Sakhalin Island

It is very difficult to find a rational connection between Russia's ad hoc rhetoric and behavior and its true intentions, as I mentioned earlier when I quoted Kissinger's *Diplomacy*.

Meanwhile, the proposal submitted by the magistrate of Nagasaki had a profound impact on the shogunate cabinet, to the extent that a scheme to "rely on Russia to block the United States" temporarily got the support of a dominant majority within the cabinet. In the end, though, because of consistent opposition from Tokugawa Nariaki, lord of the Mito-*han,* the cabinet did not endorse the scheme.

Tokugawa Nariaki argued that judging from Russia's advance to Sakhalin Island, they should not be deceived by Russia's ostensible goodwill toward Japan. This judgment might have saved Japan from a crisis. It is not hard to imagine that Russia could have demanded not only Sakhalin and the Kuril Islands but possibly also some ports on Hokkaido in compensation, claiming it had repulsed a US invasion.

In assessing the true intentions of Russia, at least during the age of imperialism, simple and straightforward fundamentalists, such as Tokugawa Nariaki in 1853 and Komura on the eve of the Russo-Japanese War, were proven correct. Those who had made more complicated calculations missed the mark. After all, one could predict Russian conduct more accurately by focusing on its overall national interest and not on its complicated rhetoric and behavior, which only confused the issue.

As a matter of fact, even while Putyatin remained in Nagasaki waiting for the shogunate's response, Muravyov-Amursky ordered the establishment of a Russian colony on the shore of Aniva Bay. He also issued orders that the Japanese dwellers along the bay be brought under the protection of the Russian government. On September 20, 1853, Lieutenant Colonel Newelskoi landed on the shore of Aniva Bay, took over the Japanese outpost, and built batteries and a Russian lookout. Hearing this, Putyatin sailed to Aniva Bay in April 1854 and ordered the withdrawal of Russian troops from the colony. Putyatin feared any friction with Japan while he was negotiating with its leaders.

Negotiations for a Russo-Japanese friendship treaty (the Treaty of Shimoda) began in Shimonoseki in November 1854. Putyatin first proposed a border settlement between the two countries and insisted that anywhere north of Itrup Island and Aniva Bay, both of which were Japanese territory, should be Russian territory. In response, the Japanese side demanded the entire Sakhalin Island, up to the mouth of the Amur River, as its territory and would not give in. In the end, it was agreed that the border would be drawn between the islands of Itrup and Urup in the Kuril Islands and that dominion of Sakhalin Island would be left undecided.

This was another occasion in which Japan showed overoptimistic judgment. It would be only natural for a powerful country to have its own way sooner or later if the border demarcation was left undecided. For example, even though the Treaty of Aigun (瑷珲条約) in 1858 stipulated that Primorsky Krai did not belong to either Russia or Qing, the latter was deprived of the territory by Russia within just two years. Because Putyatin's proposal admitted that Aniva Bay would belong to Japan, perhaps the Japanese government should have persisted in insisting on a border demarcation at 50 degrees north latitude, which Kawaji Toshiakira

(川路聖謨), Japanese signee of the Treaty of Shimoda, had initially strongly advocated.

The new Japanese government after the Meiji Restoration belatedly proposed the demarcation of 50 degrees north latitude in 1870, but Russia demanded the entire Sakhalin Island and refused to divide the island. Harry Parkes, British consul general in Japan at the time, pointed out it was already too late to do anything about Sakhalin Island and instead warned Japan about the danger of Russia's southbound advance toward Hokkaido.

Meanwhile, on Sakhalin Island, the harassment of Japanese settlers by Russian immigrants under the protection of the Russian troops became increasingly unruly. The Russians assaulted and raped the Japanese, confiscated their land to construct permanent facilities, and even obstructed efforts by the Japanese to fight a fire at Japanese facilities (the fire was suspected to have been started by Russians) by throwing the fire pumps into the fire.

Although some hardliners in Japan insisted on sending troops to Sakhalin, the argument to prioritize domestic preparedness while maintaining moderate diplomacy had become predominant within the Japanese government since the settlement of the Satsuma Rebellion. Thus, the Treaty of Saint Petersburg was signed between Russia and Japan in 1875, stipulating that Japan give up claims to Sakhalin Island in exchange for undisputed sovereignty of all the Kuril Islands.

The conclusion of this treaty was perhaps inevitable given Russia's firm intention to occupy Sakhalin Island, the circumstances that had generated on the island, and the domestic situation in Japan. It is actually more noteworthy that Russia made a concession to give the Japanese the right to possess the eighteen Kuril Islands leading up to the Kamchatka Peninsula. Russia's concession of islands that the Japanese had never occupied signifies that even Russia had to acknowledge the validity of Japan's historical claim on Sakhalin Island.

Watching for an Opportunity to Occupy Tsushima Island

Another noteworthy development around this time was Russia's territorial interest in Tsushima Island in the middle of the Korea Strait. In February 1861, the Russian consul in Japan informed the Japanese government that the British navy had been secretly surveying the seashores of Tsushima Island and warned that British ambition was unpredictable. Here again, obviously, Russia was playing the same old game—proposing that Russia put Tsushima Island under its protection in order to protect it from British territorial ambition. Around the same time, a Russian naval vessel dropped anchor off Tsushima Island and its crew members landed on it under the pretext of repairing the ship's hull. They constructed barracks on the island and ended up living there. The Russian side demanded cession of a plot on which to construct a fortress.

The fact is, in the late 1860s, Grand Duke Nikolaevich, admiral of the Russian navy, had issued an order to acquire Tsushima Island by lease and use it as the Russian navy's headquarters. The order was based on advice from outposts in the Far East. The naval vessel dropped anchor off Tsushima Island following Grand Duke Nikolaevich's order. Even when the shogunate demanded the withdrawal of crew members from the island, the captain of the vessel would not comply, insisting he and his men were there to discourage British and French territorial ambitions and they would not withdraw unless ordered to do so by their own superiors.

The shogunate negotiated with the Russian consul in Japan, but it did not make any progress. During this negotiation, Britain learned of the incident and dispatched a fleet to Tsushima. This action forced the Russian vessel to depart in July.

Although the Russian documents on this incident are scarce, Russia's intentions were self-evident. As soon as it obtained Primorsky Krai in 1860, Russia must have decided to possess Tsushima in recognition of the strategic value of the Korea Strait.

Katsu Kaishū left the following vivid description of the Russian vessel's conduct:

> When Japanese officials approached the Russian ship in a small boat, sailors got on three dinghies and surrounded them and seized their armor and spears. When the Japanese side approached the ship for negotiation, the Russians welcomed the Japanese officials on board and entertained them with lavish meals but never gave any definite answer to the Japanese inquiries. The Russians left only after they had made a full survey of the bay. But the Russian vessel returned

to Tsushima, and its crew cut down trees on the island without permission from the Japanese authority. When the Japanese patrol boat approached the Russian vessel to negotiate, its sailors pumped sea water at the Japanese boat. The Russian ship that came to Tsushima most recently dropped anchor, claiming it needed repair. Crew members landed on the island and constructed what looked like barracks, and they did not appear to leave anytime soon. . . . At this moment, Tsushima was effectively occupied by the Russians.

Given the situation, Katsu wrote that he had asked the British consul in Japan for help. This consul instructed the British consul in Beijing to dispatch the British fleet to Tsushima, which finally forced the Russian vessel to withdraw.

This incident was a typical example of the maneuvers Russia used to expand its territory under the pretext of protecting the territory in question from invasion by other countries. Russia pursued the establishment of one fait accompli after another using both violence and smooth talk.

Devious but Good-Natured Bumpkin

This Russian behavior seems to be incongruent with the good nature of individual Russians, and this puzzles me. Observing the behavior outlined above as well as many other utterances and behaviors of the Russians, you get the impression that all Russians are cruel, ruthless, and cunning, and hide venomous fangs behind smiling faces. But when you actually get to know individual Russians, they do not necessarily fit this impression.

Let me quote here an observation I once heard from Hōgen Shinsaku, who, in my judgment, knew more about Russian affairs than anyone else in the Japanese Foreign Ministry. Hōgen said: "Simply put, the Russian is a bumpkin. A country man is good natured and devious. He is cunning and kind at the same time. I know how it is because I am a bumpkin myself."

For the urban intelligentsia, consistency in logic and word is a minimum requirement. A country man, in contrast, would not say unpleasant things to a person's face. He is inclined to say something that is pleasing to the listener's ears. Nevertheless, he is fully aware of what is and what is not beneficial to him, and he has no intention of compromising his gains.

Needless to say, it never occurs to him that he may sometimes have to sacrifice his own interests for the sake of such an abstract concept as a gentleman's agreement. He will not hesitate to get hold of whatever is available to him. Thus, he always says one thing and does the opposite. Gorchakov's words in the Kissinger quote cited earlier should be interpreted in this context.

After these incidents, Russo-Japanese relations went into a state of calm that lasted until the First Sino-Japanese War. However, it might be more accurate to say that during this period Russia devoted itself to the construction and management of military bases in newly acquired colonies on the shores of the Amur River, Primorsky Krai, and Sakhalin Island. It also prepared infrastructure for an impending full-scale advance to the Far East. It constructed the Siberian Railway, connecting mainland Russia and the Far East, and built up two blue-water fleets in Europe and the Far East.

Russia's Occupation of Manchuria

—Given Russia's Intention, War Seems Inevitable—

Advancing Russian Army

"We must make Manchuria a second Bukhara." This was what Russian Minister of War Aleksei Nikolaevich Kuropatkin said to Sergei Yulyevich Witte (who later became Komura's counterpart in the negotiations for the Treaty of Portsmouth) when the Boxer Rebellion erupted in 1899. Bukhara was a Khanate located on the borders of present-day Afghanistan and Uzbekistan, and it neighbored the Khanates of Khiva and Kokando. Its capital city, Samarkand, was captured by Russia in 1868, the year of the Meiji Restoration, while Bukhara had only been a Russian territory since 1882; it remained so until the collapse of the Soviet Union in 1991.

Kuropatkin actually sounded much milder on this issue in his own memoir. Witte, on his part, was scheming to acquire Manchuria peacefully—in principle without resorting to military might—by manipulating Li Hongzhang, whom he had bought over with bribery.

Judging from the way Russia had occupied the Khanates of Khiva and Kokando, however, these episodes are minor details that are insignificant in light of the overall turn of events. Russia's ambition for Manchuria was as clear as day.

On July 9, 1900, the Russian army was ordered to advance to Manchuria, thus taking advantage of the Boxer Rebellion.

Having crossed the border in late July-August, the Russian army seized Qiqihar on August 26, Changchun on September 21, Jilin on September 23, Liaoyang on September 26, and Mukden on October 1. One city after another, Russia put all of Manchuria under its control.

As always, Russia announced it had no intention of occupying Manchuria permanently. On September 1, the Russian minister to Japan, Alexander Izvolsky, hand-delivered the note on Russia's policy toward Qing to Foreign Minister Aoki Shūzō (青木周蔵). The note contained statements that can be summarized as follows: "Our conduct this time was a temporary measure that we had to take due to circumstances beyond our control rather than being planned. It was not at all a part of our policy . . . As long as the security of the Siberian Railway is guaranteed . . . and its operations are not obstructed by other countries, Russia will not fail to withdraw its troops from the territory of Qing."[1] Despite this note, Komura, who was at that time the Japanese minister to Russia, sent a telegram to the Foreign Ministry in Tokyo as early as September 24, observing that "While Russia's immediate concern might be the security of the railroad, I suspect it will end up controlling Manchuria completely and permanently."[2] Komura also sent another lengthy telegram on October 19, predicting that "While Russia might withdraw its regular troops from Manchuria pro forma after the Boxer Rebellion is settled, Manchuria will effectively remain occupied by the Russian army."[3]

At this stage, Komura had already started pursuing a scheme to barter with Russia to gain back Manchuria in exchange for Korea. This was the scheme elder Japanese statesmen had determined to pursue as a last line of defense up until the eve of the Russo-Japanese War.

On July 20, the first day of Russia's invasion of Manchuria, Komura

---

1   *Nippon gaikō bunsho-Hokushin jihen no chū* [Boxer Rebellion: Documents of Japanese foreign policy, vol. 2], 337, quoted in Tsunoda Jun, *Manshū mondai to kokubō hōshin* [Manchurian issue and national defense policy] (Hara Shobō: Tokyo, 1967), 24–25. Text in Japanese was translated into English by the author.

2   *Nippon gaikō bunsho-Hokushin jihen no jō* [Boxer Rebellion: Documents of Japanese foreign policy, vol. 1], 735–36, quoted in Tsunoda, *Manshū mondai, 26.*

3   Tsunoda, *Manshū mondai,* 31–32.

submitted a proposal to the Japanese government that it was high time for Japan and Russia to demarcate their spheres of influence so each country could have a free hand in Korea and Manchuria respectively. On October 2, Komura visited Witte while the latter was vacationing in Yalta to sell this idea directly. Komura believed it was beneficial for Japan to secure its free hand in Korea in exchange for the early recognition of Russia's occupation of Manchuria now that Russia obviously intended to seize Manchuria no matter what it proclaimed.

Witte, however, did not buy this argument. In the conversation with Komura in Yalta, Witte responded as follows:

> It would be easy for Russia to occupy Manchuria if it wished to do so. Whether Russia occupies it or not depends solely on Russia's will. At this point Russia has no intention to do so. But circumstances beyond our control might force us to annex Manchuria as our territory, and when that happens, Japan may argue that for its part it would occupy Korea. However, that is not what will actually happen. When Manchuria becomes a Russian territory, Russia's influence on Korea will be much greater than that of Japan. Therefore, Russia cannot allow Japan to harm Korea's independence.[4]

What Witte meant by "Korea's independence" was, of course, a state in which Russia's and Japan's demarcation of their spheres of influence over Korea remained unsettled, enabling Russia to occupy Korea when the chance emerged. This was basically the same tactic that Russia had employed earlier when it left the territorial demarcation of Sakhalin and Primorsky Krai unsettled. Japan had also employed this tactic when it advocated the independence of Korea during the First Sino-Japanese War and the Russo-Japanese War.

On this particular point, Minister Chinda Sutemi (珍田捨巳), who succeeded Komura, made a similar observation in his January 1901 telegram: "Witte holds a hardliner view on Korean affairs. If and when Manchuria becomes a Russian territory, Korea will be a neighboring country sharing

---

4 Kin Masaaki, ed. *Nikkan gaikō shiryō shūsei* [Collection of documents on Japan-Korea diplomatic relations], 8: 406–7, quoted in Tsunoda, *Manshū mondai*, 34–35.

the border with Russia, and Witte seems to believe that this will make Korea all the more important for Russia. Russia's argument for Korea's neutrality is nothing but a temporary façade put forth to leave room to accomplish its ambition in the future."[5] By this time, Komura had already given up on negotiating with Russia and considered confrontation inevitable. Realizing the futility of the Manchuria-Korea bartering scheme, Komura began to confront Russia based on the premise that Manchuria and Korea were inseparable.

Why Russia Hung onto the Korean Peninsula

It would be a waste of time to prove Russian ambition over the Korean Peninsula by referring to Russian documents. This would be as futile as attempting to find North Korea's motivation for its southbound advance at the beginning of the Korean War in its official announcements. It often happens that international situations can be grasped much more accurately through common sense judgment rather than by studying documents.

Compared to North Korea at the time of the Korean War, however, statements made by Russia during this period were generally more audacious. Some of them are worth quoting. For instance, on December 10, 1901, Russian Foreign Minister Vladimir Lamsdorff wrote in his letter to War Minister Kuropatkin, "We should not conclude a new agreement with Japan if it costs us dearly. It would be too costly to give up Korea and allow Japan to take it."[6]

Two months earlier, in October 1901, Tsar Nikolai had the following to say to Prince Heinrich of Prussia, who was visiting Russia at the time: "If Japan attempts to establish a firm foothold in Korea, it will provide Russia with a reason to start a war with Japan. Japan's foothold in Korea is tantamount to the emergence of the Far Eastern version of the Dardanelles

---

5   Tsunoda, *Manshū mondai,* 35.

6   "Lamsdorff Memorandum to the Tsar, December 5, 1901," *The Chinese Social and Political Science Review* (1935): 251–52, quoted in Tsunoda, *Manshū mondai,* 113.

issue, and Russia will never allow that."[7]

In other words, Tsar Nikolai declared that Russia would not allow a situation in which the navigation of Russian vessels through the Korea Strait would be obstructed by the Japanese, thus revealing Russia's wish to control not only the southern part of the Korean Peninsula but also Tsushima Island if the situation allowed. All it takes is common sense to speculate what Russia had conspired. If you put yourself in the shoes of a monarch or a leader of a country in the age of imperialism and study the map of the Far East, you immediately know what you could and should do.

Acting French ambassador to Russia M. Boutiron sent the following observation to Foreign Minister Théophile Delcassé in October 1901:

> It is beyond doubt that Russia would not allow Japan to occupy the Korean Peninsula. If this peninsula falls into the hands of the Japanese, it would nullify as well as deadlock Russia's efforts in the region encompassing Lüshun to Beijing. It would also put Russia's sea traffic from the Liaodong region to Vladivostok at the mercy of Japan, the new owner of the Korea Strait. Russia will undoubtedly seek an opportunity to block Japan's occupation of Korea before the yellow race nation completes its war preparations and forms an alliance of nations that would be harmful to Russia. While Russia may pretend to be indifferent, it will remain very much alert and watch for the best chance.[8]

As a matter of fact, immediately before Russian Foreign Minister Lamsdorff visited Itō Hirobumi in December, he said as much to M. Boutiron: "We need Korea to be neutral. If Japan does not like the expression 'neutral,' we can change the expression—but not the state of affairs. Japan must understand that Russia will never give it Korea. If Korea is not free, all of our strategies in the Far East will be threatened. We are not at all concerned about Japan's economic activities on the Korean Peninsula,

---

7   "Bulow's Note, November 4, 1901," in *Die grosse politik der Europaischen kabinette, 1871–1914.* 19 Band, I Teil, Vol. XVIII, No. 1: 34–35, quoted in Tsunoda, *Manshū mondai,* 113.

8   "Boutiron to Delcassé, October 10, 1901," in *Documents diplomatiques Francais, 1871-1914,* 2 (1): 519–21, quoted in Tsunoda, *Manshū mondai,* 114.

but we want to keep the route between Lüshun and Vladivostok obstacle-free. If Japan does not agree to this, it should be prepared to pay the sacrifice of land and sea battles with Russia."[9] This statement should make it obvious to anyone what Russia had in mind. In fact, any ordinary person with common sense could discern Russia's intention (i.e., the neutrality of the Korean Peninsula was synonymous with Russia's refusal to allow Japan's occupation of the peninsula so that Russia could occupy it once it put Manchuria under its control). With this accomplished, a geographically stable Russian Far East, encompassing Sakhalin, Primorsky Krai, the Korean Peninsula, Manchuria, and the Liaodong Peninsula, would be complete.

Russia's Gateway to the Open Sea

As far as a gateway to the open sea is concerned, Russia is truly a hapless nation; even with the realization of this continental Russian Far East, Russia would not necessarily have free access to the high seas. On its European side, even if it controlled the Dardanelles, Russian vessels could not go out into the Mediterranean Sea, not to mention the Atlantic Ocean, if the British navy controlled the Aegean Sea. Even though some Russian vessels ventured out into the Baltic Sea during the reign of Peter the Great, the Denmark Strait denied their entry to the open sea.

In the Far East, even if Russia controlled the Korean Peninsula, its free sea traffic would be obstructed by the Japanese on Tsushima Island. The Kuril Islands in the north and the Nansei Islands (南西諸島) through Taiwan in the south also blocked Russia's free entry to the open sea.

Russia's geopolitical desire for an exit to the outer seas was partially fulfilled in 1945; during World War II its troops invaded and seized the southern half of the Sakhalin and Kuril Islands despite the Soviet-Japanese Neutrality Pact. Even this route, however, was not navigable during the winter when it was frozen over. Therefore, Russia's desire could have been realized in this corner of the world only if it occupied the northern

---

9   "Boutiron to Delcassé, December 3, 1901," ibid., 649–59, quoted in Tsunoda, *Manshū mondai,* 114–15.

half of Hokkaido Island, as the Soviet government insisted at the time of Japan's defeat in the war.

Thus, Japan's concern about Hokkaido being snatched by Russia at the eruption of the Russo-Japanese War was not groundless. It was indeed a commonsensical judgment on the part of Japan given Russia's geographical constraints.

"Japan must be forever crippled"

If the territorial expansion to secure a gateway to the open seas was indeed Russia's intention, Japan needed to be prepared for the inevitable military clash with Russia. Preparation was easier said than done when facing Russia, which was one of the two superpowers of the time, along with Britain. Japan's leaders must have become horror-struck when they speculated about what would happen to Japan if the country was defeated.

In late June 1904, half a year after the eruption of the Russo-Japanese War, Witte shared the following candid view with British Ambassador Charles Hardinge:

> Since the Russian troops occupied Manchuria, this region has become a de facto protectorate of Russia. In actuality its economy has been in the hands of Russia, which has already obtained preferential rights on all disputed enterprises and privileges. It would be impossible for other Western powers to obtain a similar position in Manchuria even if they tried. . . . Although we have signed an agreement with Qing on the withdrawal of our troops from Manchuria, we never seriously intended to withdraw our forces. Because Japan entered the war with Russia demanding the withdrawal of our troops from Manchuria and equal treatment there, I do not believe the Tsar intends to make concessions on these points when we win the war.[10]

---

10 *British Documents on the Origins of the War, 1898–1914*, eds. George Gooch and Harold Temperley (London: Foreign Office, 1926–38), 4:3, quoted in Tsunoda, *Manshū mondai*, 218.

In other words, from the beginning, Russia had no intention of making any concession to Japan's demands. Moreover, Witte went on to explain what Russia would impose on Japan as the conditions for peace after winning the war, that "apart from the question of absorption of Manchuria . . . opinion is unanimous that Japan must be forever crippled and the predominance of Russia on the Pacific Coast assured. For this purpose, Japan must be forbidden from possessing naval fleets."

Judging from past Russian conduct, making Japan "forever crippled" was only the first step toward the settlement of the issue, rather than Russia's final goal. One can imagine what would have happened to Japan if it had to face the neighboring mighty Russia after being deprived of all of its military capabilities.

According to Winston Churchill's memoir, while President Roosevelt insisted on the unconditional surrender of Japan and Germany at the Yalta Conference in 1945, Premier Stalin of the Soviet Union argued that they could demand whatever they wished from Japan and Germany once the two countries had surrendered.

In Cold War jargon, Russia's intention could be described as the "Finlandization" of Japan. But the Japanese situation could have been much worse than that of Finland. In the crisis toward the end of the Soviet-Finnish "Winter War" of 1940, General Carl Gustaf Emil Mannerheim, who is adored in Finland even today as the hero-savior of the country, insisted on the early conclusion of peace, claiming that "Our troops are still sanguine. Once our military collapses, the last chance for Finland would be completely lost." It was obvious to him that once the national military was gone, the chance for peace or even the independence of Finland would be as well.

It should be noted here that Witte made the above remarks to the ambassador of Britain, Japan's alliance partner. They could therefore be interpreted as Witte's subtle inquiry to Britain about the conditions Russia should impose on Japan after winning the Russo-Japanese War. Witte made no reference to any specific conditions Russia may have desired in order to secure "Russia's superiority on the Pacific coast," such as occupation of Tsushima and Hokkaido and the lease of military ports on Honshu Island. Witte must have constrained himself to a vague discussion of principles in fear of a possible objection or even interference from Britain. As long as Britain tolerated the condition of stripping Japan of all of its combat capabilities, Russia could do anything it wished to Japan. At the same time, predicting that Britain would have no means to interfere with Manchuria and Korea once Japan was defeated, Witte communicated Russia's intention explicitly to the British side.

To fight such a dreadful foe must have taken true fortitude and determination on the part of Japan. It could easily be argued, after Japan's victory in the Russo-Japanese War, that Japan had waged the war to seize Korea and Manchuria, which would be its gateway to advance into the Asian continent. Such a grandiose scheme must, however, have been far from the minds of Japanese leaders on the eve of the war, since they were effectively facing the peril of the loss of national independence.

The Survival of Japan

One can start a war only when one is convinced that evading it is at least as bad as being defeated in it. If Japan does not fight Russia now, the latter will sooner or later advance to the southern tip of the Korean Peninsula. If this happens, and if Russia starts making unreasonable demands on Hokkaido and Tsushima, Japan must confront Russia because these demands would threaten the very survival of Japan. If we end up fighting a war with Russia anyway, we might as well fight it now before Russia's military buildup in the Far East becomes impossibly formidable. This must have been how the thinking went at the time.

Judging the international situation in those days objectively, the above was probably the correct conclusion. Nevertheless, it still took tremendous courage to put this thinking into practice as a policy. There was no better person than Komura to do this.

In retrospect, the year 1901 was the turning point for Russia's fortunes. That year, Itō Hirobumi, according to Alexander Izvolsky almost the only person who could promote a mutual compromise between Russia and Japan, resigned from the prime ministership in May, and Li Hongzhang, whom Russia had got under its thumb, passed away in November. In the Katsura cabinet that succeeded Itō's government, it was Komura who served as foreign minister.

Komura's hard-line view on Russia and his perception of Russia's true intentions was shared by the second-generation Meiji Restoration leaders, including Prime Minister Katsura Tarō and Katō Takaaki, who was foreign minister before and after Komura.

As soon as Russia had nearly completed its occupation of Manchuria, Witte sent a secret envoy to Li Hongzhang with the purpose of making Qing approve the de facto occupation of Manchuria by Russia. As pro-Russia as Li was, he could not quite give in that far and suggested, as a tentative measure, a local agreement on the Russian occupation instead of a formal agreement between the two governments. Consequently, the Second Sino-Russian Secret Treaty was concluded in November 1900. In a nutshell, this treaty stipulated that the Qing troops stationed in Manchuria would be put under the de facto command of Russian generals after being disarmed. Naturally, Qing officials in Manchuria showed reluctance at first. In response, Russia detained the Qing negotiators and demanded unconditional approval of the secret treaty as a condition for their safe return to Mukden. Thus, this secret treaty was finally signed.

Initiation for Japan

In response to the signing of the Second Sino-Russian Secret Treaty, Foreign Minister Katō of the Itō cabinet (in office from October 1900 to May 1901) demanded an explanation from the Russian government. Minister Izvolsky reported to his home office on this incident, analyzing it as a revelation of "a conflict between the moderates within the Japanese government headed by Lord Itō on the one hand and the young bureaucrats headed by Foreign Minister Katō on the other . . . as I have repeatedly called to the attention of the home government."[11]

The Japanese minister to Russia, Chinda Sutemi, executed the order from the foreign minister and demanded an explanation from Russian Foreign Minister Lamsdorff, who replied flatly that "Because the Manchurian issue is a matter between Russia and Qing, the Russian government is not obliged to explain its position on this affair to a third party."[12] Simply put,

---

11 "Izvolsky to Lamsdorff, January 27, 1901," *The Chinese Social and Political Science Review* (January 1935): 577, quoted in Tsunoda, *Manshū mondai*, 46–47.
12 *Nippon gaikō bunsho: Hokushin jihen*, 34: 107, quoted in Tsunoda, *Manshū mondai*, 50.

Lamsdorff's message was that Japan should not meddle with what Russia had agreed on with Qing.

Subsequently, Katō requested support for Japan's protest from the British and German governments, who had advocated the open door policy for Qing, but neither of them had any intention of intervening in the Manchurian affair. They seemed resigned to letting Russia do whatever it wished in Manchuria.

Meanwhile, Russia applied increasing pressure on Qing. The Russian intragovernmental conference on November 13, 1900 adopted a set of eighteen demands on Qing to be imposed as the draft treaty. This draft treaty demanded Qing expel all foreign concessions in Qing's territory north of the Great Wall and leave the defense of Manchuria entirely to the Russian troops. According to this draft, no Qing official or policeman was allowed to be appointed in Manchuria without Russian approval.

The content of this draft treaty was immediately communicated to Japan by the Qing government, which had already been keenly aware of the Russian threat and expected help from Japan. Meanwhile, Qing's political leaders secretly warned the Japanese side, in Tokyo as well as in Beijing, that the Japanese government should be aware of Li Hongzhang's special relations with Russia.

Foreign Minister Katō once again requested the British and German governments' cooperation, but they remained undecided. This situation finally prompted the Itō cabinet to adopt Katō's proposal for the Japanese government to protest to Russia single-handedly. On March 25, 1901, the Japanese government instructed Minister Chinda in Saint Petersburg to convey a protest to Russian Foreign Minister Lamsdorff, who once again brushed off Japan's protest by saying the situation was an affair between two independent sovereignties. In response, Katō immediately sent a telegram to Lamsdorff on April 5 to communicate his disagreement with the Russian view. The telegram was preceded by the Japanese Foreign Ministry's strong protest to Russian Minister Izvolsky in Tokyo, denouncing Russia's unlawful conduct of not only occupying the Liaodong Peninsula but also the much larger Manchuria after having opposed Japan's seizure of the Liaodong Peninsula at the end of the First Sino-Japanese War six years earlier.

At this point, Russia abruptly changed its attitude and recalled the Second Sino-Russian Secret Treaty. While Lamsdorff himself stated, "I had no idea that Japan attached such great importance to the Manchurian affair, which surprised me." What Russia really realized was the reality of power relations at the time.

Judging from the letter Lamsdorff sent Kuropatkin later, it appears that the true reason for Russia's abrupt change in attitude was the realization that the Russian army and navy in the Far East were relatively much weaker than their Japanese counterparts. Moreover, Russia feared that hasty remedial attempts to strengthen its army and navy in the region would prompt an early attack on Russia by Japan before its war readiness was complete.

Russian historian Boris Romanov described Japan's single-handed and frontal protest to Russia without British support as "an act of unprecedented boldness."[13] And, according to British historian Ian Nish, forcing Russia to retreat in this way was like a rite of initiation for young Japan.[14]

From beginning to end, the Russo-Japanese War was essentially a competition between Russia, which planned to overpower Japan after expanding its military strength in the Far East, and Japan, which attempted to expel Russia from the Far East before the latter's war preparations were complete.

Once Russia made a full-scale advance into Manchuria, Japan could never rival it. This was widely understood in Japan, as Ozaki Yukio's (尾崎行雄) criticism of the proposal to expand Japan's naval buildup during the Diet session following the First Sino-Japanese War reveals. Ozaki, a long-time parliamentarian who was later called "the father of parliamentary government," said, "Japan's government revenue is 250 million yen, while that of Russia is 2 billion yen. Japan has absolutely no chance of winning an arms race with such a great power." Since the Napoleonic wars, Russia had maintained the world's largest army, boasting 2 million regular troops compared to 200,000 troops for the Japanese Imperial Army.

If 1 million Russian troops had been concentrated in Manchuria and then

---

13 B. A. Romanov, *Russia in Manchuria 1892–1906* (English translation), 217, quoted in Tsunoda, *Manshū mondai,* 72.

14 Ian H. Nish, *The Anglo-Japanese Alliance: The Diplomacy of Two Island Empires, 1894–1907* (London: Athone Press, 1966), 119, 123, quoted in Tsunoda, *Manshū mondai,* 73.

advanced southward, as Kuropatkin had envisioned, Japan really would not have had any chance of defeating Russia anywhere between Manchuria and the southern tip of the Korean Peninsula, no matter what it tried.

The only problem for Russia was the underdevelopment of the transportation infrastructure, which would have enabled the delivery of such a massive force to the Far East across Siberia. Thus, it was self-evident that the situation would become increasingly unfavorable for Japan as time went on.

Tsar Nikolai II's Ambition to Rule the Far East

The idea of constructing the Siberian Railway had already been conceived when Russia annexed Primorsky Krai and Vladivostok in 1860. Around that time, the transcontinental Union Pacific Railroad in the United States was being extended steadily toward its full operation in 1869. While the extension of the railway from the Ural Mountains to Siberia was a natural course for Russia to take in order to facilitate its eastbound advance, it was actually Tsar Nikolai II and Sergei Witte who promoted its full-scale construction.

Tsar Nikolai II visited Japan as the crown prince and attended the cornerstone-laying ceremony for the new railway in Vladivostok in 1891 on his return trip home.

Incidentally, while he was visiting Japan, Nikolai II was assaulted with a sword by a constable named Tsuda Sanzō, who was one of the guards on duty for the Russian prince. The assault left Nikolai II with a lifelong scar on his forehead. It is believed that after this incident, Nikolai II bore an intense hatred toward Japan and the Japanese.

Throughout the entire process leading up to the start of the Russo-Japanese War, there had naturally been a variety of arguments, both hard and soft, within the Russian government on policies toward Japan. Witte stressed in his memoir how hard he had constantly tried to avoid the tragic Russo-Japanese War. Witte's memoir also reveals that leading up to his final decision on the war, the tsar had almost always sided with the hardliners.

In fact, it would not be an overstatement to say it was Tsar Nikolai II who had driven the turn of events toward a final showdown. The British government correctly predicted that "Russia will simply abolish its international commitment when it becomes inconvenient. Who in Russia could restrict and criticize the deeds of the great tsar?" Indeed, in those days, no one in Russia could resist the wishes of its absolute ruler. Friedrich von Gentz, who was advisor to Austrian Minister of State Klemens Wenzel von Metternich around the time of the Congress of Vienna (1814–15), had the following to say about the Russian tsar: "There exist no constraints on the Russian tsar, such as division of powers, constitutional restrictions, or public opinion, that have forced other monarchs to restrain themselves or abandon their desires. He can even carry out in the morning what he dreamed the night before."

On top of possessing absolute power of such magnitude, Tsar Nikolai II consistently remained highly opinionated and, moreover, positively engaged in policies toward the Far East. Even though he had traveled to the Far East only once, this experience was a great asset for Tsar Nikolai II in those days, when people knew little about the region.

Besides, it appears that Tsar Nikolai II empathized with the "yellow peril" argument of Prussia's Wilhelm II. Surprised to find that Japanese military officers stationed in Beijing had been put in charge of the reorganization of the Qing army, Wilhelm II sent the following private note to Tsar Nikolai II: "We must not overlook the emergence of twenty to thirty divisions of powerful Qing troops supported by six Japanese divisions under the command of dauntless, fearless, and anti-Christian Japanese officers with the unforgivable purpose of expelling all the foreigners from Qing. Nevertheless, the day may come when this kind of situation actually emerges. In fact, the situation has already emerged. Although I warned about the danger of the yellow peril years ago, most people ignored me." According to Romanov, Witte regarded these remarks by Wilhelm II as a German stratagem to lure Russia into adventures in the Far East in order to reduce the threat from Russia. Of course, Wilhelm II genuinely believed in the danger of the "yellow peril" to a certain extent, which found its echo in Tsar Nikolai II, who had an "uncontrollable desire to advance into the Far East and conquer various locations in the region." Tsar Nikolai II's notion was to "utilize this opportunity to prevent Korea from becoming a Japanese territory before the yellow race completes its war readiness," as predicted by a French diplomat stationed in Saint Petersburg. Thus, a logical consistency is found between Wilhelm II's "yellow peril" argument and Tsar Nikolai II's expansionism.

The Approaching Rumble of Cossack Horses

At this point, Russia's advance into the Far East depended on the completion of the Siberian Railway. According to American historian Denis Warner, after Prince Nicolai's cornerstone-laying ceremony in 1891, the railway had been extended at an average speed of 620 kilometers a year between 1892 and 1895. In 1895 alone, Witte ordered the construction of a full 1,338 kilometers, prompted by Japan's victory in the First Sino-Japanese War.

But the Siberian Railway was incomparably more difficult to construct than the American intercontinental railway. For more than half a year, the land's surface was frozen up to two meters deep, defying any attempt at pile driving, while during the summer it turned into a sea of mud. Fighting these surface conditions, construction had to go across great rivers, including the Yenisei and Ob Rivers, and over frigid mountains. Until the very end, the greatest obstacle of all was the route bypassing Lake Baikal. South of the lake, which would be a shorter route, is impassable because it is lined with a sheer cliff. To pass the northern shore required a detour of as much as 700 kilometers, where the frozen ground of the tundra posed another difficulty. Workers were forced to rely on the ferryboat across the lake for transport, but it too became unavailable when the lake froze over completely during the winter. To switch to transport on sleighs, they had to wait until the ice became thick and hard enough. An army of convicts was mobilized as labor. They were motivated to work speedily because of a special incentive system that made eight months of labor for the Siberian Railway equivalent to a year's labor in prison.

The Japanese side watched this steady construction of the Siberian Railway with a sense of fear, as if hearing the approaching rumble of horses' hooves made by massive numbers of Cossack troops.

In 1892, the year after the construction of the Siberian Railway commenced, Lieutenant Colonel Fukushima Yasumasa of the Japanese Imperial Army traveled alone across Siberia to observe the construction. Through subsequent intelligence activities, the Japanese side was able to judge, based on the information it had collected, that the transportation capacity of the single-track Siberian Railway could not exceed seven trains per twenty-four hours, which was exactly the same capacity the Russian side had envisioned.

Once the Russo-Japanese War erupted, however, Russia zealously strove to expand the railway's transportation capacity. The southern route around Lake Baikal was completed within seven months after the start of the war. The Russians even resorted to such extreme measures as abandoning cargo trains without deadheading them back, something totally unimaginable for a poor nation such as Japan. In the end, a total of 1,294,566 troops, 230,269 horses, and 9.5 million tons of cargo were transported to Harbin via the railway during the war according to *Kindai Nippon sensō-shi* (History of Modern Japanese Warfare). They were all ordered to the battlefront, forcing Japan to face an uphill battle.

Because Russia's transportation capacity was greatly expanded toward the end of the war, it is obvious that Japan could not have won the war had it been prolonged any further.

It should be obvious from the above observations that Komura's decision to hasten the start of the Russo-Japanese War was a smart move. One could even go so far as to say it was Komura's decision that saved Japan.

CHAPTER
7

The Anglo-Japanese Alliance

*—Komura's Memorandum Settles the Dispute over
an Alliance Partnership—*

A Blank Space on the World Map

Japan's relations with Britain date back 300 years. The first Briton to
come to Japan was William Adams, a navigator of the Dutch vessel *De
Liefde* who was washed ashore on the island of Kyushu in 1600. Adams
was a veteran sailor who, during the reign of Queen Elizabeth I, had distinguished himself as a captain in the British navy against the Spanish
Armada. Tokugawa Ieyasu heavily favored Adams and treated him as a
domain lord, granting him a domain and subjects.

Hearing that Adams had been treated well in Japan, Britain dispatched
King James I's envoy to Edo and opened a trading house in Hirado,
Kyushu, in 1613. The British trading house, however, lost the competition with the Dutch in Nagasaki and was closed down in 1624. When
the British officials left Hirado, they entrusted the building, storehouse,
and pier to the care of the Hirado-*han* and pleaded for permission to trade
under the same conditions when the trading house reopened. Thus, Britain
was not exactly expelled from trade with Japan, unlike Spain or Portugal,
who were both suspected of seeking to expand their influence by means of
Catholic missionary activities.

In any event, Britain in those days was much more interested in the

Qing market, which was incomparably larger than the Japanese one. Britain neglected its trade with Japan until the nineteenth century.

Meanwhile, the great British explorer, Captain James Cook, explored the entire Pacific basin between 1768 and 1770, including Australia and New Zealand. It was during his preparations to explore the last destination, the North Pacific, that he was killed by natives in Hawaii. Because his successor, Charles Clark, also died of sickness shortly thereafter, the North Pacific ended up remaining unexplored. For these reasons, the region north of the Japanese archipelago was a blank space on the world map of the time.

King Louis XVI of France, who had been watching Captain Cook's exploration closely with a sense of rivalry, ordered naval officer Jean-François de Galaup, comte de La Pérouse, to explore the Sea of Japan in 1783. As a result of this expedition, Sōya Strait (宗谷海峡) between Sakhalin and Sapporo became known internationally as La Pérouse Strait. However, it was not until Mamiya Rinzō's 1808–9 expedition that Sakhalin was finally determined to be an actual island.

Two Great Powers Dividing the World

The Far East around the time Japan opened its doors was a bipolar world centered around Russia, which expanded its sphere of influence from the north, and Britain, which expanded from the south.

Watanabe Kazan (渡辺崋山; 1793–1841), an enlightened thinker, statesman, and painter who lived toward the end of the Tokugawa shogunate, was anxious about Japan's future in the world, having studied Western sciences since his younger days. In one of his written works, Watanabe pointed out that while Japan persisted with national isolation, Russia and Britain might resort to forcing Japan's doors open and, in due course, attempt to seize its territory. He stressed that the "resourceful British are good at naval warfare, while Russians under the benevolent government are excellent land fighters."

Hashimoto Sanai (橋本左内; 1834–59), an otherwise brilliant philosopher who met a premature death by execution during the Ansei Purge (安政の大獄; 1858–59) carried out by Ii Naosuke (井伊直弼) toward the end of the Tokugawa shogunate, argued that two master spirits (i.e., Britain and Russia), could not exist together and insisted that Japan should collaborate with Russia. In a pair of China-style antitheses, Hashimoto analyzed, "It will be most likely that either Britain or Russia will dominate the world. While Britons are fierce and greedy, Russians are calm but mighty and tough, and it will be Russians who will be more trusted in the end."

Due to the stylistic constraints of classical Chinese, with which Hashimoto had to comply when fitting the characters of the Britain and the Russians into a pair of antitheses, the accuracy of the descriptions leaves much to be desired. Nevertheless, they must have been based on information obtained from the Netherlands, and moreover, they might have been generally accepted ideas in the world in those days.

After Britain and Russia became the two major victors of the Napoleonic Wars, they grew into great powers and divided the world into two. The situation was somewhat analogous to the emergence of the US-Soviet Union bipolar world after the Allied Forces annihilated Germany and Japan in World War II. Comparing the fierceness of Admiral Horatio Nelson, who completely destroyed the French-Spanish armada off the Cape of Trafalgar, with the depth of General Mikhail Kutuzov, who prevented the invincible Napoleonic army from winning a decisive victory at the Battle of Borodino, and comparing the British capture of former French and Dutch colonies after the war with Russia's attempt to restore the legitimacy of European monarchs by forming the Holy Alliance at the Congress of Vienna, it might have been only natural for continental countries, especially a British rival such as the Netherlands, to side with Russia.

It was the Opium War that first gave Japanese political activists in the twilight of the Tokugawa shogunate a sense of crisis about the future of Japan. After this war that was devastating for Qing, these activists began to worry about when Britain would reach out for Japan and whether Japan could really resist a British offensive. Thus, the greatest threat for Japan at that time was Britain and, therefore, it was only natural for the Japanese to place their high hopes in Russia, Britain's archrival. In fact, Qing never lost its faith in Russia until the very end—which cost it not only the vast Siberian territory but also Manchuria. Qing's trust in Russia put its very existence at risk.

As I pointed out in chapter five, the Tokugawa government came very close to being lured by Russia's smooth talk when Commodore Perry and

Admiral Putyatin visited Japan one after another in 1853. Despite political upheaval, Japan was able to steer through the age of imperialism, with its gaping, unfathomable pitfalls everywhere, by relying on its own strength and judgment.

When the Tokugawa government was on its death bed, France was active in offering its help, and some in the shogunate argued that it should accept the French offer. But Katsu Kaishū (勝海舟), the shogunate's chief negotiator at the time, adamantly rejected this argument. Britain also offered assistance to the Imperial Court in rivalry with France, but Saigō Takamori (西郷隆盛), commander of Satsuma-*han* troops in Kyoto, declined the offer without hesitation, saying it would be dishonorable to ask for foreigners' help to promote Japan's reform, because reform should be carried out by the hands of the Japanese themselves. And it was these two, Katsu and Saigō, who helped accomplish the Meiji Restoration by agreeing on the peaceful surrender of Edo. Had it not been for these two, Japan could have been an arena of British-French strife, like India.

According to Katsu's memoir, Russia offered a loan to Katsu, who was obliged to financially support numerous former vassals of the shogunate after its fall. This must have been partly because Hokkaido at the time was still under the control of the shogunate. Katsu reminisces: "I say nobody else had a harder time during the transition from the old regime to the new. At the time of the Meiji Restoration, I had to take care of as many as 150,000 former vassals of the shogunate with limited funds of a mere 500,000 yen. It was a tall order because, after all, they had to be fed. When Russia offered me a loan, however, I turned it down immediately. Had I offered Hokkaido as collateral, Russia would have gladly lent me 5 million yen or so. If I had embezzled 1 million yen out of it, I could have had an easy retirement. Oh, don't take me seriously, I am not that vicious." In contrast to Li Hongzhang, who had been easily bribed by Russia, Katsu declined Russia's offer for help without hesitation. It was the samurai spiritual tradition behind Katsu's behavior that saved Japan from Russia's ambition.

Even though Japan was forced to accept unequal treaties with the Western powers, it somehow managed to ride out the turbulent transition from the shogunate to the Meiji government without interference from foreign powers.

After this brief contact with Japan, Western powers in the late nineteenth century began to concentrate on areas other than East Asia, including the division of the Ottoman Empire, the division of Africa, and the conquest of Central Asia, allowing Japan to devote energy to its modernization without being bothered too much by international relations. Meanwhile, Qing's military might become a serious threat to Japan at one point as a result of Qing's own modernization after taking advantage of the Western powers' temporary absence from the Far East. But Japan was able to overcome this threat on its own through the First Sino-Japanese War.

Entering the twentieth century, with the completion of Russia's Trans-Siberian Railway just around the corner, Japan was finally forced to make a choice to side with either Britain or Russia, the two greatest powers in the world.

It was around the time of the Boxer Rebellion that the idea of an Anglo-Japanese alliance began to take concrete form.

An alliance with Britain vis-à-vis Russia's eastbound advance had, of course, already existed as a theoretical possibility even before the rebellion. For instance, Mutsu Munemitsu wrote the following editorial for the magazine *Sekai no Nippon* (世界之日本), which was published after the Triple Intervention:

> Many people have high hopes for the Anglo-Japanese Alliance. But Britain is not a Don Quixote that would empathize with other countries' woes. If the alliance requires Britain to guarantee Japan's security, Britain needs to be compensated for its own security. Is Japan capable of helping the British Empire defend its extremely long line of defense? Britain does not believe that Japan as an ally is capable of fighting wars in the Asian continent and dispatching its fleet further away than Singapore. If Britain had only referred to Japan as its ally during the Triple Intervention, the Itō cabinet might have made a historic decision to commit Japan's fate to an alliance with Britain. Because Britain did not mention such an alliance, however, we had no other choice but to accept the Triple Intervention.

This quote clearly shows Mutsu had understood the truth: an alliance would not be formed unless both sides found it beneficial.

In any event, Mutsu's judgment was accurate. At the time of the Triple Intervention, Japanese naval power was so pathetic that the only battleship Japan owned was the battered *Zhenyuan* (鎮遠), which it had captured from Qing. It was after Japan became one of the leading naval nations in the world, procuring battleships one after another during the *Gashin Shōtan* (persevering through hardship for the sake of revenge) period, that Britain decided to form an alliance with Japan. At the first renewal of the Anglo-Japanese Alliance in 1905, which made it a complete offensive and defensive alliance, Japan committed itself to the defense of India, which was far west of Singapore.

According to the journalist Sakazaki Sakan (坂崎斌), the true reason behind Itō Hirobumi's proposal to greatly expand the Japanese navy and army at the ninth session of the Imperial Diet (1895–96) was his support of Mutsu's argument that Britain would not agree to conclude the Anglo-Japanese Alliance unless Japan was powerful and influential enough to meet British expectations.

Arms expansion during the period of the *Gashin Shōtan* ideology that followed in the wake of the Triple Intervention was truly remarkable. While the wartime naval budget for 1895 was 13 million yen, it was tripled to 38 million yen in the 1896 peacetime budget, and further doubled to 76 million yen in 1897.

Of course, the Japanese government had to resort to a massive tax increase. According to the Japanese elders who have lived through the hundred years since the Meiji Restoration, the hardest time for them in terms of day-to-day living was during and immediately after World War II, but life during the *Gashin Shōtan* period and the Russo-Japanese War had been just as tough.

Besides, the Japanese government devoted almost 90 percent of some 300 million yen war redemptions from Qing to military buildup. One way of looking at this is that the margin Qing had failed to spend for the war with Japan was spent by the Japanese government to prepare for its war with Russia, which resulted in preventing Russia from taking Manchuria from Qing.

Germany Acts as an Unintentional Go-Between

During the period between March and April 1901, acting German ambassador to London Hermann von Eckardstein frequently visited Japanese Minister Hayashi Tadasu (林 董). The German diplomat hinted at the possibility of forming a triple alliance between Japan, Britain, and Germany, and he assured Hayashi that some in members of the British cabinet also supported this scheme.

The true intention behind Eckardstein's suggestion is unknown even today. When Eckardstein brought the same suggestion to Britain, its foreign minister at the time, Henry Charles Keith Petty-FitzMaurice, fifth Marquess of Lansdowne, inquired of the German ambassador to London as to whether the idea was truly Eckardstein's personal opinion, as he had claimed it to be, or whether he was acting on a secret order of the German government to sound out the British.

Whatever Eckardstein's true intention might have been, he acted as a go-between to promote the prompt signing of the Anglo-Japanese Alliance. When Foreign Minister Katō Takaaki received Hayashi's report, he asked for an opinion from Komura Jutarō, who was the Japanese minister to Qing at the time. In response, Komura strongly supported Eckardstein's proposal, saying this alliance would "bring an immense benefit to Japan." Hearing this, Foreign Minister Katō issued instructions to Hayashi, stating that "Although the Japanese government currently cannot express its official position on this issue, I hereby grant Minister Hayashi the authority to explore the intention of the British government on this matter at his own personal initiative." Following these instructions, Hayashi discussed the possibility of an Anglo-Japanese Alliance with the British foreign minister. Although no concrete progress was made during this initial contact, this was possibly the first occasion on which Japan's attitude toward the alliance was conveyed to the British side.

A few months later, in July 1901, Sir Claude MacDonald, British minister to Japan who was on leave in London, visited Hayashi to share the following view: "Recently, I had a chance to talk with top authorities of the British government (Edward VII and Prime Minister Robert Cecil, 3rd Marquess of Salisbury) and both agreed that an alliance had to be made between Britain and Japan in order to cope with future problems in the Far

East.[1] Both held the view that, when a partner of the alliance went to war with a third country, the other partner had to remain neutral. Each partner had to cooperate with the other, however, when one of them was engaged in war with two or more enemy countries."

MacDonald visited Hayashi once again on the following day to tell him that the British government had every intention of forming an alliance with Japan, although launching the alliance might take some time because it was against the traditional policy of Britain. Meanwhile, MacDonald told Hayashi emphatically that the Japanese government should never conclude a bilateral cooperation arrangement with Russia.[2]

Finally, toward the end of July, the British foreign minister, the fifth Marquess of Lansdowne, declared to Japanese Minister Hayashi that it was high time for the two countries to seriously consider forming a bilateral alliance, revealing British intentions quite explicitly.

Japanese Soldiers: The Best by Far

Prior to his assignment to the ministership in Japan, Claude MacDonald had been stationed in Beijing as British minister during the Boxer Rebellion. It appears that one of the driving forces behind the Anglo-Japanese Alliance was the trust MacDonald had developed for the Japanese military while in Beijing.

When the Qing government declared war on the Western powers in June 1901, rebels besieged foreign missions. It was indeed the calm and level-headed conduct of MacDonald and Lieutenant Colonel Shiba Gorō of the Japanese Imperial Army that saved the lives of foreign residents.

At that time, no Western power stationed its regular forces in Beijing, forcing its foreign mission to rely on volunteer forces composed of foreign residents and Chinese Christians oppressed by the Boxers for protection.

One of the British volunteers, B. Simpson, had the following to say in praise of Lieutenant Colonel Shiba: "Although the Japanese embassy

---

1 *Nippon gaikō bunsho* [Documents of Japanese foreign policy], 34: 19–20, quoted in Tsunoda, *Manshū mondai,* 82. Text in Japanese was translated into English by the author.

2 Ibid.

could muster only a few dozen volunteers to defend the wall of the imperial palace, which easily took 500 soldiers to defend, they were endowed with an excellent commander. This small man somehow found a way to bring order to the chaos. He organized his volunteer forces and reinforced the defense of the front line of the battle. He did everything he could and should. I have already become an ardent admirer of this man and it won't be too long before I willingly enslave myself to him. For reasons unknown even to me, I was unable to distance myself from the Japanese military post." Lancelot Jayle, a clerk at the British

Lieutenant Colonel Shiba Gorō (©The Aizu Bukeyashiki)

legation, also praised Shiba as follows: "Japanese soldiers are no doubt the most superior warriors, and Lieutenant Colonel Shiba is regarded as the most excellent officer of all. The courage and audacity of the Japanese soldiers are simply amazing. British sailors may be the distant number two. Japanese soldiers are the best by far." At the international conference that was convened when the Eight-Nation Alliance forces arrived in Beijing, British Minister MacDonald announced that half the success of the defense of the Legation Quarter was attributable to the distinctly courageous Japanese officers and soldiers, which was a fair assessment.

Words of Appreciation from the British Navy

Subsequently, MacDonald was appointed as British minister to Japan. It is not hard to imagine that in the course of briefings on the situation in East Asia during his temporary stay in Britain, he persuasively stressed to British leaders how trustworthy the Japanese and the Japanese officers and soldiers were.

There were other sources of British trust in the Japanese. When Russia occupied Lüshun in 1898, it became necessary for Britain to open a military base along Bohai Bay to counter Russia. During the question and answer period in the British Parliament on May 17, Prime Minister Robert Cecil, third Marquess of Salisbury, stressed the need to demonstrate Britain's firm determination that Russia not be given a free hand in Lüshun lest the Chinese become desperate, allowing foreign powers to annex their territory at will.

While this explanation was self-contradictory in the face of Britain's own annexation of others' territories, it must have sounded reasonable enough to the British people in those days. The British sphere of interest in China originally centered around the Yangtze River basin, starting from Shanghai; Britain, therefore, did not have great stakes in Bohai Bay. However, if Britain gave Russia a free hand in the area around the capital city, Beijing, the Qing Chinese might fall into a state of defeatism that could eventually lead to the fall of their own country. Since Britain did not possess the military or political means to block Russia's control of Lüshun, the only thing it could do was establish its own military base on the opposite shore of Bohai Bay as a counterbalance.

It should be recalled that Weihaiwai (威海衛) had been occupied by Japan as collateral for Qing's war redemption. Thus, the first thing the British government did was to inquire whether the Japanese government had any objection to Britain's lease of Weihaiwai after the Japanese troops withdrew. The Japanese minister to Britain, Katō Takaaki, recommended to the head office in Tokyo that the Japanese government should actively support the British lease of Weihaiwai in order to promote Anglo-Japanese cooperation, and the Japanese government accordingly responded to the British government that it had no objection. As a result, Britain was able to obtain the Qing government's agreement to lease Weihaiwai under the same conditions as Russia's lease of Lüshun.

When British troops arrived in Weihaiwai, they found the barracks in order and in pristine condition, with a lot of equipment still intact. The commander in chief of the British fleet requested that the British minister to Japan officially express his gratitude to the Japanese military for its consideration, which benefited his troops greatly.

An obsession with cleanliness and tidiness, as well as the custom to clean up a place before leaving, is uniquely Japanese. Even today, Korean tourists marvel how "sickeningly clean" Japanese towns are. Although the reason for this cultural trait is uncertain, it might be attributable to sanitary needs during hot and humid summers. This pragmatic need has been refined by Japanese perfectionism, typically manifested in the tea ceremony, and it became embedded in all layers of Japanese life as civic society matured during the 300 years of the Tokugawa shogunate.

Korean Peninsula Decides Japan's Fate

On September 21, 1901, Komura was appointed as foreign minister, and he granted Minister Hayashi in London the authority to negotiate with the British side on October 8, signifying the beginning of formal negotiations on the Anglo-Japanese Alliance.

In a nutshell, what Japan sought through the negotiations was to block the Korean Peninsula from falling into the hands of an enemy force. Japan's security was always threatened when the southern part of the Korean Peninsula fell into the hands of an adversary. The threat from a superpower on the Asian continent reached the southern shore of the Korean Peninsula when Tang troops defeated the Baekje Kingdom (百濟) in the seventh century and when the Mongols conquered the Kingdom of Goryeo (高麗) in the thirteenth century. In its long history, Japan had reinforced the defense of its mainland only for these two occasions, thus constructing fortifications on Kyushu. Furthermore, when the Communist army threatened Busan on the southern tip of the peninsula during the Korean War, the National Police Reserve (警察予備隊), predecessor of today's Self-Defense Force, was established—even after Japan had abandoned all of its armed forces as a result of its defeat in World War II.

Japan's need to secure the Korean Peninsula by its own hand created two other needs. One was to put the peninsula under Japan's control, beyond the simple neutralization of the peninsula. Whenever Russia in particular spoke of the neutralization of a territory, it meant only that it wished the territory to remain neutral until Russia was prepared to take it. Even if neutralization was guaranteed by other Western powers, including Britain and the United States, none of them would have been capable of dispatching their armies to maintain the neutrality had Russia militarily advanced to Korea against the agreement. That scenario would have been a rerun of the Western powers' inaction vis-à-vis Russia's forceful occupation of northern Manchuria despite John Hay's Open Door Note and the British and German declarations on the open door policy for China.

Also, although it is rude to the Korean people today to mention this, it was generally believed in those day that Koreans lacked the capability to govern themselves. Even as recently as after World War II, it was seriously discussed whether Korea should be put under UN trusteeship until it gained self-governing capability. It was, therefore, international common sense at the height of the age of imperialism in the early twentieth century to doubt the self-governing capabilities of the Korean people.

That being the case, mere "neutrality" would make the future of Korea highly uncertain—and thus Japan felt compelled to assert its special rights on the peninsula with respect to the Western powers. This Japanese policy on Korea remained consistent and culminated in the annexation of the peninsula in 1910.

Japan's second, more proactive, need was to block Russia's control of Manchuria. During the negotiations on the Anglo-Japanese Alliance, the Japanese side insisted that while Japanese interest in Manchuria was only indirect, it was imperative to protect Manchuria's territorial integrity and keep its doors open lest Russia should monopolize Manchuria, which would be a prelude to Russia's advance to Korea. Given Russia's ambitions in those days, which I have repeatedly discussed in previous chapters, this apprehension on the part of Japan appears only natural.

As far as territorial integrity and Manchuria's open door policy were concerned, Japan's interests were perfectly aligned with Britain's from the beginning. When it came to the recognition of Japan's special right in Korea, however, the British side was hesitant to include such a clause in the treaty, although it had agreed with the Japanese argument in substance from the early stages of the negotiations. Because the British side had agreed with Japan's position in substance, it made a compromise in the wording of the treaty to satisfy the Japanese side.

The End of Splendid Isolation

British interest in the Far East in those days was concentrated in the area of the Yangtze River basin, and Britain did not have a major interest in Manchuria or the Korean Peninsula. Above all, British interest was in the conclusion of a military alliance itself (i.e., a guarantee that the alliance partner would immediately participate in a war Britain started with two or more enemy countries). This is more clearly understood if "two enemy countries" is replaced with Russia and France, Britain's rivals in those days.

The table below shows the naval balance in the Far East among major powers as of April 1901.

Table 1. Naval power in the Far East in April 1901 by country

	Number of Battleships	Number of Armored Cruisers	Number of Cruisers	Number of Destroyers	Total Tonnage
Japan	5	4	10	13	200,000
Britain	4	2	11	7	170,000
Russia	5	6	2	6	120,000
France	1	1	6	1	80,000

* Translated from the table in Tsunoda, *Manshū mondai*, 88.

Previously, British sea power had single-handedly overwhelmed the combined naval power of all other countries in the world; this had provided the foundation for the *Pax Britannica* in the nineteenth century. Subsequently, the naval armaments race among nations intensified. In a key move, Russia deployed newly built ships to the Far East after the Triple Intervention. As a result, by January 1901 the British naval force in the region was surpassed by the sum of Russian and French naval power, both in terms of the number of ships as well as total tonnage.

Thus, while Britain could handle either Russia or France separately, it would need Japan's assistance if it had to engage the two countries at once. If, moreover, an entente was formed between Japan and Russia ahead of the Anglo-Japanese Alliance, Britain would be powerless in the Far East; this was the biggest worry for Britain throughout the period. In this sense, one could argue that Itō's approach to Russia for bilateral entente in 1901 (as we will see shortly) contributed to the early conclusion of the Anglo-Japanese Alliance by making Britain anxious about the possibility of a Russo-Japanese alliance.

When the draft treaty of the Anglo-Japanese Alliance was discussed at the British cabinet meeting, Chancellor of the Exchequer Michael Hicks Beach astutely observed that "if any benefit could be gained from this treaty, it would go to the Japanese navy and, in case of unexpected development, it could reduce the burden imposed on our own navy."[3] This statement should be understood with the above context in mind.

---

3   "Hicks Beach to Lansdowne, January 2, 1902," in *The End of Isolation: British Foreign Policy 1900–1907*, G. W. Monger (London: Nelson, 1963), 59, quoted in Tsunoda, *Manshū mondai*, 99.

After the majority of the cabinet approved the draft treaty of the Anglo-Japanese Alliance in November, Prime Minister Robert Cecil, third Marquess of Salisbury, reported the result to the king and added that "this will be the end of the isolation."[4] Thus ended the splendid isolation that had characterized British diplomacy in the nineteenth century. Military expansion throughout the period of *Gashin Shōtan* made Japan powerful enough to be a player in international politics.

Whether to Side with the Anglo-Saxon or the Slav

At this point, the last hurdle for the conclusion of the Anglo-Japanese Alliance was the domestic situation in Japan (i.e., how Japan could break away from the notion of cooperation with Russia), which Britain had repeatedly expressed its concerns about during the treaty negotiations with Japan.

Advocates of cooperation with Russia included such elder statesmen as Itō Hirobumi and Inoue Kaoru (井上馨), as well as Kurino Shinichirō (栗野慎一郎), Japanese minister to Russia. The pro-British camp included Katsura Tarō and Komura Jutarō, among others.

According to Katsura: "The pro-Russian argument was based on the assessment that it would be impossible to fight against Russia. This assessment was quite understandable considering Japan's bitter experiences since the Meiji Restoration. But the peace with Russia would be short-lived because Russia would most certainly advance to Korea after conquering Manchuria—in which case it would be inevitable that Japan confront Russia. Not doing so meant that Japan would have to submit meekly to Russia's will." In contrast, Britain already had territories all over the world, and there was no need for it to come to Japan to conquer another one. Therefore, Katsura argued, it would be better for Japan to team up with Britain.

Itō and Inoue, however, never dropped their idea of cooperating with Russia. When Itō visited the United States to receive an honorary doc-

---

4   "Salisbury to the King, August 16, 1901," in *The Anglo-Japanese Alliance: The Diplomacy of Two Island Empires 1894–1907*, Ian H. Nish (Athone Press: London, 1966), 160, quoted in Tsunoda, *Manshū mondai*, 89.

torate from Yale University in the fall of 1901, Inoue enthusiastically encouraged him to visit Russia on his way home, a proposal with which he concurred. The purpose of Itō's visit to Russia, as envisioned by Itō and Inoue, was to reach a settlement on the Korean issue with the Russians. Itō and Inoue belonged to the generation that had vivid memories of a weakling Japan who was utterly powerless against the Western powers' fleets. As such, as Katsura pointed out above, they felt quite uncomfortable with the argument advocated by the younger generation, including Komura, for a war with such a formidable foe as Russia.

Itō was briefed by Japanese Minister to Britain Hayashi Tadasu on the progress of the negotiations for the Anglo-Japanese treaty in Paris while he was on his way to Russia. Nevertheless, Itō sent a telegram to Tokyo requesting the postponement of the final decision on the treaty until after he exchanged views with the Russian side.

By that time, however, negotiations on the Anglo-Japanese Alliance had reached such a stage, both in Tokyo and London, that, according to Katsura and others, they could not be terminated "without damaging the honor and dignity of Japan." Although Itō was informed of this situation, he persisted in exploring the possibility of cooperating with Russia and met Sergei Witte and Foreign Minister Vladimir Lamsdorff in Saint Petersburg in early December.

Russia had taken the position that its decision on whether or not to occupy Manchuria depended solely on its own will and that it had absolutely no intention of bartering its free hand in Manchuria for Japan's control of Korea; this negotiation with Russia was doomed from the very beginning.

In short, Britain succeeded in forming the Anglo-Japanese Alliance by approving Japan's control of the Korean Peninsula, while Russia had to take the path of confronting Japan because of its own ambitions to control the peninsula.

Komura Memorandum

On December 7, 1901, in the midst of the critical time when negotiations on the Anglo-Japanese Alliance were in the last stretch—and Itō was still negotiating on the possibility of cooperating with Russia—a conference among elder statesmen was convened in Hayama near Tokyo. The so-called Komura Memorandum submitted to this conference is a historical document that exhaustively explains Komura's diplomatic strategy. The gist of this document is as follows.

First, on the situation in the Far East, Komura deliberated on the view he had cherished since his days as Japanese minister to Russia, saying that "Even though a day may come when the Russians are made to temporarily withdraw, it is beyond doubt that Manchuria will be effectively occupied by Russia sooner or later because Russia has been steadily expanding its control of Manchuria and it has already established the right to station troops in Manchuria to protect the railway." Komura continued to discuss the futility of the scheme to barter Manchuria for Korea with Russia, as was advocated by Itō, Inoue, and Kurino, analyzing that "if Manchuria is conquered by Russia, Korea will not be able to defend itself." Subsequent history as well as Russia's internal documents have clearly proven that Komura's assessment was accurate.

Stressing the need to ask for Britain's cooperation to forcefully control Russia, Komura compared the merits and demerits of concluding the Russo-Japanese entente and those of the Anglo-Japanese alliance as follows:

(1) While British objectives in the Far East are to maintain the status quo and protect the country's trading interests, Russia has territorial ambitions. Any peace with Russia will inevitably be short-lived, but peace with Britain will be longer-lasting.

(2) The economic value of Siberia, if any, would be realized only in the long term, incomparable with the immense benefit Japan could gain from trade with the British Empire, which has colonies all over the world.

(3) It will be far easier to team up with British naval power to counter Russia than it would be to team up with Russia to face British sea power.

(4) While cooperation with Russia will hurt Chinese feelings, teaming up with Britain benefits the expansion of Japan's interests in China.

(5) Japan can expect financial benefits from an alliance with Britain.[5]

---

5   *Nippon gaikō bunsho* [Documents of Japanese foreign policy], 34: 66–69, quoted in Tsunoda, *Manshū mondai*, 128–130.

This is an exhaustive as well as realistic analysis, showing how bright a man Komura really was. His judgment was far more accurate than Itō's at that time, and this was indeed the argument that finally put an end to the debate on whether to side with the British or Russians—a debate that had haunted Japan since the last days of the Tokugawa shogunate.

Although Itō's telegram, which arrived on December 8, still requested postponement of the final decision on the conclusion of the Anglo-Japanese Alliance, Katsura and Komura proceeded as previously planned, ignoring Itō's request. On December 10, imperial sanction of the Komura Memorandum was granted, clearing the last hurdle before the signing of the treaty.

The first Anglo-Japanese Alliance was signed in London on January 30, 1902, and its contents were publicized on February 12.

Komura's penetrating assessment of the international situation, as well as his iron will, enabled him to accomplish his initial goal and lead the Anglo-Japanese Alliance this far, despite opposition from elder statesmen.

Eruption of the Russo-Japanese War

—The Anglo-Japanese Alliance Makes Up for Japan's Weakness—

Russia Refuses to Withdraw Troops from Manchuria

As soon as the long-desired Anglo-Japanese Alliance was signed, the Katsura government, under the initiative of Foreign Minister Komura Jutarō, started demanding the Russian government officially withdraw its troops from Manchuria. At the same time, the Japanese government encouraged the Qing government to resist demands from Russia, whose ambitions for Manchuria were becoming increasingly evident.

As early as October 5, 1901, immediately after he became foreign minister, Komura sent the following request to the Qing government: "When Japan had previously dissuaded Russia from concluding a new Sino-Russian treaty, the Qing government expressed its gratitude for Japan's forceful assistance and declared that it would consult with Japan immediately if Russia approached Qing with a new demand. It is critically important for Qing to continue to do so." In those days, Sergei Witte was still at the center of Russia's Far Eastern policies, and he continued to pursue the policy of expanding Russia's sphere of influence in Manchuria by cajoling Qing instead of using force. Russia had made a variety of proposals to Qing as a condition for the withdrawal of Russian troops from Manchuria, aiming to monopolize rights and interests in the region. Every time a new proposal arrived from Russia, the Qing government did not fail to notify the Japanese government of the content, upon which Komura advised the Qing side to resist the pressure from Russia.

In the end, Russia went as far as proposing to put the entire Manchurian economy under the control of the Russo-Chinese Bank (露清銀行), but the Qing side, encouraged by advice from Japan, succeeded in rejecting such tenacious demands.

It was on the day after Qing's final rejection of the above proposal that Russia was informed of the conclusion of the Anglo-Japanese Alliance. These two developments came as a tremendous shock to the Russian side; testimony to what a well-kept secret the negotiations for the alliance had been.

All of the cabinet members in the Katsura government were honored with aristocratic titles from Emperor Meiji in recognition of their contribution to the successful conclusion of the alliance with Britain. When some complained about the lavishness of the reward, Komura laughingly stated, "Anyone deserves to be honored with a title just by keeping the secret." According to B. A. Romanov's *Russia in Manchuria 1892–1906*, Russia's scheme to monopolize Manchuria was totally crippled by these two developments.

Russia was, as a consequence, forced to withdraw its troops from Manchuria without any special compensation. Nevertheless, Russia was careful enough to attach a condition for withdrawal: "Russia shall withdraw its troops from Manchuria as long as there emerges no unexpected upheaval and as long as Russia's withdrawal is not obstructed by the conduct of any third party." This condition allowed Russia to reserve the right to call off the withdrawal when even a minor incident took place in Manchuria, even if it was obviously engineered by Russia, or when a third country took action elsewhere.

Although the Qing side resisted the inclusion of this condition until the very end, Witte succeeded in bribing Qing's negotiators. With this agreement, Russia committed itself to the withdrawal of its troops: from the southern Shengjing Province within six months of signing the agreement; from northern Shengjing Province and Jilin Province in the ensuing six months; and from Heilongjiang Province in the next six months after that. In other words, it was agreed that all Russian troops would be withdrawn from Manchuria except for those that had been granted the right to be stationed along the Chinese Eastern Railway, which Russia had obtained earlier.

This agreement was signed on April 8, 1902, and the first withdrawal was carried out on October 8, six months after the signing. While Russia had committed to the second withdrawal from central Manchuria, which included withdrawal from the city of Mukden (presently Shenyang), by April 8, 1903, Russia had no intention of abiding by this commitment, thus betraying those who had pinned their hopes on Russia's sincerity.

In fact, Russian troops in central Manchuria had already been reinforced by March. While a token withdrawal was staged by a small number of troops on April 8, the bulk of the Russian army marched to the Mukden railway station and subsequently returned to their barracks, a scornful action against the international community.

United Front between Japan, Britain, and the United States

In May 1903, US Secretary of State John Hay sent a memorandum to President Theodore Roosevelt on Russia's sabotage of the second troop withdrawal. In this memorandum Hay said: "Although Russia claims to the US government, both in Washington, DC, and Saint Petersburg, that it has not made any additional demands on Qing, there is no doubt that it indeed has. When I voiced my concerns to Russian ambassador to the United States Cassini that Russia's continued pursuit of its act of aggression would prompt a division of China by the Western powers, he openly pronounced that Russia is entitled to have its own share when the Western powers have already been engaged in the division of Qing, which has long been in the process of collapse." Because what Russia demanded of Qing went against the British and US open-door policy in China, Komura notified both the British and the US governments of the Russo-China negotiations and advised the Qing government to reject Russia's demands. While Britain and the United States initially hesitated to join in the direct protest to Russia, they collaborated with the Japanese government in the joint recommendation to the Qing government to reject Russian demands. Thus, a de facto united front emerged among Japan, Britain, and the United States in order to maintain the open door policy in China.

It should be noted, however, that hidden behind this demand for open doors in China was the implicit threat that Britain and the United States would also demand similar concessions if Russia was to be given exclusive rights in Manchuria. While this might appear to be a cruel warning to Qing in today's context, it was only commonsensical conduct during the age of imperialism. The United States was no exception to this jungle law, and there was a rumor in Washington, DC that the United States would follow suit with other Western powers in case the open-door policy failed. This worried Qing so much, it dispatched representatives to confirm the rumor. Judging from its proposal in 1900 to lease Samshawan Port, it was indeed obvious that the United States harbored the intention of encroaching on Qing. At that time, Qing was on the verge of being divided and colonized by the Western powers.

On Qing's part, too, there were some who actually welcomed foreign pressure. For example, when Japanese Minister to Beijing Uchida Kōsai advised the Qing government to reject the agreement concerning the role of the Russo-Chinese Bank on February 5, 1900, he declared that if Qing signed the Russo-Chinese Bank agreement, thus neglecting its obligations to other countries as stipulated in the treaties, the Japanese government would have no other choice than to pursue the "correction of inequalities" (i.e., to demand comparable rights and interests from Qing). In response to this rather threatening message, the Qing government sent back a reply in which Uchida detected "their sense of gratitude and reliance on us." It must have taken a message containing a certain degree of threat to move the Qing court, which had been completely cajoled by Russia since the time of Li Hongzhang. It is not hard to imagine, therefore, that the administrative authority of Qing secretly welcomed this type of clear foreign pressure to persuade the court.

Russia's Advance to the Korean Peninsula

Meanwhile, Russian conduct had become increasingly aggressive since August 1900. In September and October, the East Siberian Railway, on the pretext of damaged railroads, refused to handle regular cargo, allowing it to concentrate on transporting reinforcement troops and military supplies. The Russian navy also dispatched a considerable number of naval vessels, including battleships, to the Far East.

Later, during the Cold War era, the US military developed an early-warning system to detect the eruption of war. This system regarded restrictions on handling regular cargo by a railway as an important sign of an imminent military attack. Applying this analysis, war was already on the verge of breaking out in the autumn of 1903.

In November, Russia sent its soldiers across the border into Korean territory, on the pretext of lumbering, to occupy Yongam Inlet (the Amnok / Yalu River estuary) and demanded that the Korean government lease the inlet. Hearing about this incident, Komura advised the Korean government to reject Russia's request. The Korean government, for its part, was determined to restrict Russia's conduct in its territory even if doing so called for the use of force. Nevertheless, the Russian side totally ignored the Korean government's rejection and accumulated faits accomplis to justify its continued presence. Finally, Russia succeeded in coercing Korea's forest administration authority to sign a lease contract with Russia's lumber company. Despite the Korean government's pronouncement of the invalidity of this contract, with strong backing from Komura, the Russian side continued to occupy Yongam Inlet and construct facilities there.

Prior to this incident, a cabinet meeting attended by the emperor was held on June 23. Five Meiji elder statesmen were at this meeting: Itō Hirobumi, Inoue Kaoru, Yamagata Aritomo, Ōyama Iwao, and Matsukata Masayoshi, as well as Prime Minister Katsura Tarō, Minister of War Terauchi Masatake, Minister of Navy Yamamoto Gonbei, and Komura Jutarō. Komura submitted a lengthy opinion paper to this meeting, which was eventually adopted as Japan's basic policy toward Russia after hours of deliberation. Most noteworthy in this paper was the resolution that the Japanese government would not allow any part of Korea to be ceded to Russia under any condition whatsoever, and that this goal should be achieved at all costs.

Japan's position vis-à-vis Russia was thus confirmed at this cabinet meeting. Russia's occupation of Yongam Inlet was by itself sufficient grounds for Japan to start a war with Russia, unless the latter withdrew its troops from the occupied territory.

Having firmly made up their minds to resort to war if necessary, the Japanese leaders at this meeting also decided that the possibility of a peaceful settlement with Russia should be explored one more time.

In a nutshell, the Japanese side proposed that Japan should approve Russia's special interest in the region along the Chinese Eastern Railway in Manchuria, that Russia should support Japan's prominent position in

Korea, and that both countries should guarantee territorial integrity and equal opportunities for Qing and Korea. Japan formally submitted this proposal in August, but it was not until October that Saint Petersburg finally sent back its response. Russia's long-awaited counterproposal was highly unsatisfactory to Japan, focusing as it did on the issue of Korea, denying Japan any voice on Manchuria, and refusing to make any commitment to Manchuria's territorial integrity or to equal opportunities. Moreover, the counterproposal attached various restrictions to Japan's prominent position in Korea.

Komura met with the Russian minister to Japan Roman Rosen four times to discuss this matter, and toward the end of October, he sent back the Japanese response. Again, Russia did not respond immediately despite Japan's repeated urgings. The response from Russia, which came at last in December, was basically the same as the first one and was, if anything, even more unyielding on some points.

It became obvious from these interactions that as long as it had ambitions in Manchuria, Russia would never promise to guarantee Manchurian territorial integrity or equal opportunities. Meanwhile, behind the scenes, Russia had mobilized its military forces, including some 30,000 tons of fleet reinforcements that had departed Russian ports and reached the Mediterranean Sea.

Britain and the United States Get Cold Feet

In his journal on January 5, 1904, US Secretary of State John Hay wrote, "The Russians now have obviously decided that they will make no concession to Japan. They are convinced that the time has come to annihilate Japan and wipe out all of Japan's strongholds in the Far East."

In parallel with the negotiations with Russia, Komura informed the British and US governments of the progress of the negotiations in the hopes of obtaining their diplomatic support. The two countries, however, remained lukewarm in their attitude toward Russia.

The primary objective of Britain in the Far East was to prevent Japan and Russia from collaborating to reduce British naval power in the region to a position of absolute inferiority in strength. Since this objective had already been achieved with the signing of the Anglo-Japanese Alliance,

Britain did not particularly wish Japan to go into an all-out war with Russia. Instead, Britain was concerned about how the situation in the Far East would evolve if Japan was defeated in the war with Russia.

The United States also got cold feet. By 1902, Hay had already given up on maintaining Manchuria's territorial integrity and had retreated to a position whereby, no matter who became dominant in Manchuria, the United States would be in a position to seek the dominant country's protection of US trade interests.

In a May 31, 1903 letter to President Theodore Roosevelt, Hay wrote: "We are not in any attitude of hostility toward Russia in Manchuria. On the contrary, we recognize her exceptional position in northern China. What we have been working for two years to accomplish . . . is that, no matter what happens eventually in northern China and Manchuria, the United States shall not be placed in any worse position than while the country was under the unquestioned domination of China."[1] In other words, Hay was saying it would not matter if Manchuria was under Russian domination or Chinese domination as long as the terms of trade for the United States were protected; so much for the declaration on territorial integrity.

In August, Hay clearly stated to Russian Ambassador Cassini, "As long as freedom of US trade and American corporations in Manchuria are guaranteed, the US government shall not obstruct Russia's conduct in Manchuria."[2]

This remark was made only two years after Hay's own declaration on Qing's territorial integrity, and it was a far cry from the American rejection of everything Japan would acquire during the Manchurian Incident thirty years later. This difference in US attitude should be attributed to the difference of power between Russia at the beginning of the twentieth century and Japan at the time of the Manchurian Incident. While it has become a cliché in recent US diplomatic documents to say that the traditional policy of the United States is not to approve any one power's domination of the Asian continent, the United States obviously approved Russia's hegemony in Manchuria in those days.

---

1   A. L. P. Dennis, "John Hay," in *The American Secretaries of State and Their Diplomacy*, ed. Samuel Flagg Bemis (New York: Alfred A. Knopf, 1929), 9: 150–51.
2   Edward H. Zabriskie, *American-Russian Rivalry in the Far East, 1895–1914* (Philadelphia: University of Pennsylvania Press, 1946), 85, quoted in Tsunoda, *Manshū mondai*, 191. The Japanese text was translated into English by the author.

Under Komura's instructions, the Japanese minister to the United States Takahira Kogorō (高平小五郎) had been attempting in various ways to make the United States join hands with Japan in protest against Russia. But his efforts had not been successful, and in his report to the Foreign Ministry on October 26, he had to admit: "The US government's attitude toward the Manchurian issue has been gradually changing and, today, it appears as if it is content with the present situation as long as the open door policy in China is guaranteed even if Manchuria's territorial integrity is not maintained."[3]

Although President Roosevelt had not officially opposed Hay's policy, in his mind he was furious about Russia's conduct and was sympathetic toward Japan. But Roosevelt believed public opinion would not be on his side.

In response to Hay's report, Roosevelt had the following to say: "An unwelcome symptom for us if the perception that the United States would not fight Russia to keep Manchuria open" (May 22, 1903); "I have no objection whatsoever to Russia's knowing that I am furious about its conduct in Manchuria, . . . and I have no intention to make any concession" (July 18, 1903); and "As far as the Manchurian issue is concerned, I wish to go as far as our people support me" (July 29, 1903).[4] These personal comments notwithstanding, it was utterly unthinkable for the American people (i.e., the US Congress) to support a war with Russia. Judging that the Senate would never pass an international commitment that purported to restrict Russia's invasion of Manchuria, it can therefore be concluded that Hay had no intention of actually carrying out the principle of territorial integrity he had proposed.

The Eve of War

The situation had come this far, and war was inevitable. On January 12, 1904, a cabinet meeting, with the emperor in attendance, endorsed Komu-

---

3   *Nippon gaikō bunsho* [Documents of Japanese foreign policy] 36, no. 1: 411, quoted in Tsunoda, *Manshū mondai*, 194. The Japanese text was translated to English by the author.

4   *The Letters of Theodore Roosevelt*, ed. Elting E. Morison (Cambridge: Harvard University Press, 1951–4) 4: 478, 520, 532, quoted in Tsunoda *Manshū mondai*, 233–34. The Japanese text was translated into English by the author.

ra's proposal to seek Russia's reconsideration once again and, if Russia still delayed its response or gave unsatisfactory answers, to notify Russia that Japan would discontinue negotiations, reserving the right to take necessary actions of its own. As soon as Russian Minister Rosen received the ultimatum from Komura, he sensed Komura's firm determination and immediately warned Foreign Minister Lambsdorff of the urgency of the situation. Lambsdorff, however, did not pay much attention to this report from Tokyo.

Three weeks passed, but there was still no response from Saint Petersburg. Allegedly, Witte testified after the Russo-Japanese War that Tsar Nikolai had been ready to make a major compromise with Japan in order to avoid the war at the last minute, but the validity of this rumor remains uncertain. After all, people are bound to say they should have done this and that after defeat in a war.

In fact, the Russian side did propose minor amendments after the Japanese announcement of the discontinuation of negotiations on February 5, but they were too minor to be called "a major compromise." As far as Russia's strategy was concerned, naturally, it was more advantageous for Russia to delay the eruption of war as long as possible while building up its forces in the Far East, and this minor amendment proposal should be considered as a maneuver toward this end.

On the Japanese side, Yamagata and Itō remained cautious until the very end. But, at the council among cabinet members and elder statesmen on January 30, even Itō, who had preferred an alliance with Russia, had to admit that war with Russia was inevitable. In the end, Itō wrote: "Now that Russia's aggressive intention is manifest, it is obvious that confrontation with Russia is inevitable sooner or later no matter what temporary compromise we might make. At this point we have but two choices—either to seek a temporary peace in recognition of Japan's feebleness or to block Russia's invasion, thus putting Japan's fate on the line." At this point, the differences between the cautious elder statesmen and the aggressive younger generation, including Katsura and Komura, within the Japanese government were reconciled.

Meanwhile, by the end of January, Russia had transported its menacing troops and massive military supplies to the Yalu River region and issued a new mobilization order in Russia's Far Eastern states and Siberia. The governor of Vladivostok ordered Japanese residents to leave Khabarovsk.

The Russian fleet stationed in Lüshun was ordered to deport, except for one vessel that was under repair. These actions were tantamount to a state of war readiness.

On February 5, the Japanese government wired its negotiators to discontinue negotiations with Russia. This was followed by an official telegram to the Russian Foreign Ministry conveying a severance of diplomatic relations and withdrawal of the Japanese diplomatic missions from Russia. Officials at the Japanese mission decoded the telegram and translated it into English overnight; Minister Kurino hand-delivered the telegram to Foreign Minister Lambsdorff at 4:00 p.m. in the afternoon on February 6.

Receiving the ultimatum from Japan, Tsar Nikolai II sent the following instructions to Yevgeni Alekseyev, the Russian viceroy in Lüshun, on February 8: "It would be desirable to have the Japanese side initiate military action. If, however, the Japanese fleet crosses over the 38th parallel along Korea's western coast, whether or not accompanied by landing parties, you are permitted to attack the enemy fleet before it starts the offensive." The Japanese navy attacked Russian fleets off Incheon and outside the Lüshun Port (Port Arthur) on February 8. Imperial Proclamations of War were issued on February 9 in Russia and February 10 in Japan.

Diplomacy at the Eruption of War

After the announcement of discontinuation of negotiations, Komura devoted his energies to securing the understanding and support of Britain and the United States. In consultation with Itō and Katsura, Komura decided to dispatch his old classmate at Harvard, Kaneko Kentarō, to the United States and Suematsu Kenchō, son-in-law of Itō, to Britain. Komura instructed them to stress Japan's justification for starting the war in order to obtain support from both governments and the general public. Komura's diplomacy vis-à-vis Britain and the United States was indeed thorough.

The primary issue immediately after the start of the war was to forestall interventions by other Western powers. The longer Japan spent in diplomatic interactions with other countries, the more time Russia could spend on improving its war readiness, which would benefit Russia and impair Japan's chances of winning the war. The first thing Komura did, therefore, was to request Britain and the United States to forestall interventions from third-party countries. As Komura had feared, France, which had granted a massive amount of credit to Russia and feared being involved in its war with Britain, showed its intention to intervene. But both Britain and the United States turned a deaf ear to the French proposition. Qing was also apprehensive of Manchuria being the battleground, but again, neither Britain nor the United States paid any attention to Qing's plea. At the request of the Japanese government, the German government also agreed not to intervene. Thus, Japan was able to completely neutralize the risk of interventions by other powers.

Moreover, as soon as the war started, Britain and the United States, which had both been neutral before the war, became highly sympathetic to Japan. President Roosevelt's change in attitude was particularly remarkable. Upon hearing of Japan's victory in the early stage of the war, he wrote to his son Theodore Roosevelt, Jr. on February 10, 1904, "I am extremely pleased with Japan's victory because they are playing our game in our place."[5]

Furthermore, Roosevelt told Kaneko Kentarō, special envoy of the Japanese government that "Since Japan is now fighting for the sake of civilization, my sympathy is entirely with Japan"[6] on March 20 and wrote to Kaneko on April 23 that he had long believed that it would be a good omen for the entire world for Japan to join the club of civilized nations.[7] He also shared a similar view with Secretary Hay.

On his part, Hay highly praised Japanese diplomacy on the eve of the Russo-Japanese War. He shared the following thought with Japanese Minister Takahira: "Reviewing the Japanese attitude during its negotiations with Russia, I am struck by Japan's fairness and solidness. Japan made necessary and moderate concessions without hesitation and without giving an inch when it came to national security. This is quite unheard of not only in other countries but even in US diplomatic history." While Britain remained strictly neutral in compliance with international law, it tacitly extended various kinds of assistance to Japan as its ally, including the provision of critical information.

---

5   Ibid., 724, quoted in Tsunoda, *Manshū mondai*, 234. The Japanese text was translated into English by the author.

6   Ibid., 726, quoted in Tsunoda *Manshū mondai*, 235.

7   Ibid., 710, quoted in Tsunoda *Manshū mondai*, 235.

For instance, Britain helped Japan purchase warships. Since it took at least two and a half years to build a battleship, both Japan and Russia were driven by an avid need to acquire newly constructed vessels. Around the time of the Russo-Japanese War, there was an ongoing naval armament race between Argentine and Chile, with both countries commissioning the construction of warships to shipyards in the Western powers' own countries. Because both had commissioned more than they could afford, there were vessels that had been completed but undelivered.

Chile was on the verge of selling two battleships to Russia that it had commissioned at a British shipyard. The British government informed the Japanese government about these two vessels, implying that Japan should purchase them. But Japan could not come up with the required 20 million yen deposit. Hearing this, the British government immediately bought up these two vessels for the British navy, paying for them in cash, rather than letting them fall into the hands of the Russians. Moreover, the British government also informed the Japanese government of two heavy cruisers that were about to be completed in an Italian shipyard. Referring to this incident, Itō Masanori, a Meiji-Shōwa journalist and military commentator, wrote that it was "a historical fact that reminds us how fortunate it is to have an ally."

Russia learned of these two heavy cruisers only one day after Japan did. Although Russia attempted to purchase these ships by bidding up the price, they ended up in the hands of the Japanese at the last moment on December 31, 1903. Even though the vessels were cruisers, they were armed with guns that had a higher elevation, giving them a much longer range than any other vessel in either navy. These cruisers, *Nisshin* and *Kasuga*, played a major role in the Russo-Japanese War, particularly during the bombardment of Lüshun, when they were the only two vessels to shell the enemy's main batteries from outside their range.

However, the transportation of these two vessels to Japan was a headache for the Japanese navy. It would be natural for the Russian fleet to attempt to capture or sink them if the war erupted before they reached Japan. In contrast to Russia, which was already a global naval nation at the time, Japan had no naval capability with which to protect its vessels outside the Far East. Throughout the time spent fitting the equipment on these two cruisers, Russian vessels were constantly anchored inside the port, and a Russian fleet was standing by at the French colony of Bizerte Port.

On January 8, the vessels departed the shipyard with only the fighting equipment on board and entered the Mediterranean Sea. The Russian fleet tried to intercept the vessels and broke up into two groups: the battleship *Oslabia* dropped anchor at Port Said in northeast Egypt to wait for the arrival of *Nisshin* and *Kasuga*, while the rest of the fleet sailed along with the two vessels. But *King Alfred*, the British navy's state-of-the-art heavy cruiser, sailed from the British naval port of Malta and cut in between *Nisshin* and *Kasuga* and the Russian fleet, effectively protecting the Japanese vessels.

In Port Said, where all facilities and equipment, from coal to barges, belonged to Britain, the British side offered subtle assistance that did not violate the rule of neutrality to the Japanese side. For instance, when the *Oslabia* requested coal, the British port authority told the Russians that all the barges had already been reserved by the Japanese side and gave higher priority to the Japanese vessels so they could sail out of the port first. After that, the British port authority leisurely attended to the Russian vessels. Disheartened, most of the ships of the Russian fleet returned to their home port from there. Still, three ships continued to follow the Japanese vessels tenaciously up to the Red Sea, from where they too returned home. In the middle of the Indian Ocean, *King Alfred,* upon completion of its escort duty, signaled the *Nisshin* and *Kasuga* and said, "We believe and pray to God that both ships will arrive home safely," and headed for Australia. Itō Masanori described this incident as "an episode that brings home the preciousness of friendship."

When the *Nisshin* and *Kasuga* arrived in Japan after completing their treacherous voyage they were welcomed as if their arrival were a national celebration. According to the journal kept by Lieutenant Painter, a British navy reserve officer who commanded *Kasuga*'s transportation, all the transportation crews were taken to Tokyo on a special train after being welcomed in Yokosuka and Yokohama. They were treated as if they were generals returning in triumph, with welcome gates raised in several places, soldiers forming lines, and streets filled with well-wishers. After the welcome ceremony in Hibiya Park in central Tokyo, the transportation crews were granted an audience with the emperor. Lieutenant Painter wrote, "In retrospect, I realized that I have accomplished a life-time task by this single voyage." It is not hard to imagine how proud and pleased the Japanese people were to receive these two warships.

Sources of Funds and Information

Of all the assistance and cooperation Britain and the United States extended to Japan, the most welcome by far was their financial assistance. Coming up with the idea of issuing government bonds in Britain in October 1903, about a year before the war, the Japanese government negotiated with Samuel Samuel & Co. in Yokohama on the issuance of bonds in London for the amount of 10 million yen. Because Samuel Samuel & Co. basically agreed to respond to the Japanese request on the condition of the British government's guarantee, the Japanese government sounded out British Foreign Secretary Lord Lansdowne for help. Showing an encouraging attitude, Lansdowne promised he would earnestly consider the issue if formally approached by the Japanese government.

The foreign secretary's encouraging attitude notwithstanding, the fiscal authority of the British government frowned upon the provision of a government guarantee to the Japanese bond issue because the London financial market had already been saturated with British government bonds to finance the Boer War. This war had caused a fiscal deficit, forcing the British government to float its own government bonds. Hearing this, the Japanese government decided to give up on the British government's guarantee and to float bonds in its own right.

After the severance of diplomatic relations with Russia, the Japanese government dispatched Takahashi Korekiyo (高橋是清), deputy governor of the Bank of Japan, to London to float the public debt. The plan that the Japanese government had commissioned Takahashi for reflected the dire reality of the fiscal situation in Japan at that time.

According to this plan, the total war expenditure was estimated to be 450 million yen, 150 million of which had to be financed by foreign currency. This amount was based on Japan's experience during the First Sino-Japanese War, in which one-third of the war expenses had to be raised abroad. Because the foreign reserves available at the Bank of Japan for the war with Russia were only about 50 million yen, the remaining 100 million yen, or about 10 million pounds according to the exchange rate in those days, had to be raised by issuing government bonds overseas. However, the amount of 450 million yen was estimated to give Japan one year to eliminate the Russian troops from the Korean Peninsula. If the battle continued beyond one year, and beyond the Yalu River, additional funds would have to be raised. Thus, the Japanese government had to raise funds urgently, within a year, by issuing external bonds.

In actuality, the war expenditures ballooned to 2 billion yen by the end of the war, and the amount of public debt floated in London exceeded 100 million pounds, far exceeding the initial estimates.

At first, raising funds in Britain with a government bond issue was a challenging task. Because Britain was hesitant to single-handedly side with a nation of the yellow race in a strife between the white and yellow races and because there was no guarantee that Japan would win the war, harsh conditions were imposed on the issue of Japanese bonds.

When Takahashi was dispatched, he was instructed to limit the annual interest to below 5 percent. However, it ended up being set at 6 percent, and the Japanese government was requested to mortgage its tariff revenue. Although British banks insisted that Japanese customs should be put under the control of British officials, as they had demanded of Qing, Takahashi adamantly refused this, stressing that "the Japanese government has never defaulted on the interest on foreign bonds."

Nevertheless, it was still a tall order to raise 10 million pounds in Britain alone, and the Japanese government was forced to raise half of the amount by issuing bonds in the United States. In those days, Jews in the United States were sympathetic toward Japan, resenting the Russian oppression of Jews. Thus, Jewish capital, particularly from Kuhn Loeb & Co., greatly helped the Japanese government to successfully issue bonds for the amount of 5 million pounds in the United States.

As Japan continued to defeat Russia in one battle after another, however, the number of holders of Japanese bonds increased and the conditions imposed on them gradually relaxed, until the annual interest rate dropped to 4 percent without collateral by November 1905, the moment when Japan's victory became decisive.

Komura wrote in the Komura Memorandum that one of the advantages of an alliance with Britain would be the financial assistance Japan could obtain. It would have been impossible for Japan to wage the Russo-Japanese War had it not been for the help of the financial markets in Britain and the United States. The war was only possible because of Japan's friendly relations with two of the day's richest countries in the world.

Table 2. Issue of Japanese government bonds during the Russo-Japanese War

	Amount Issued (£)	Annual Interest (%)	Floatation price per face value of £100	Government revenue per face value of £100	Handling fee per face value of £100	Collateral	Term for redemption
1st Issue (May 1904)	10 million	6.0	£93 10s	£90 00s	£3 10s	Tariff revenue	7 months (3 months deferment
2nd Issue (November 1904)	12 million	6.0	£90 10s	£86 15s	£3 15s	Tariff revenue	7 months (3 months deferment)
3rd Issue (March 1905)	30 million	4.5	£90 00s	£86 15s	£3 5s	Profit of tobacco monopoly	20 months (5 months deferment)
4th Issue (July 1905)	30 million	4.5	90 00s	£86 15s	£3 5s	Profit of tobacco monopoly	20 months (5 months deferment)

Finally, what Japan greatly benefited from the Anglo-Japanese Alliance, along with the financial assistance, was the critical information provided by the British. As soon as the alliance was formed, the British government proposed that Anglo-Japanese military consultations be launched, and they started discussions in Yokosuka in May. In June, Major General Fukushima Yasumasa, director of intelligence of the Japanese Imperial Army, and Lieutenant Colonel Shiba Gorō, were dispatched to London to represent Japan at the negotiation for the Anglo-Japanese military agreement, accompanying Prince Komatsu Akihito, who was to attend the coronation of Edward VII.

In 1892, Major General Fukushima, on his way home from Germany, where he had served as the military attaché, traveled across Siberia alone on horseback for fourteen months to observe the conditions there, particularly the construction of the Trans-Siberian Railway. Fukushima was one of the most experienced intelligence specialists in the entire Japanese military. And Lieutenant Colonel Shiba for his part was the commander of the Japanese troops dispatched to Beijing during the Boxer Rebellion, and he was highly respected in Britain as the savior of foreigners in Beijing.

The Anglo-Japanese military agreement was signed on July 10 by Major General Fukushima and Lieutenant General William Nicholson, director general of the Intelligence Bureau of the Ministry of War. An elaborate agreement was made, specifically about the exchange of information.

The quality of information that Japan collected during the Russo-Japanese War was far superior to that collected during World War II. For one thing, Japan in those days was still a minor player who was not capable of proactively influencing the international situation, and yet it was about to challenge Russia, one of the world's superpowers at that time. It was only natural for the Japanese military to devote itself to collecting as much accurate information as possible.

Interaction with the British intelligence organizations must have had a tremendous effect on the Japanese military. The accuracy of the information was greatly improved simply by comparing the information it had collected with that from Britain, through which Japanese officers were able to obtain the know-how for information processing. Nothing is more important in information processing than the ability to make comprehensive and well-balanced judgments. Simply by constantly having dialogue with the country that dominated the Seven Seas and monopolized all the world's information, the capability to judge the importance and value of each piece of information would be acquired. One cannot help but reflect on how many erroneous assessments Japan made after the abolition of the Anglo-Japanese Alliance and up until its defeat in World War II and how many of those errors could have been avoided had Japan consulted with the Anglo-American countries.

In ordinary life, too, those who are befriended by an elite group in the school or office—in other words, those who possess quality information—will not be distracted by dubious information and, therefore, will be spared from unnecessary study or work. It is as simple as that.

In a nutshell, the key to maintaining the quality of intelligence is to construct a relationship of friendship and mutual trust with the Anglo-American world.

Thus, by supplementing war finances and intelligence, two of Japan's weakest points, through the Anglo-Japanese Alliance, Japan went on to confront the superpower Russia to the best of its ability.

CHAPTER

9

Rise of Japan

—Japanese Patriotism Amazes the Entire World—

Race against Time

The gap between the military strengths of Russia and Japan on the eve of the Russo-Japanese War was certainly great enough to say that it was indeed foolhardy for Japan to start a war with Russia. The population of Japan was about one-third that of Russia, and its steel and pig iron production was only tens of thousands of tons compared to 1.5 million tons and 2.2 million tons respectively for Russia.

Some forty years later, on the eve of World War II, Winston Churchill asked Japanese Foreign Minister Matsuoka Yosuke how Japan could dare to plot a war with the United States and Britain, which produced 75 million tons and 12.5 million tons of steel respectively, when Japan produced only 7 million tons annually. The gap between Russia and Japan at the beginning of the twentieth century was much larger than that.

According to Australian war writers Denis and Peggy Warner, in January 1904 the Russian army had a wartime mobilization capability of 3.5 million personnel, including 1,135,000 troops on active duty plus army reserves and second reserves. In contrast, the Japanese Imperial Army in those days had 180,000 troops on active duty, 200,000 army reserves, and another 200,000 in the second reserves.

Table 3. Comparison of Japanese and Russian military strength before the Russo-Japanese War

Army	Infantry	Cavalry	Cannons	Total Force Strength
Japan	156 battalions	55 companies	636	approx. 158,000
Russia	1,740 battalions (90 battalions)	1,085 companies (—)	1,200 (172)	approx. 2,070,000

Navy	Battleships	Armored Cruisers	Cruisers	Total Tonnage
Japan	6	6	12	approx. 260,000 tons
Russia's Baltic Fleet	11	12	12	approx. 800,000 tons
	(7)	(4)	(—)	(approx. 190,000 tons)

Numbers in parentheses are Russian forces in the Far East

It could be misleading to compare the war capability of armies on the basis of the number of divisions. During the Cold War, for instance, a division of the Soviet army was considered to be the equivalent of two to three divisions of the Japan Ground Self-Defense Force. This is because numbers of soldiers, tanks, and cannons in a division differ from one army to the next.

Instead, the number of infantry battalions that can immediately participate in battle is the measure used to compare the war capability of armies. The size of a battalion does not differ much from country to country. Using this yardstick, Russia had 1,740 battalions, or more than ten times the 156 battalions that Japan had on the eve of the Russo-Japanese War.

In terms of total tonnage of naval vessels, the Russian navy had 800,000 tons, of which 190,000 tons had been stationed in the Far East. In comparison, the Imperial Japanese Navy with 260,000 tons.

The above table clearly shows that Japan appeared to have no chance of winning the war with Russia. The only advantage for Japan was the great distance between the European center of Russia and the Far East. Such great distance meant that it took a long time to transport reinforcements and military supplies, making logistics and replenishment highly challenging. In this sense, the Russo-Japanese War was a race against time.

The Battle of Mukden on March 10, 1905 was one of the largest showdowns in the history of ground warfare. Some 250,000 Japanese troops—all that Japan had at the time—fought against 320,000 Russian troops.

By that time, Russian troops were fully benefiting from the East Siberian Railway, which enabled the arrival of monthly reinforcements of 50,000 troops. Toward the end of the war, monthly reinforcements of 60,000 troops became possible via this railway.

Had the Battle of Mukden been delayed by half a year, therefore, the number of Russian troops would have nearly doubled, leaving Japan no chance of winning. Had the battle been fought half a year earlier, the Russian side would have had to fight with a strength of only 220,000 troops. Since this was approximately the same strength the Russians had mustered for the Battle of Liaoyang (遼陽会戦) in September of the previous year, annihilation of the main Russian force might have been possible.

In this sense, Komura's effort to trigger the eruption of the war as early as possible was, strategically speaking, highly appropriate.

Miscalculation in Delay Tactics

The race against time was an important factor in the Russo-Japanese War, not only in the grand strategy but also in every aspect of the war. In a way, it is even possible to interpret every strategy and tactic employed throughout the war as having used this variable. The most urgent issue for Japan at the beginning of the war was how to wipe out Russian troops and cripple Russian ambitions on the Korean Peninsula. Subsequently, it was imperative to sever the line of communication between the Russian troops based in Liaoyang in southern Manchuria and those in the Lüshun fortress. After that, the imperative was to annihilate the Russian army assembled in Liaoyang before it grew into a massive force.

The key to accomplishing these missions was to send as many soldiers as possible to northern Korea and southern Manchuria.

The fastest way to dispatch troops to northern Korea was to transport them to Incheon on boats. This would be about one month faster than landing the troops either at Busan or Wonsan on the east coast and marching them across treacherous roads. This method of transport, however, required Japan to secure command of the Yellow Sea. This was why the first military operation of the Japanese side was the bombardment of the Russian squadron in Lüshun.

The Russian military plan in 1901 called for concentrating the bulk of troops in Mukden and Liaoyang, then from there withdrawing all the way to Harbin—while defending Lüshun and Vladivostok with a limited number of troops. The plan was to delay Japanese advances in the course of withdrawing, and then turn to offensive tactics as repeated reinforcements tipped the military balance in Russia's favor. The revised plan of 1903 was basically the same: first withstand the Japanese attacks and then go on the offensive after massive reinforcements arrived to expel the Japanese troops from Manchuria and Korea. The plan, which had received imperial endorsement from the tsar before the start of the war, also envisaged the initial withdrawal to Harbin.

This military strategy was behind the mysterious withdrawals of the Russian troops during the Battles of Liaoyang and Mukden—when one more push would have destroyed the Japanese troops. The Russians felt they could surely win sooner or later if they continued to amass reinforcements as they withdrew. While Russia might have had a fifty-fifty chance of winning a face-to-face showdown, it was not at all necessary to gamble against a Japanese army known for its intrepidness. All the Russian troops had to do was fight the Japanese enough to delay their operations and then, once that mission was accomplished, withdraw their main force to preserve its strength. Some may criticize this strategy, but commanders would not be denounced too harshly as having only followed the basic grand policy that was decided in the tsar's presence. Seen from this angle, it could be said that ground battles during the Russo-Japanese War proceeded almost exactly as Russia had planned.

In retrospect, however, this delay tactic was the greatest cause of Russia's defeat in the Russo-Japanese War.

To begin with, troops fighting at the forefront were put in the difficult position of having to decide whether to fight a battle all the way, which meant risking their lives, or end the battle at an appropriate time; this allowed death-defying Japanese soldiers to take advantage of the situation.

But the far graver impact was on Russia's domestic politics. Reporting on one withdrawal after another damaged the prestige of Russia, which in turn encouraged the activities of antigovernment subversives and separatist movements run by minorities. Just as the revolt of American intellectuals and students during the Vietnam War (1965–75) and the slowdown of the Soviet economy as the result of the war in Afghanistan (1979–89) damaged the capabilities of the United States and the Soviet Union to continue those wars, the outcome of the delay tactics became a critical obstacle for Russia trying to continue the Russo-Japanese War.

A Bold Personnel Change Affected the Fate of a Nation

It seems appropriate to spend a few pages here portraying the leaders of the Japanese military at the time of the Russo-Japanese War.

Kodama Gentarō (児玉源太郎) guided the strategy of the whole campaign during the Russo-Japanese War. An elite from among the elite of the Chōshū-*han*, Kodama had been a prime minister hopeful early in his life. He was an attractive man of sharp wits, dauntless actions, and decisiveness, and he had an abundant sense of humor.

Kodama first participated in military action at the age of sixteen during the Boshin War (戊辰戦争) in 1868–69. He was already deputy chief of staff at Kumamoto Garrison when he was twenty-five years old; he successfully defended Kumamoto Castle from the fierce charges of Satsuma rebels. During the First Sino-Japanese War, Kodama supported Kawakami Sōroku (川上操六), then de facto chief of general staff of the Imperial Army, attending to military administration as the vice-minister of war. Kodama was appointed as minister of war in the fourth Itō cabinet at the age of forty-eight. In the subsequent Katsura cabinet, he was appointed as minister-of-home-affairs-cum-governor-general of Taiwan; he was also in charge of supervising the planning of strategies against Russia as de facto deputy prime minister.

The chief of the general staff at that time was Ōyama Iwao (大山巌)—who was succeeded by Yamagata Aritomo when Ōyama was appointed to commander in chief of the Japanese army in Manchuria after the eruption of the Russo-Japanese War—one of the Meiji elder statesmen and a man of tremendous presence. While it was actually the deputy chief who managed General Staff affairs, Kawakami Sōroku met a premature death as a result of exhaustion from the First Sino-Japanese War. He was followed by a brilliant successor, Tamura Iyozō (田村 怡与造), who also passed away in October 1903, half a year before the Russo-Japanese War, exhausted by operational preparations for the war. After these two deaths, no one had any brilliant ideas about who the next deputy chief of the General Staff should be.

After careful consultation, the bewildered Prime Minister Katsura, Kodama, and Komura all decided that there was nobody else but Kodama to assume the post. For Kodama it would mean a demotion of two levels, from a cabinet minister and de facto deputy prime minister to deputy chief of the General Staff, but Kodama paid no heed to that. Among those who appointed Kodama, and for Kodama himself, the only consideration in their minds was the fate of the nation.

Tōgō Heihachirō was appointed as commander in chief of the Combined Fleet of the Imperial Japanese Navy, which surprised some people. With such brilliant leaders in the Imperial Navy as Hidaka Sōnojō and Shibayama Yahachi—who, some thought, might be more qualified to be commander in chief—voices questioning the wisdom of appointing Tōgō reached even the Imperial Court. When asked by Emperor Meiji about this appointment, Navy Minister Yamamoto Gonbei replied, "Because Tōgō is a man of good fortune, Your Majesty." To be sure, Tōgō had played a vital role at various key points during the First Sino-Japanese War as commander of the superannuated *Naniwa*. It appears that Tōgō's promotion was attributable to his restraint, calm composure, and ability to stay focused.

Blockading Russia's Lüshun Squadron

Emperor Meiji always hesitated to decide on whether to wage war until the very last minute. At the time of the First Sino-Japanese War, the emperor said, "It is a war of Our cabinet members. It is not Our war," and he remained in a bad mood for a few days.

On the eve of the Russo-Japanese War, when even the cautious Itō Hirobumi decided that war was inevitable, Emperor Meiji repeatedly said, "We do not know how to apologize to our people if the war turns out to be a disaster." Because the emperor of Japan is ultimately responsible to the state, its people, and the spirits of the ancestors, it must have been the graveness of his responsibility that made him make these comments.

But, on February 3, the Japanese government received a telegram reporting that all the vessels of the Lüshun squadron had left port, which could only mean that Russia was in a state of war readiness. While there was no knowing where the squadron was heading, the worst possible sce-

Sailors seeing off the torpedo squadron for blockading Lüshun, February, 1904. Battleship *Asahi* in the front, Battleship *Mikasa*, the flagship of the Japanese Combined Fleet on the left, with Captain Tōgō on board.

nario for Japan would be for the Russian squadron to capture Jinhae Bay, which faced the Korea Strait. Located in the southeast of the Korean Peninsula, Jinhae is a good harbor where later, at the time of the Battle of Tsushima, the Japanese Combined Fleet would anchor to wait for the arrival of Russia's Baltic Fleet. If Jinhae Bay was captured even temporarily, traffic through the Korea Strait would be cut off, disabling the transport of Japanese ground troops to the Asian continent. Even if the Japanese side were able to recapture the bay shortly, the delay in the transportation of troops caused by the initial Russian capture may have proven fatal.

The urgency of the situation notwithstanding, Emperor Meiji still did not endorse the war, not even at the cabinet meeting held in his presence on February 4. It was on February 5 that imperial sanction was at last given to dispatch naval vessels. Departing Sasebo Port in Nagasaki on February 6, the Japanese Combined Fleet immediately headed for Jinhae Bay and attacked the Russian squadron off Lüshun Port on February 8.

Anchored in Incheon Port were two Russian vessels, the gunship *Korietz* and the cruiser *Variag*. These two vessels sailed out of port on February 8 but soon returned to port, having encountered the main force of the Japanese fleet. They ventured out once again on February 9 only to be routed by the superior enemy forces. Both ships scuttled backed to Incheon Port.

Deep in the night of February 8, the fleet of Japanese destroyers spotted and assaulted the Russian fleet anchored off Lüshun Port, seriously damaging the battleships *Tsesarevich* and *Retvisan* and the cruiser *Pollada*. Although the Japanese Combined Fleet challenged its Russian opponents to a duel on February 9, the entire Russian squadron, intimidated by the surprise attack from the night before, retreated deep into Lüshun Port and never came out.

For about one year after this, Russia's Lüshun squadron concentrated solely on preserving its force until reinforcements arrived from Europe. Other than one vain attempt to escape to Vladivostok, the fleet's activities were confined to the region around Lüshun Port. Thus, the Japanese Combined Fleet was able to accomplish its original goal of gaining command of the Yellow Sea and protecting the safety of its naval transports.

Sea battles between the two sides during this period hardly affected the big picture of the war, so I would be justified in forgoing a detailed description. However, the operation of blockading Lüshun Port merits some explanation, because it was an operation that was very visible to the Japanese people, generating a lot of heroic stories—in fact, for quite a few elders, this blockade would be the first thing to come to mind from the entire Russo-Japanese War.

Noblesse Oblige

The blockade had already been tried by the US Navy during the Spanish-American War (1898), and the tactic had been incorporated into the operational plans of the Imperial Navy before the start of the Russo-Japanese War. The blockade was aimed at obstructing the passage of Russian vessels by sinking old transport ships in the narrow channel near the mouth of Lüshun Port. This tactic would not be effective unless vessels were sunk accurately at the intended spot. But it would be challenging to spot the right point during the night, while the attacking vessel would be easy prey to the garrison's salvos during the day. In the end, Commander in Chief Tōgō decided to carry out the mission at night out of concern for the safety of his men, but it would still be a highly risky, death-defying operation, sailing through shells from hundreds of enemy guns.

When sixty-seven volunteer sailors and noncommissioned officers were called for on February 18 for the first attempt, as many as 2,000 volunteered. Some even sealed their applications with blood.

Blockade attempts were made three times in vain on February 24, March 27, and May 2, each time piling up casualties. Nevertheless, as many as 6,800 still volunteered for the next attempt, testifying to the high morale among officers and sailors. As abortive attempts were repeated, many involved naturally started arguing that those who had experienced the operation before should be given preference in the recruitment. Tōgō, however, single-handedly rejected this argument, saying that "While it might be applicable to officers, no same sailor should go twice." This was a manifestation of Tōgō's spirit of noblesse oblige, urging the elite to volunteer for dangerous tasks ahead of others.

First Victory at the Battle of Yalu River

During the blockade of Russia's Lüshun squadron, the Japanese First Army, under the command of General Kuroki Tamemoto (黒木 為楨), successfully landed on Incheon in mid-March. The Second Army, under General Oku Yasukata (奥 保鞏), subsequently landed on Liaodong Peninsula.

Meanwhile, the Russian squadron in Lüshun Port would not take the offensive, except for small-scale operations around Liaodong Peninsula. Basically, the Russian squadron in Lüshun took the option of preserving its strength until the arrival of the Baltic Fleet from Europe, a very passive decision that inadvertently made it easier for the Japanese side to concentrate its forces.

The Japanese victory at the Battle of Yalu River (鴨緑江の戦い), which determined the outcome of the early stage of the Russo-Japanese War, was primarily the result of the speed at which the Japanese side was able to concentrate its forces. While the Russian side had estimated that about 20,000 Japanese troops would arrive at Yalu River in mid-May, it was actually in late April that Kuroki's First Army reached the southern bank of the Yalu River—and 20,000 Russian troops found themselves up against 40,000 Japanese troops.

Kuroki's troops started crossing the Yalu River on May 1. In anticipation of the Japanese crossing in the vicinity of Andong (present-day Dandong) at the estuary of the river, the Russian troops had built defense lines there. But the Twelfth Division of Kuroki's army took a northern detour and completed the crossing.

As a matter of fact, Imperial Headquarters had proposed postponing the river-crossing operation for three days so as to synchronize it with the Second Army's landing on Liaodong Peninsula. General Kuroki turned down the proposal on the grounds that preparations were already too far advanced to put off the river crossing. Heavy rains began falling after Kuroki's army crossed the river on May 1; these rains would have made the crossing impossible for another week. Thus, it turned out that General Kuroki's decision was a priceless one in this war that was a race against time. Had the river crossing been delayed for another week, the Russian troops would have had that much more time to gather reinforcements and strengthen their defenses.

The Japanese army was superior to its Russian opponent on several points. The number of troops was one, as we have seen, but the power of the Japanese 12 cm howitzer, which had been a well-kept secret, proved particularly effective, simply overwhelming the Russian troops.

The topography of the region favored the Russians defending their stronghold and led to expectations that the Japanese side would suffer heavy casualties upon attacking. In fact, army surgeons attached to Kuroki's army had been instructed to prepare themselves to attend to some 6,000 wounded. As it turned out, however, Kuroki's army succeeded in capturing the Russian stronghold within a day and with little more than 900 casualties.

In order to escape being besieged and annihilated by the Japanese troops, the Russian troops started to retreat. En route, they were confronted by First Lieutenant Makisawa's company, which was defending a gorge. Even though the company suffered devastating damage, losing half of its soldiers in the battle, it succeeded in defending its stronghold from the Russian attacks until reinforcements from the Japanese main forces arrived. The result was the destruction and surrender of two Russian regiments. This battle was reported to various Western powers by their military observers, who unanimously praised the heroic conduct of Makisawa's company.

The commanders of the Japanese Manchurian Army gathered in Mukden, on July 26, 1905, the Chief of General Staff Yamagata Aritomo in attendance. From left, General Kuroki Tamemoto for the First Army, General Nozu Michitsura for the Fourth Army, Chief of General Staff Yamagata Aritomo, Commanding General of the Japanese Manchurian Army Ōyama Iwao, General Oku Yasukata for the Second Army, General Nogi Maresuke for the Third Amy, The Chief of Staff for the Japanese Manchurian Army Kodama Gentarō, and General for the Yalu River Army Kawamura Kageaki. (Photo: Kyodo News)

Although this Battle of Yalu River was not as large in scale as the subsequent Battles of Liaoyang and Mukden, its psychological impact on both the Japanese and Russian sides was tremendous.

In regard to this victory, Major General Nagaoka Gaishi (長岡外史), who later succeeded Kodama Gentarō to become deputy chief of the General Staff, wrote to Kuroki that "I know that 'happy enough to dance despite myself' is a figure of speech, but this was exactly what happened when the news of your victory reached the Imperial General Headquarters." Minister of War Terauchi Masatake sent a congratulatory telegraph saying that "The whole nation is in a state of boundless jubilation."

At that time, Toyokawa Ryōhei of Mitsubishi Bank was engaged in the flotation of the Japanese government bond issue in Britain and the United States under the special command of Prime Minister Katsura. Toyokawa reminisced: "While we had been suffering from a dearth of purchasers of our bonds no matter how favorable the conditions were before the Battle of Yalu River, we have had so many purchasers since the victory on May 1 that we were forced to turn some of them down." The amount of bonds issued also shot up from 2 million yen before the May 1 victory to 50 million yen overnight.

Kuroki Tametomo: Overnight World Hero

The Battle of Yalu River was the first combat in which a nation of a colored race, using modern weapons, overwhelmed the white race. *The Times* of London praised Japan's victory, stating: "There is no word that can sufficiently praise the morale, courage, and perfect organization of the Japanese Army. This battle has proven that Japanese staff officers are endowed with supreme military capabilities. Its soldiers are also excellent, moving precisely like a machine." In her book about the Hsinhai Revolution in China, Eiko Woodhouse introduced the following overseas episodes that can only be described as "Kuroki Fever":

> Kuroki became an overnight hero. In Mexico they renamed their most productive mine General Kuroki Mine for good fortune. Kuroki fever was also witnessed in Canada where the Northern Land Railway named a newly opened station in Saskatchewan province after Kuroki, . . . while the Department of Communication of the provincial government of Ottawa also named a newly opened post office after him . . . To some in the United States it might have been unbearable for this hero Kuroki to be a mere Japanese, and a rumor was going around that Kuroki was actually a descendant of a Pole by the name of Kroski.
>
> In Russia, rumor has it that Kuroki was actually part Russian because his grandfather was born in a Siberian village. The Kuroki Army's great victory at the Battle of Yalu River, the rumor says, owes it to the Russian blood of its commander.[1]

---

1   Eiko Woodhouse, *The Chinese Hsinhai Revolution: G. E. Morrison and Anglo-Japanese Relations, 1897–1920* (London: Routledge, 2013).

Those were the days when no one believed that a colored race could defeat a white race.

In the subsequent Battle of Nanshan (南山の戦い) as well, the quick concentration of troops by the Japanese was the decisive factor. Nanshan is a 3 km wide mountainous region in the narrowest part of Liaodong Peninsula. Because the landing of the Japanese Second Army on Liaodong Peninsula had been carried out much more smoothly than expected, the Russian side had no time to request reinforcements from Liaoyang or Lüshun, forcing it to defend Nanshan with a solitary regiment.

Still, the Japanese troops found Russian defenders, protected by trenches and armed with machine guns, tough opponents. They showed a caliber of fighting suited to a modern state military—a far cry from Qing soldiers during the First Sino-Japanese War, who had fled without putting up any respectable resistance. In retrospect, the hardship the Japanese troops experienced in the Battle of Nanshan was a precursor to the fierceness of the battle at Lüshun. While Russian gunships dispatched from Lüshun bombarded the advancing Japanese troops, causing heavy casualties, the Japanese Combined Fleet also bombarded the Russian strongholds, contributing to their eventual fall.

The Times of London reported on the Battle of Nanshan and lavished praise on the "marvelous courage and patience" of the Japanese troops.

Subsequently, Japanese forces captured the region around Dalian Bay. Dalian became Japan's logistics base throughout the war.

All of Kuroki's Bold Initiatives Hit the Mark

Having succeeded in isolating Lüshun, the next requirement for the Japanese military was to dispatch as many troops as promptly as possible to Liaoyang to engage in a decisive battle with the Russian army before its main force was joined by reinforcements.

To the west of Liaoyang lies the great plain of Manchuria, which stretches until it meets the sea at Bohai Bay. Now that the Japanese army had conquered Dalian, it could use the branch line of the Chinese Eastern Railway to transport troops northward. In contrast, east of Liaoyang—the region between the Yalu River and Liaoyang—is mountainous. A dividing ridge connects eastern Manchuria and Liaodong Peninsula, a con-

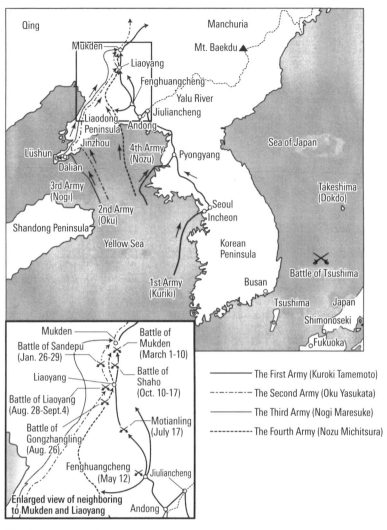

The Japanese army's course

figuration that was easy for the Russians to defend but difficult for the Japanese troops to attack. In light of this natural handicap, therefore, it was commendable that Kuroki's army broke through the Russian defense much faster than expected and advanced further to threaten the east side of Russia's main force.

Kuroki's army was always a step ahead of the Russians from one occasion to the next. Moreover, Kuroki was even a step ahead of the operations of the Imperial General Headquarters. After the successful crossing of Yalu River, General Headquarters instructed Kuroki to stay put for a while, holding off on a further advance deep into Manchuria. General Kuroki, however, asked for General Headquarters' permission to attack Fenghuangcheng (鳳凰城) on the grounds that his current station was too narrow for 40,000 troops and too difficult to defend. Headquarters replied that he could proceed at his own risk. While his staff officers were furious at this reply, Kuroki remained calm, telling his men, "No need to be so upset. Naturally, I will take full responsibility." Kuroki's troops attacked Fenghuangcheng on May 12. Because the Russian side was caught in the middle of constructing defense facilities, Fenghuangcheng, a point of strategic importance on the Korea-Manchuria border, fell easily into the hands of Kuroki's army.

Now that Fenghuangcheng was conquered, the only thing Kuroki's army had to do to reach Liaoyang was to take the rough mountainous road that goes through the natural stronghold of Motianling (摩天嶺). When Kuroki realized that the Russians, quite unaware of the strategic importance of Motianling, had not yet fortified it, he had his army capture it, again going beyond the instructions of General Headquarters. Belatedly realizing Motianling's importance, an elite division of the Russian army challenged Kuroki's army in a hand-to-hand fight to retake it. The Japanese troops successfully repulsed this challenge. Thus, the preparations for Japan's First Army to proceed to Liaoyang were completed.

The above episode shows that each time a new situation emerged, the Japanese troops always made the first move—before the Russian side had even made an action plan. The Russians had to convene a war council to decide how to cope with each new situation. From the beginning, there had been a difference in views between Quartermaster General of the Third Manchurian Army Mikhail Alekseyev, who insisted on defending, on Russia's honor, the territories Russia had captured on the Korean and Liaodong Peninsulas, and Aleksey Kuropatkin, commander in chief of the Russian land forces in Manchuria, who was mindful of strategic sustainability. The differences between these two resulted in unnecessarily long war councils and halfhearted compromise plans.

One of the Most Astounding Feats in World Military History

Kuroki achieved many distinguished military feats during the Russo-Japanese War, but the night raid of Gongzhangling (弓張嶺) was, according to the military historian Itō Masanori, one of the most astounding feats in world military history.

Although the Japanese army had secured the dividing ridge of the road that connects the Korea-Manchuria border and Liaoyang by conquering Motianling, it still had to break the defensive line on the mountain range put up by the robust Russian Tenth Army. At the heart of this defensive line was Gongzhangling. Unless this defensive line was broken, Kuroki's army would remain locked in the mountains, unable to contribute to the general attack on Liaoyang.

Faced with this task, Kuroki received a telegram from General Headquarters informing him that no additional rounds of cannon fire could be supplied for the time being, and therefore, his army had to make do with what ammunition it already had to win this battle. Except for engaging in close combat with swords and bayonets after sneaking into the enemy stronghold under the cover of darkness, it was simply impossible to seize an enemy fortress without shell protection.

But a night raid was a tactic adopted by smaller troops, a battalion at the largest, and a night raid by a full army division was unheard of in world military history—nor was it guaranteed to succeed. Accomplishing tactical goals in the dark would be extremely challenging, and there was always the risk of friendly casualties. Opinions on the wisdom of this operation differed among his staff officers, but Kuroki brilliantly put an end to the dispute, saying: "What's most important is the opinion of the field commanders who will be actually engaged in the battle. Unless they are wholeheartedly supportive of the plan, this operation can never succeed. If field commanders agree with the plan, let's carry it out, but if they appear doubtful, we will revise the plan. Summon the division commander and the brigade commander at once." The Second Division from Sendai was in charge of the Gongzhangling front. The commander, accompanied by two brigade commanders under him, came to see Kuroki and his staff officers. Upon hearing the plan, he immediately said, "Let's give it a try."

A night raid called for special preparations. First, all of the officers had to be made completely familiar with the topography of the region. Thus, officers snuck into the mountains in their areas of responsibility to thoroughly study the terrain and returned to their respective bases, all before dawn. One foreseeable problem on the night of the raid, which would have a full moon until 3:00 a.m., was the reflection of moonlight on the bayonets, but the solution was found when a soldier suggested wrapping the bayonets in sorghum leaves. The password was agreed on, and it was decided that all the raiders would wear white armbands as a mark. Kuroki's army was under a severe time constraint to reach Liaoyang in time for the showdown, but somehow the troops managed to complete their preparations in time.

Thus, on the night of August 26, 12,000 troops from the Second Division started marching silently toward the mountain peak that was protected by 17,000 Russian troops. Soldiers were even prohibited from batting at the mosquitoes swarming around them.

It was an operation in the pitch dark with no verbal commands. Nobody knew how their fellow soldiers were fighting. If some fell behind, they would go unnoticed. Under these circumstances, one could only trust the patriotism and sense of duty of each and every soldier. In retrospect, all the officers and soldiers of the Second Division gallantly lived up to Kuroki's expectations. Some participated in the raid in spite of high fevers. One officer was recuperating from the loss of his right arm in the previous battle, but he also took part in the raid, claiming he wished to die honorably with his still-serviceable left arm and two legs.

The valor of Captain Miura, one of the sword masters among the rank and file, during this night raid became legendary. While cutting down one enemy soldier after another in a dogfight, Miura spotted enemy trenches that were effectively shooting down Japanese soldiers. Dashing toward the gunfire, he immediately cut down several enemy soldiers. All of a sudden, he felt his body become astonishingly heavier. With no way of knowing what had happened in the darkness, Miura continued to cut down enemies around him, as he felt the extra weight had been lifted. He continued to swing his sword in the darkness to save his division. Finally, he collapsed.

One of Miura's men rushed to rescue him and found the point of a bayonet sticking out from his back. Picking up a stone, this soldier struck the point of the bayonet and pulled it out from Miura's chest. In retrospect, it is believed that as Miura charged at Russian soldiers, one of them, having no time to shoot, threw his bayoneted rifle at Miura, which penetrated his chest and that was the moment when he felt an extra heaviness on his body. As he continued to cut down enemies, the hilt of the bayonet must have broken off, making him feel suddenly relieved of the weight of the rifle. It was after the battle was won that Miura fainted from loss of blood.

Miura miraculously recovered from this injury. For his distinguished service, he was later promoted to major general, the highest rank a non-graduate of the Army War College could reach.

The night raid began at 3:30 a.m., after the moon had set. By 11:30 a.m., having suppressed the fierce firepower of the Russian defenders, the Japanese flag stood at the summit. From the summit of the mountain, massive numbers of Russian troops were seen retreating, like an outgoing tide. Itō Masanori pointed out that a successful night raid involving a full army division was unprecedented. It will almost certainly not be repeated easily in the future.

War is the Foundation of All the High Virtues and Faculties of Men

According to *Nichiro sensō* (Russo-Japanese War) by the Japanese author Kojima Noboru, Lieutenant General Ian Hamilton, a British military observer with Kuroki's forces, left the following impression of this battle in his memoir: "I wish to stress at least ten times that Japanese soldiers are endowed with splendid qualities. They are innocent like young children and intrepid like lions and think only of fulfilling their duties to their ancestors and the emperor."[2] Believing that the Japanese is "a born soldier," bred with the "milk of patriotism," Hamilton continued to quote John Ruskin, his compatriot art critic and social theorist, who said, "All the pure and noble arts of peace are founded on war; no great art ever yet rose on earth but among a nation of soldiers. . . . War . . . is the foundation of all the high virtues and faculties of men." Hamilton expressed his great admiration for Japan's refined samurai ethic and culture, with its balanced emphasis on liberal and military arts, contrasting this tradition with that of embattled China, which "discouraged their best from adopting the military

---

2   Ian Hamilton, *A Staff Officer's Scrap-book During the Russo-Japanese War* (London: Edward Arnold, 1906), 14–15.

career, and thought their worst were good enough for the army."

Moreover, Hamilton expressed concern about the future of his own country, noting that "English women do not teach their children even one-tenth of traditional spirit that Japanese mothers do."

It was not only the British who worried about their country's future in light of the patriotism manifested by the Japanese during the Russo-Japanese War. In his *Shufu shu-u hito o shosatsu su*, Japanese author Takeda Taijun quoted *Waga dōhō ni tsugu* (Message to My Fellow Compatriots) by Qiu Jin, a Chinese revolutionary, who said she felt like "dying of envy" at the sight of young, sweet children waving small national flags as they saw young soldiers off to the battlefield when she visited a friend in Yokohama in the fall of 1904.

She continued to comment:

> Ah my fellow people, it is because the Japanese unites so solidly in giving unqualified esteem to fighting men that soldiers can give up their lives so selflessly in battle. . . . Families of soldiers in the battlefield are provided with subsidies, and it is a great honor for family members to have husbands, sons, and brothers in the battlefront. Shops carry a signboard saying "special half-price service to military personnel."
>
> Alas, have pity on our own soldiers. They are forced to support themselves and their families with scanty rations that are already skimmed every month, and they are cursed and sworn by their superiors when they make even the slightest error. Those in power look down on soldiers as if they were lowly slaves, refusing even to sit with them. Soldiers are despised as the most inferior of the inferior. Even when a war is won, it is only senior officers who monopolize all the credit.

Qiu Jin also touched on women's education, observing that "women's schools are increasingly flourishing in Japan," and proposed that Chinese women should consider studying in Japan because, "a state like Japan, where women support their parents, assist their husbands, educate their children, and try to eradicate idlers, must become a mighty nation." Thus, it was not only soldiers but also women in Japan whom Hamilton and Qiu Jin praised in admiration.

What Is This Thing Called War?

What is this thing called war? As the saying goes, "Thousands die to raise one hero to fame." Soldiers in the field are not the only victims of war. From ancient times onward, there is nothing that makes people suffer more than a war.

Yet, from the viewpoint of a history of civilization, it is undeniable that many of the arts that are so moving have been founded on war, as Ruskin said. Particularly during the period when a nation is rising, war becomes a source of people's energy; war could even nurture a great civilization. It is needless to recall that the "Golden Age" of Athens under Pericles flourished after the Greco-Persian Wars and that Elizabethan England prospered as a result of the annihilation of the Spanish Armada. Incidentally, Pericles was around twenty years old at the time of the Battle of Salamis, and William Shakespeare was twenty-five years old when the Spanish Armada was destroyed in the Anglo-Spanish War. This is testimony to the fact that it was those who were young during the heroic age of a war who became the driving forces of the subsequent rise of culture.

In Japan, many aspects of the so-called prewar culture that present-day Japanese admire and feel nostalgic about have been cultivated by people whose youth was spent in the days of the Russo-Japanese War, a period that saw the rise of a new Japanese Empire. In fact, the high standards of present-day Japan, not only in science and technology but also in literature, the fine arts, and many other areas, owe much to the people of that age.

The times have changed and people are different. Contemporary Japan is not what it was during the Russo-Japanese War. Nor is today's Great Britain the same as England during the reign of Queen Elizabeth I. Still less is contemporary Greece Pericles' Greece. However, for a nation, this kind of heritage is a part of its history and traditions, and it should never be forgotten.

CHAPTER

10

Bloody Battle

—The Bitter Epic of the Siege of Lüshun Port—

Death-Defying Battles

Day by day, the Russo-Japanese War became increasingly bloody. Defenders entrenched themselves in fortifications made of stone and cement and dug trenches during field operations. From these points, they fired rifles and machine guns at the charging enemy. Attackers shelled enemy fortifications, crawled forward low on the ground, and then charged at defenders for the last few meters. Naturally, quite a number were gunned down in the course of a charge, but that was to be expected. The important thing was for the remaining chargers to rush into the enemy fortifications to fight with swords and bayonets. For both friend and foe, there was a fifty-fifty chance of being killed. Thus, whichever side succeeded in sending more soldiers inside the fortifications, defying the barrage, would have the better chance of winning. And whichever side had more soldiers who were prepared to die would have a better chance of winning in hand-to-hand combat. Once the winner took over the enemy's stronghold, the loser would try to retake it, either with a counteroffensive—repeating the tactics of the winning side—or by first bombarding the captured stronghold with cannons pre-positioned for that purpose.

This was the typical pattern of ground battles during the Russo-Japanese

War. Being the height of the age of imperialism, both Japanese and Russian soldiers were animated with patriotism and ready to die to protect their honor and that of their countries. Concentrated charges by well-built foot soldiers had traditionally been the most favored tactic employed by the Russian army. Although initially the Japanese side attempted to employ a tactic centered around open-order deployment and firepower, based on its successful experience during the First Sino-Japanese War, it became increasingly entangled in the Russian tactic and found itself also engaged in hand-to-hand combat. Consequently, the Russo-Japanese War was filled with bloody hand-to-hand clashes wherever the two sides met.

The Battle of Liaoyang began with 134,000 Japanese troops charging at Russia's 225,000 ground troops. Given the difference in strength between the two camps, the charge by the Japanese troops seemed suicidal, but the Japanese side had no other option. Although it was obvious that it was overwhelmed by its opponent in terms of troop strength, a day's delay in attacking would further tip the balance in Russia's favor because reinforcements continued to arrive. If left unchallenged, heavily reinforced Russian troops would advance south to launch a pincer attack on the Japanese troops that were besieging Lüshun—and the Manchurian-Korean border that the Japanese army had managed to capture earlier would become highly vulnerable. Thus, the Japanese had no choice but to attack the 225,000 Russian troops in Liaoyang. Objectively, the only thing the Japanese side could rely on in this situation was the courage and boldness of its soldiers, who did indeed fight beyond the call of duty.

Lieutenant Colonel Tachibana: A War Hero

Of the four Japanese armies mobilized for the Russo-Japanese War, the Third Army, which had been assigned to besiege Lüshun, did not take part in the Battle of Liaoyang. This battle was fought by the Second and Fourth Armies, which attacked the Russian's southern front, and the First Army, which advanced from the Yalu River to attack the eastern flank of the Russian forces. The Second and Fourth Armies made frontal attacks on the Russians, who stubbornly resisted the offensive and refused to retreat even an inch.

Meanwhile, the Russians steadily bolstered their preparations for a combined counterattack. It was also reported that some Russian troops were advancing south from the western flank, where the Japanese defense was the weakest due to a shortage of troops. If those troops turned west and besieged the Japanese troops, it would have marked the end of the Japanese soldiers there. Objectively speaking, the Japanese Manchurian Army would have been annihilated if the Russian side had switched to an offensive at this point.

It was, again, the First Army under the command of General Kuroki Tametomo that rose to meet the Japanese army's crisis. Kuroki's army was indeed the only hope the Japanese side had. On September 1, Commander in Chief Ōyama Iwao sent Kuroki a telegram saying, "With the frontal attacks by the Second and Fourth Armies at a standstill, prospects for this desperate battle remain bleak. Our only hope to turn back the tide of war is your army's bravery."

On the eastern front, Kuroki's army was facing Russian troops across the Taizi River. Numbering 78,000 men, the Russian army was more than twice the size of Kuroki's. Unless the First Army crossed this river, it would become an idle force, exercising no influence on the state of the war. Anticipating this river-crossing operation immediately after the successful raid on Gongzhangling, Kuroki had transported all the equipment and materials his army had used to cross the Yalu River all the way to the Taizi River. Once again demonstrating his quick thinking and action, one of his best qualities, Kuroki immediately moved his army far to the northeast while feinting a frontal attack and succeeded in having it cross the river in the forenoon of August 31. As soon as it crossed the Taizi River, Kuroki's army marched toward a hill called Manju Yama (饅頭山; or Hsi-kuan-tun), which was a point of strategic importance.

Hearing that Kuroki's army had crossed the river, Aleksei Kuropatkin initially reacted with fury at his men for having allowed the enemy to cross the river so easily. Then he resolutely changed his plan and ordered the main division on the southern front to move east to besiege and destroy their sworn enemy, the First Army. The Russian division that was directed to move initially resented the order because it was about to crush the Japanese Second and Fourth Armies. However, the division had no choice but to follow the order, and in doing so, it inadvertently helped the Japanese troops survive and continue their advance.

The outcome of the battle on the eastern front depended on which side conquered Manju Yama. Along with the above change of plan, Kuropatkin ordered that this hill be defended to the last, but Kuroki's army had already headed for it.

As a result of the night battle on September 1, during which possession of the hill passed back and forth between the two sides, Kuroki's army succeeded in capturing Manju Yama. It was not until after dawn that the 37,000 foot soldiers and 140 cannons hastily dispatched by Kuropatkin finally arrived at the scene and immediately launched a massive counterattack. Again, Kuroki's moves proved to be one day ahead of the enemy.

Short of ammunition supplies, the Japanese side had no choice but to hide in the trenches and endure the enemy bombardment. Regarding this battle, Lieutenant General Hamilton wrote in his memoir that "It seemed as if the hill had been flattened and all the heroes of Gonzhangling were buried alive." The following episode demonstrates that Kuroki was a man of quick and clear decision. In the middle of the enemy's blistering bombardment of the hill, Kuroki decided to take a nap for about an hour, believing there was little point in actively commanding the situation. Seeing Kuroki lying on the grassy ground, his staff officer rushed to pick him up and found him in a deep sleep.

Although Manju Yama was temporarily seized by the Russians, who wrapped the hill with a chorus of "Ura" (Hurrah), the Japanese troops charged the hill after sunset and retook it after mortal combat. A Russian countercharge immediately followed. It was at this moment that a Japanese trick went into play. In the middle of the enemy's fierce attack, Japanese soldiers were ordered to cease fire. The fact the soldiers followed this order at once testifies to the amazing degree of discipline among the Japanese soldiers, because firing at the enemy was the only means for soldiers to protect their own lives. By not firing, the Japanese side was able to clearly locate the enemy forces, which were firing in the dark. Taking advantage of the situation—the Russian forces judged that the Japanese side must have retreated—Japanese soldiers poured out of their trenches at the sound of the trumpet, rushed at their enemies, and wiped them out. At this point, the Russians abandoned any attempt to retake Manju Yama. The battleground was reportedly filled with the corpses of the Russian soldiers, as if they were tuna fish displayed at a fish market.

After this battle, the Second Army from Sendai earned a name as the bravest division in the Japanese Imperial Army, until its annihilation at Guadalcanal during World War II.

Even though the Russian army was overwhelmingly superior in terms of troop strength, Kuropatkin ordered its retreat by way of precaution, seeing how his troops had unexpectedly faced an uphill battle. He judged that given the confidence of Kuroki's tactics, the Japanese side could have hidden an extra reserve force. If his troops in the eastern front were defeated, Kuropatkin feared that the supply route between Mukden and Liaoyang would be severed and his entire force could be besieged and destroyed.

During the Battle of Liaoyang, the Russian side suffered about 20,000 casualties, while casualties on the Japanese side ran as high as 23,500. The Japanese troops were so exhausted, they lacked the energy to chase after the retreating Russians. Because it was the Russians who had technically withdrawn from the battlefield, the Japanese side won the battle. But because it had been the Russian strategy from the beginning to delay the advance of the Japanese troops, the Russians had accomplished their strategic goal through this battle. Thus, the Russians lost the battle but conserved their reserve power, while the Japanese managed to win but completely exhausted their energy. And that was what the Battle of Liaoyang was all about.

Desperate Battle that Lasted 130 Days and Nights

The Siege of Lüshun Port (Siege of Port Arthur) was the bitterest epic during the Russo-Japanese War. At the beginning, nobody anticipated it would become such a bitter battle. When a full-scale offensive at Lüshun Port was announced on August 19, all the Japanese newspapers set up tents within the Ministry of War compound so that they could put out an extra on the fall of the Lüshun naval port ahead of their competitors.

However, for the next five months, every full-scale attack failed one after another. Meanwhile, the Baltic Fleet, into which almost all of Russia's fleets (except for the Black Sea Fleet) had been integrated, was advancing closer to the Far East day by day, and at the same time, the Russian troops in Mukden grew more powerful as reinforcements arrived. It was therefore under a growing feeling of impatience, agitated by the possibility that the outcome of the siege might critically affect the overall prospect of the war, that the Japanese soldiers engaged in a 130-day-and-night hand-to-hand battle at Lüshun Port. In the end, the port was captured by the Japanese side, but at the cost of heavy casualties of 60,000 soldiers, of which 15,000 lost their lives.

The progress of this battle was closely watched by the entire Japanese nation, which oscillated between anticipation and disappointment. It was not only the families of the injured and the dead but also the entire population that learned of the gruesomeness of a modern war. People discussed wars and strategies, while countless demonstrations of patriotism and the spirit of self-sacrifice were repeated every day on the warfront.

It was during the siege of Lüshun Port that the poet Yosano Akiko (与謝野晶子; 1878–1942) wrote her famous poem: "Oh, younger brother mine, for thee I weep, . . . So I prithee, do not die, though Lüshun's fortress should perish, should it be saved, what of that?"

It amazes me to realize how lively the Meiji spirit was. Of course, some people criticized the unpatriotic poem by Yosano, but the criticism remained within the bounds of literary commentary, and Yosano was not socially blacklisted for freely expressing her sentiments. In Japan, not only before World War II but even today, one should be prepared to be ostracized by society, including the mass media, when voicing an opinion that is contrary to what the overwhelming majority of people believe. Against this background, it is refreshing to know that there was such a liberal atmosphere in the Meiji era. Yosano Akiko henceforth remained a woman Japanese men admired throughout the Meiji and Taishō eras.

Still, a perpetual spring of patriotism among soldiers on the battlefront, as well as the powerful support of the people back home, was called for to bolster the soldiers' spirits to fight through the hand-to-hand battle that lasted 130 days and nights. Even though Yosano lamented as above, she did not have even the faintest doubt that her younger brother would fulfill his duty for his country. That was the zeitgeist of the time. This is a poem by a woman who pled for the safety of her brother because she was fully aware that he was willing to die for his country.

It is a Japanese ideal to possess a perfect combination of heart and mind, as reflected in a famous poem, *Ohyakudo mōde* (One Hundred Prayer Visits), by the contemporary poet Ōtsuka Naoko (also known as Kusuoko; 大塚楠緒子):

Should a woman be denounced
If she thinks of her husband at the first step

Her country at the second step
But her husband again at the third step?

Those were the days when the spirit of each and every Japanese was uninhibited by any exogenous coercion or manneristic education and freely realized itself as it pleased.

Strategic Dilemma for Japan and Russia

Because there are too many individual episodes concerning the siege of Lüshun Port, let me confine myself to some discussion of the strategic significance of the siege.

Many criticize the battle for having wasted more time and more human lives than originally expected. Below, I will attempt to analyze this battle mostly along the lines of the treatise by Kuwata Etsu (桑田悦), who presented a relatively detached view of the combat, which is included in the first volume of *Kindai Nippon sensō-shi* (近代日本戦争史).[1]

In the course of the Russo-Japanese War, the main theater of which was the Manchurian plain, the presence of Lüshun became a strategic dilemma for both Japan and Russia.

Being a small and weak nation, Japan had no other option than to first defeat the Russian navy and army stationed in the Far East and then to set up favorable conditions for peace negotiations, with the help of mediation by friendly nations. Japan needed to do this while crushing Russian reinforcements one by one as they arrived from Europe.

Russia's strategy was completely the opposite. Lüshun Port was a military base that the Russians wished to defend until the arrival of the Baltic Fleet. At the same time, if the defense of Lüshun Port required the presence of most of the Russian army in Manchuria, the entire army would become extremely vulnerable if and when the Japanese army attempted a full-scale offensive before further reinforcements arrived from Europe.

---

1   Dōdai Keizai Konwakai, ed., *Kindai Nippon sensō-shi* [Military history of modern Japan] (Tokyo: Dōdai Keizai Konwakai, 1995).

Due to this dilemma, the Russian war council on the eve of the Battle of Liaoyang was divided between those who argued for sending forces to Lüshun, as advocated by Yevgeni Alekseyev, Russian viceroy in Port Arthur, and those who argued for withdrawing troops to Harbin, as advocated by Kuropatkin. This impasse between the two sides resulted in a series of halfhearted compromises.

From the Japanese navy's viewpoint, it was imperative to destroy the Russian squadron that had locked itself up in Lüshun Port before the Baltic Fleet arrived. From the army's point of view, however, it would be deprived of a force that was vital to crushing the Russian army in Manchuria at an early stage if it had to dispatch a large force to besiege Lüshun. Its true wish was for the force to be deployed to Liaoyang after the occupation of Jinzhou, where the Liaodong Peninsula is the narrowest. In fact, the Japanese army had already missed the chance of pursuing the retreating Russians in Liaoyang once owing to a shortage of soldiers.

Japan had difficulties supplying not only troops but also munitions, being forced to divide meager resources between two major operations. There had at first been no plan to promptly capture Lüshun. The decision to attack Lüshun was taken in late May, more than three months after the eruption of the war, at the strong request of the Imperial Navy, which had realized the futility of the blockade operation. The first full-scale offensive was launched on August 19.

In retrospect, it turned out that this delay of half a year, although it was nobody's fault, crucially influenced the entire war.

Beton (Cement) as Hard as Steel

Although the Russian side had been in the process of executing a long-term plan by constructing a modern fortress in Lüshun, it completed a new and more operationally oriented fortress within half a year after the start of the war. Under the direction of the brilliant General Roman Kondratenko, as many as 10,000 laborers were employed to build the fortress. Reinforcements of some 20,000 soldiers were also delivered in the three months while the Lüshun-Mukden railway was still serviceable.

In retrospect, if the Japanese army divisions had advanced straight to Lüshun immediately after the eruption of the war in February at a speed comparable to that of Kuroki's army, the occupation of Lüshun might have been much easier.

Partly because the siege of Lüshun had been originally requested by the navy, the army did not have sufficient information on the target, not to mention a workable operational plan. This explains why the Japanese Imperial Army had scarcely any valid information on Lüshun. It should be recalled that the Japanese army had earlier made such a thorough and accurate study of circumstances in regions along the Trans-Siberian Railway and in northern Manchuria that it differed only a little from the Russian records published after the war. However, the Japanese army was totally unaware of the modern fortress that had been constructed with scrupulous care in Lüshun.

Therefore, the Japanese side had assumed the entire city of Lüshun would fall easily with a conventional frontal attack. This misguided assumption was the principle cause of the grave damage that Japanese forces later suffered, as well as the greatest reason why the attack on Hill 203 was not carried out when the Russian defenses were still undermanned.

Once the Japanese troops started attacking Lüshun, however, they soon realized that the strength of the Russian defense was far beyond their imagination. The fortifications were consolidated with beton, which withstood the shelling of the Japanese guns. Having passed the barbed wire that surrounded the fortification, attackers had to deal with trenches, which were 6 to 9 meters wide and 3 to 10 meters deep, with almost vertical walls, making easy targets for the Russians from the numerous gun ports set up within the fortification. This setup resulted in a wretched spectacle on the part of the Japanese troops that was described by the Meiji literary giant Mori Ōgai (森鷗外) as, "Despite the valor of our brave warriors, the steel-hard cement wall of the enemy fortification became splattered with human flesh." During the first full-scale offensive between August 19 and 24, the death toll on the Japanese side reached 16,000 soldiers. It was a miserable defeat, with the Japanese failing to take even a single fortification.

Based on this failure, the Japanese side abandoned its initial plan to destroy enemy fortifications at a stroke and rush to Lüshun Port and instead adopted the orthodox tactic of taking up a position and closing in on the enemy via breaches.

Despite this change of tactics, all-out offensives in September and October only resulted in piles of Japanese soldiers' corpses in and around the trenches due to the fierce resistance put up by the Russian defenders. The only good news for the Japanese side during this period was that its 28 cm howitzers proved highly effective against the enemy defense because of their long-range and heavy warheads. The Japanese side succeeded in transporting eighteen 28 cm howitzers, which had been previously installed in fortresses in Japan, to Manchuria and making them operable in only two weeks, with the prompt completion of gun platforms, which normally would have taken one to two months.

Nogi Maresuke: Commander of the Japanese Third Army

Meanwhile, the Baltic Fleet had sailed out of the Baltic naval port of Libau on October 15, 1904. At the earliest, it was expected to arrive in the Far East by early January. Because the Combined Fleet of the Imperial Japanese Navy had been stationed outside Lüshun Port to police the Russian squadron since the early stages of the war, all of its vessels needed to be docked and fitted out at least two months before a major sea battle. From the beginning of the war, the Japanese navy had hoped to capture, not Lüshun Port itself but Hill 203, from which Russian vessels could be bombarded and sunk, and it had repeatedly submitted its request to the army through General Headquarters.

The Japanese Third Army was criticized for not having responded to this request from the navy promptly, which was counted as one of the causes of the failure of the operation. As days idly went by without any hopeful progress in the war, people's disappointment and frustration reached a limit, with daily reports on failed operations and the miserable deaths of countless young soldiers.

People showered the residence of General Nogi Maresuke, commander of the Third Army, with stones and verbal abuse; Mrs. Nogi had to pay a visit to Ise Grand Shrine in Mie prefecture and pray for the fall of Lüshun in exchange for her and her husband's lives. Even though some in General Headquarters

Nogi Maresuke
(Photo: Kyodo News)

argued for Nogi's dismissal, it never materialized. Everyone knew that if he were dismissed, he would take his own life by disembowelment.

Until the end of World War II, General Nogi had been the god of war and an icon for the Japanese, so much so that any play or movie on General Nogi was guaranteed to become a big hit. General Nogi ended up being a legend himself, and numerous folktales depicted his superhuman capabilities—for example, Nogi appearing by the bedside of an impoverished sick person to solve all his problems, and so on. Of course, most of those tales must have been mere fantasy.

Although the failure of the operation in Lüshun was mostly attributable to inadequate planning before Nogi was appointed commander of the Third Army, and thus was something for which Nogi could not be held responsible, Nogi was, as the commander at the time, naturally blamed for all failures. Nevertheless, Nogi was a man of integrity and nobody ever doubted his selflessness.

During the encampment, Nogi declined any special treatment and insisted on being treated just like an ordinary soldier. While he never allowed *ondol* (underfloor heating) in his room to be fired up, he did not forbid others from firing up theirs. He would not touch anything other than the same rations given to the rank and file. Even when he had indigestion, he declined the offer of a rice porridge his aide-de-camp had prepared and ate ordinary rations.

During the First Sino-Japanese War, one division commander sent Nogi an overcoat with a woolen lining during encampment, which was to be worn in the severe winter, but he instructed one of his men to return the coat immediately to the sender. Reminded by his subordinates of the rudeness of this act in the face of the kindness of the sender, Nogi ordered the coat to be sent to a hospital as bedding for patients.

There are countless other episodes that reveal Nogi's kindness to his subordinates and strictness toward himself. His life in peacetime was also simple and honest. He generously gave away money to his subordinates that had been accumulated during expeditions or that came from imperial grants for his service. Nogi died almost penniless when he disemboweled himself after the death of Emperor Meiji.

War, however, is not won by the personal virtue of a commander alone. After repeated abortive attempts in Lüshun, frustration reached a peak in Tokyo, and on the eve of the all-out offensive scheduled for November 26, an imperial edict was issued wishing for the success of the operation. Such an edict was highly unusual. Now that the emperor had voiced his wish for the success of the operation, Nogi would have to die if he failed again. Just before commencing the full offensive, Nogi announced to his senior officers that if the offensive did not go as planned this time, "I intend to lead the Seventh Division myself and charge the central line of the enemy fortress, and I beg for your approval." This could only mean that Nogi intended to be the first to be killed, and it took his staff officers two hours to dissuade him from this plan.

Instead, a special detachment known as the Shirodasuki-tai (White Sash Company) was organized. Members of this detachment were told that "Although it is the greatest honor to be a member of this special detachment, . . . you should not expect to come back alive. You are expected to accomplish the mission at the sacrifice of your life." The detachment's mission was to launch a bayonet charge at the enemy under the cover of darkness and not to fire a single shot. Members all wore white cotton sashes across their shoulders for identification. Members spent their last minutes on this earth preparing for the departure, entrusting others with their farewell notes and tufts of their hair to be sent to their families at home. One of the notes reads, "I will depart to heaven with great glee. Never should you deplore my departure."

But even this suicide squad failed to bring a breakthrough. When the squad charged at the enemy, the majority of its members were gunned down within a few initial steps, except for a few who somehow managed to reach the wall, only to be shot to death there. In the end, some 3,000 members of the Shirodasuki-tai were wiped out.

Death-Defying Struggle for Hill 203

At this point, Nogi finally made up his mind to shift the major target to Hill 203. The charge at the hill had to be launched immediately, while Russian attention was still concentrated on the Japanese frontal attack. The failure of the third full-scale offensive at Lüshun became obvious before dawn on November 27, and Nogi had already ordered the attack on Hill 203 at 10:00 a.m. in the morning of the same day.

Meanwhile, the Russian side had not paid too much attention to Hill

203, preoccupied as it was with the defense of Lüshun. As the war progressed, however, the strategic importance of Hill 203 became more clearly recognized, and the Russians started constructing strongholds on the hill. These hastily constructed strongholds were not permanent establishments like the other fortifications in Lüshun.

It was against this backdrop that the most gruesome battle in the history of land warfare took place. There never has been and never will be another battle like this. When the initial success of the night raid led Nogi's army to capture a part of the plateau, Tōgō Heihachirō, commander in chief of the Combined Fleet of the Imperial Japanese Navy, immediately dispatched a messenger to convey his congratulations. But the Japanese troops occupying the captured territory were soon wiped out by a Russian counteroffensive, marking the beginning of incessant death-defying struggles between the two armies, during which this territory changed hands sixty-seven times.

Colonel Nikolai Tretyakov, commander of the Fifth East Siberian Rifles Regiment defending Hill 203, reminisced that "It is rare to take part in such a gruesome battle . . . those who had already lost guns tried to strangle their opponents with bare, bloody hands. . . . The gruesomeness of the battlefield was enough to make you cover your eyes." In the end, the Japanese side launched a last offensive with all of its remaining soldiers on December 5 and succeeded in capturing the top of the hill. By that time, the Russian side had lost all the reserve forces it needed to launch another counterattack, and silence returned to the hill.

Having captured Hill 203, the Japanese side was astonished by its strategic importance. Beneath their eyes were all the vessels of Russia's Lüshun squadron, whose whereabouts had been unknown, as if they were model ships in a miniature garden. Taking advantage of the newly acquired vantage point, Nogi's army started bombarding the Russian squadron as early as the afternoon of December 5. Within thirty minutes, the battleship *Portava* was sunk, followed by the destruction of all the other vessels in the squadron in three subsequent days.

With the elimination of the Russian squadron in Lüshun, Tōgō led the Combined Fleet back to Japan in order to prepare for the imminent showdown with Russia's Baltic Fleet.

Although the main force of the Russian troops continued to resist for another month, nailing down the Third Japanese army, their morale visibly

General Nogi and General Anatoly Stessel, after the Meeting in Shuishiying (Photo: Kyodo News)

deteriorated after General Roman Kondratenko, the central person in the Russian defense of Port Arthur, was killed by a Japanese 28 cm howitzer on December 15. The Russians surrendered on January 1, 1905.

After surrendering the fortress, the commanding generals on both sides, General Nogi and General Anatoly Stessel, met on January 5. An American movie crew had been dispatched to cover the war, a highly unusual scene in those days, but Nogi declined its offer to take pictures of the meeting, explaining that doing so would dishonor the defeated opponent, which was against samurai ethics. After repeated pleas by the Americans, Nogi finally allowed one picture to be taken of him and Stessel—wearing swords, sitting next to each other as friends, and surrounded by their respective staffs. After the meeting, it is said that Stessel uttered, "Although I had expected General Nogi to be a pitiless demon, I came back convinced that it was not a shame at all to be defeated by such a modest and kindhearted warrior." This meeting between the two generals was vividly captured in "*Suishiei no kaiken*" (Meeting in Shuishiying), a song composed for elementary school pupils of the time.

Humble even in victory, the Japanese side treated the Russians with courtesy and humility. When the commanders of the two sides met, they treated each other with mutual respect, as fellow warriors who had fought

through a battle of unprecedented feroc-
ity, albeit on opposite sides: "[The enemy
general] sitting straight, started by saying, 'I can only feel how dishearted Your
Excellency must have been with the loss
of your two sons in this war'" (Verse 5);
"In response, our General replied, reas-
suringly, 'I am happy that both my sons
found their own place to die. This is truly
an honor to a military family'" (Verse 6).

General Nogi had two sons. The elder
one, First Lieutenant Nogi Katsusuke, was
killed in the Battle of Nanshan. When his
staff endeavored to assign his younger

First Lieutenant Nogi Katsusuke
and Lieutenant Nogi Yasusuke

son, Lieutenant Nogi Yasusuke, to headquarters so as to keep him away
from frontline duty, Nogi rejected the idea and dispatched his younger and
only remaining son to the battle of Hill 203, from which he never returned.
Of course, not only the Nogis but tens of thousands of Japanese families
lost their sons and husbands in this war. An Edo-style popular song with
the 7-7-7-5 syllable pattern composed around this time laments: "It is pre-
sumptuous to cry over the loss of your only son / When some noble persons have lost two." Nogi expressed his feeling in the form of a Chinese
poem he composed on the occasion of the triumphant return:

"One million soldiers of the Emperor's Army conquered arrogant
barbarians
During field operations and attacks on enemy strongholds, mountains of corpses were built
I am so ashamed, how could I meet the elderly fathers of the
fallen soldiers
How many of them have returned today with the triumphant song."

Honor to a Warrior

General Nogi continued to look for a place to die in the subsequent Battle
of Mukden, always positioning himself at the head of charges. When he

disemboweled himself after the death of Emperor Meiji in later years, it must have been the occasion he had long waited for.

Shizuko, the general's wife, died with her husband as she had wished for at the Ise Grand Shrine. The recent, iconoclastic historic view tends to see her death as a suicide coerced by General Nogi, although this view lacks any hard evidence. The only remaining evidence about Nogi's death is the general's written will. While its first clause—about his long journey to look for a place to die ever since the humiliation of having lost his regimental banner to the enemy during the Satsuma Rebellion—was a moving account of his view on the honor of a warrior, the ninth clause contained meticulous instructions on how Nogi's wife was to be looked after in her advanced age. The third clause and the end note instructed that Shizuko should be consulted on anything that was not covered by the will.

Nogi was by birth a typical, feudalistic macho man, and, as such, dying with his wife was utterly foreign to his beliefs. Here, we should take pity on Shizuko's determination to take her own life using a sword, with which she would not have been familiar, after sending her husband off.

Nogi's will concluded with the instruction that there should be no adoption and that the Nogi family line should become extinct when Shizuko passed away.

Prelude to the Fall of Tsarism

The fall of Lüshun had a tremendous international impact. While Japan did not come off with a clear victory in the Battle of Liaoyang, and some say Russia was not necessarily defeated, the outcome of the battle in Lüshun was obvious to everyone. In a nutshell, a Caucasian commander raised a flag of surrender to Asian troops.

The Times of London stressed the significance of the siege of Lüshun by saying, "Port Arthur was not a mere fortress. It was a symbol of Russia's power."

The most direct influence on the war at this point was the psychological impact of this defeat on the Russian people. An Austrian newspaper predicted "the fall of Port Author would ignite dissatisfaction and frustration among Russian people as if throwing fire into a powder keg," a statement which later proved to be accurate.

Vladimir Lenin characterized the fall of Port Arthur as "a prelude to the fall of Tsarism." On January 22, only twenty days after the fall of Lüshun, the "Bloody Sunday" massacre took place. Witte described it as "the first bloody festival of the Russian Revolution in 1905."

Although the incident was triggered by a trivial difference of opinion, like the beginning of many other revolutions, 1,216 citizens lost their lives due to army gunfire. Whatever the cause, bloodshed ignites a revolution. The year 1905 thus became a prelude to the 1917 Russian Revolution. These domestic events, as well as other issues, were behind the attempts of Witte and others to promote peace negotiations with Japan despite the tsar's strong wish to continue the war.

Had there not been the threat of revolution within Russia, the tsar would not have listened to offers of mediation from President Theodore Roosevelt, and as a result, Japanese troops would have been driven away from the Liaodong and Korean Peninsulas and the entire Asian continent. This would have put not only Korea but also the entire northern half of China at the mercy of Russia—a horrifying prospect.

Japan's Intelligence War during the Russo-Japanese War

Behind the domestic unrest in Russia was, among other factors, Japan's secret service. Because it was undertaken in a strictly confidential manner, no General Headquarters documents on this operation remain, except for the debriefing report of Lieutenant Colonel Akashi Motojirō (明石元二郎), allegedly a central figure in this operation. Thus, what was actually done and how effective it really was remains a mystery. Because antigovernment factions in Russia would not and could not admit they had received financial assistance from the Japanese government, the truth never came out.

By order of General Fukushima Yasumasa, director of intelligence of the Imperial Japanese Army, Lieutenant Colonel Akashi undertook a secret operation to support revolutionary movements in Russia while he was assigned to the Japanese embassy in Stockholm as a military attaché. Because General Headquarters had provided Akashi with a bold sum of 1 million yen, out of which only 270,000 yen was left unused at the end of the war, the size of Akashi's operations can be more or less conjectured.

First, having succeeded in making contact with Finnish national independence activists, Akashi continued to expand his connections to various other nationalist activists and, finally, to the Russian Social Democratic Labour Party led by Lenin, which was later to become the Communist Party of the Soviet Union. Akashi aimed to cultivate a sense of unity among them based on broad common interests.

On October 1, 1904, several secret societies in Russia got together for the first time in Paris and agreed on plans of action, including antiwar demonstrations and antiwar strikes at military arsenals. It is believed that Lieutenant Colonel Akashi's swift but clandestine maneuvering, as well as the war chest he had offered, were behind this collaboration. The second meeting was convened in Geneva in April 1905 after the Battle of Mukden, after which countless riots and insurgencies continued to erupt in Russia until the end of the war. During this period, Akashi not only helped organize meetings but also purchased a massive number of weapons and supplied them to the revolutionary groups within Russia.

Akashi was not the only Japanese engaged in subversive activities. Taking advantage of their appearance, which made them indistinguishable from the Mongolians or the Chinese in the eyes of the Russians, Japanese agents snuck into northern Manchuria and engaged in spying and subversive activities. The Trans-Siberian Railway was so tightly guarded that minor damage was soon fixed, but they nevertheless were able to temporarily delay the transport of reinforcements by damaging parts of the railway. Thus, for Japan, the Russo-Japanese War was truly an all-out effort, involving not only soldiers at the battlefront but also everyone else, including secret agents behind the scenes.

The Japanese side also used *bazoku* (馬賊; mounted bandits), who were rampant in Manchuria in those days, to their advantage. While both Russia and Japan tried to win the hearts and minds of these bandits, many of them started to seek personal advantage by helping the Japanese troops as the war situation became increasingly favorable for Japan, thus overcoming their initial doubts about Japan's prospects. Behind the winning of widespread support from the bandits, which allegedly annoyed the Russians tremendously, was the personal character of Major Hanada Nakanosuke (花田仲之助), the Japanese army officer in charge of *bazoku* relations. Nicknamed Hua Daren, Hanada rallied *bazoku* clans, while leading a bunch of firebrands from the Japanese ultranationalist society Genyōsha (玄洋社). Eventually, the bandits started admiring Hanada, and some even treated him as a living saint. This was attributable to Hanada's humility and his willingness to give all the credit to his men.

It should be recalled that most of the officers and soldiers engaged in the most dangerous behind-the-scene activities had given up the honor of being killed in the battlefield and were fully aware that their accomplishments would go unsung and be forgotten. Because their spirits were so noble, they left no clue of their existence, and it is difficult for us to trace their accomplishments today. We can only be thankful for their self-sacrifice and pray for the repose of their souls.

11

Turning Point in World History

—*Miraculous Victory at the Battle of Tsushima*—

Ammunition Running Low

The Japanese army's advance stalled after the Battle of Liaoyang in September 1904. This was attributable, above anything else, to a shortage of ammunition. Night raids with bayonets, which required no shelling of the enemy, had determined the outcomes of the aforementioned battles of Gongzhangling and Manju Yama. The Japanese army in Manchuria, in contrast, was unsure of its capabilities in daytime battle on the plain. In fact, it had been unable to do anything to chase after the massive Russian forces that were withdrawing.

While sparse ammunition reserves had always been criticized as a traditional shortcoming of Japan's national defense, the situation faced by Japan was essentially the fate of a poor nation that had overextended itself to expand its armaments.

During the Cold War, Japan had graduated from the status of a poor country, but its military budget had been confined to within 1 percent of its gross national product (GNP) despite the Soviet threat. When asked by the Finance Ministry if they wished for more fighters or more ammunition, the Japan Self-Defense Forces (SDF) had to choose the former because, if the Soviet Union was to attack Japan with, say, one hundred fighter jets, the

SDF needed enough fighters to counter the attack. To begin with, this question is about as absurd as asking if your child in college wants tuition money or bus fare. Now that the child is in college, you should be prepared to provide both, and it is nonsense to make your child choose between the two.

However, it is another story when you have financial constraints. And when you have to choose between fighters and ammunition, you must choose fighters because they take a long time to develop and manufacture, whereas ammunition and missiles could be manufactured in an emergency given Japan's industrial capabilities. When an emergency does occur, however, everything is needed at once, and thus, ammunition might not be given top priority. Repeat this process several times, and you will have a highly distorted military.

After the conclusion of the First Sino-Japanese War, Japan expanded its army by adding six army divisions, two cavalry brigades, and two artillery brigades. It is not hard to imagine that attention was not given to ammunition under such a hasty expansion, in which priority had been given to the quick fulfillment of personnel and equipment requirements. Consequently, the short supply of ammunition became a common headache for all the troops in the Imperial Japanese Army.

At first, the Russian side was puzzled as to why the Japanese troops did not pursue the withdrawing Russian troops on many occasions, missing the best opportunity to deal a serious blow to their enemy. Because the objective circumstances were such that it was obviously wisest for the Japanese to attack the Russians before their reinforcements arrived, the Russians expected that the Japanese would and should attack at any moment. The Japanese troops, however, did not move. At last, the Russians realized the Japanese had been suffering from a shortage of ammunition, making them decide to counterattack before the Japanese side received more ammunition supplies. The Russians intended to defeat the Japanese troops and rush immediately to Lüshun to relieve its defenders.

By the end of September, 220,000 Russian troops had advanced south. This formidable force was met by 150,000 Japanese troops. Since defensive operations had never been the Japanese army's strong point, it adopted what was known as an offensive defense—baffle the attacking troops at the outset of a battle by first taking the offensive.

After several days of fierce battle, in which no side came out as the clear victor, the Russian side finally gave up on the offensive and started to withdraw. This presented the Japanese side with the golden opportunity to chase after the Russians, but the shortage of ammunition prevented the Japanese from grabbing this chance. Instead, both sides dug trenches within a few hundred meters of the opponent over the distance of a few dozen kilometers along the battlefront and faced off against each other. This was the Battle of Shaho (沙河の会戦), and it became a forerunner of the trench warfare on the western front during World War I.

In January 1905, the Russian side once again planned an offensive and started assembling troops toward the western end of the battlefront, facing the left wing of the Japanese troops. Although the Japanese side correctly judged the Russians' intentions and dispatched a division of its own in the direction of the enemy's advance, it immediately faced an uphill battle against the enemy's massive forces. Seeing this, the Japanese commanders dispatched an additional three divisions from the central force, resulting in a death-defying battle in a snowstorm between 100,000 Russians and 50,000 Japanese soldiers. The battle, which was later known as the Battle of Sandepu (Heikoutai; or 黒溝台会戦), lasted for three days and nights, resulting in 10,000 casualties on each side.

If the Russian central force had taken the offensive during this three-day battle, the Japanese leftwing battlefront would have been inevitably destroyed because further reinforcements were impossible. Nevertheless, Russia's central force under the command of Aleksei Kuropatkin, commander in chief of the Russian land forces in Manchuria, did not move. It was later discovered that the Russian offensive had been an arbitrary decision on the part of Oskar Gripenberg, commanding general of the Russian Second Manchurian Army, despite opposition from Kuropatkin, who, instead of moving his forces to aid Gripenberg, decided to see how well Gripenberg could do on his own. After this abortive offensive, Gripenberg slammed his letter of resignation down on Kuropatkin's desk and returned to Harbin.

The Third Army to the Rescue

Meanwhile, Lüshun fell into Japanese hands. The day after the triumphal entry into the city on January 13, 1905, 70,000 soldiers from the Third Army, under the command of Nogi Maresuke (乃木希典), started marching northward. One month later, they reached Liaoyang. After completing preparations for a further advance, they departed for Mukden on February 28, where they took part in the Battle of Mukden. Even so, some units of the Third Army were unable to arrive in Mukden in time for the battle, indicating how most of the Third Army had barely made it to the scene.

A war is bound to be full of wisdom on both sides after the event. In the case of the Russo-Japanese War, the Russian side must have had many regrets—many should haves and should not haves. If the Lüshun squadron had to be annihilated anyway, why was it not deployed more aggressively at the outset of the war, which could have considerably disturbed the Japanese transport of troops. They could have easily defended the Lüshun fortress for one or two more months, which would have made the arrival of Nogi's 70,000 troops from the Third Army too late for the Battle of Mukden, even though it would have been a tall order to keep the fortress until the Battle of Tsushima in May 1905. History shows that Nogi's army played such an important role in the Battle of Mukden that it influenced the course of the entire war.

The Russo-Japanese War's "Battle of Sekigahara"

The domestic situation in Russia became increasingly restless after the fall of Lüshun. It would no longer allow the Russian military the luxury of losing a few battles before gathering one million soldiers in Harbin and crushing the enemy for good.

In early February, some ten days after the futile offensive in Sandepu (Heikoutai), which coincided with the Bloody Sunday incident in Saint Petersburg, the Russian government sent a wire to Kuropatkin stating, "Situations both within and outside the country require a major victory of our troops at the earliest possible occasion."

Both warring sides agreed, independently, that it was an opportune moment to launch a major operation—before the Shaho River thawed and turned the battlefield into a sea of mud. The Russian side decided on the offensive at the war council on February 19, and the command to attack was issued on February 21. The Japanese side issued the command to attack on February 20 and decided to start the battle by launching a containing action at the eastern flank of the Russian troops on February 27.

It was a grand battle, extending over one hundred kilometers, between

250,000 Japanese soldiers—all the troops of the Japanese army that could be mustered—with 990 canons versus 320,000 Russian soldiers with 1,200 canons. At the outset of the offensive, Japanese Commander in Chief Ōyama Iwao declared to his men that this battle would be the Battle of Sekigahara[1] in the Russo-Japanese War. At the same time, Ōyama did not fail to remind his men that any waste of ammunition had to be avoided. The Japanese troops used 120,000 shots in the Battle of Liaoyang, 100,000 in the Battle of Shaho, and 300,000 in the Battle of Mukden. Even though they tried to conserve ammunition as much as possible, the stock was about to run out toward the end of the war.

The containment action to Russia's eastern flank proved to be effective. While Kuropatkin had at first plotted an attack on the western flank of the Japanese troops, expanding on the tactic he had employed in Sandepu (Heikoutai), the Japanese attack on Russia's eastern flank forced him to modify his plan, which unintentionally made it easier for the Japanese troops to advance north from the western flank, thus affecting the outcome of the battle as a whole.

A chain of bitter experiences inflicted by Kuroki Tamemoto's First Army, plus the Japanese feint operation, which made the advance from the Yalu River of one division of Nogi's Third Army deliberately conspicuous, must have given the Russian field commanders the impression that Nogi's army would attack from the eastern flank.

On the contrary, Nogi's army was positioned on the western-most end of the battlefront with the mission of besieging Russian troops from there. Nogi, as an army general, was more a man of integrity than ingenuity, and he could inspire his subordinates to sacrifice their lives to accomplish his mission. As such, he seemed to be more suited for open battles. Besides, Nogi always dashed forward ahead of his troops, looking for an honorable death; his men had no other choice than to follow closely after him.

Thus, a competition of enclosure was fought between Nogi's army, which was constantly advancing north, and the Russian troops, which continued to move north in order to avoid being besieged by the opponent

---

1   The Battle of Sekigahara (関ヶ原の戦い), popularly known as the Battle for the Sundered Realm (天下分け目の戦い), was a decisive battle on October 21, 1600, which cleared Tokugawa Ieyasu's path to the shogunate. Sekigahara is widely considered to be the unofficial beginning of the Tokugawa bakufu, the last shogunate to control Japan.

from the northwest. In the end, Nogi's army managed to win this competition by a slim margin, allowing it to occupy, ahead of the Russians, the position north of the city of Mukden, which could allow them to then threaten the Mukden-Changchun railway. This scared Kuropatkin, who feared his troops' retreat would be cut off by the enemy, one of the key factors behind his final decision to withdraw.

The Battle of Mukden began on March 1 along the entire battlefront. Fierce seesaw battles lasted for six days and nights, with no clear winner. The Japanese army's battle capability had long peaked, and it began to go downhill. Had the Russians hung on for one or two more days, it could have ended in a draw, like the earlier Battle of Shaho.

It seems universally true, be it a battle or an athletic competition, that when the going is toughest for you, it is also tough for your opponent. Whoever can hang on longer wins. At the risk of oversimplification, this seems to summarize the seven days of the Battle of Mukden. As I have repeatedly pointed out, the Japanese side could not afford to lose any of the battles, while the Russian side could spare a battle or two because the longer the war lasted, the stronger the chain of reinforcements would be for the Russians.

On March 8, Kuroki's First Army sent a wire to General Headquarters saying, "The enemy is about to retreat and we intend to pursue its forces." General Headquarters immediately issued the command to chase after the retreating enemy.

On March 9, in a blistering sandstorm characteristic of the Manchurian plain, a fierce battle was fought between the advancing Japanese forces and the Russian troops, who struck back in an attempt to secure their retreat. On March 10, the Russian troops withdrew from Mukden.

Corpses from Both Sides Stain the Manchurian Plain with Blood

Japanese casualties during the Battle of Mukden totaled 70,000, while those on the Russian side reached 60,000 plus 30,000 who were missing in action (20,000 of whom were prisoners of war). The Manchurian plain was stained with their blood. One of the most popular war songs among the Japanese—"Sen-yū" (戦友; Brother in Arms)—was composed after this battle.

Immediately after the end of World War II, I saw a war veteran in white robes getting on a train. He was wearing an artificial leg and a charity donation box hung around his neck. In those days, the entire nation was impoverished: Nobody could afford to help anybody. The other passengers on the train looked away from the invalid soldier. When he started playing *"Sen-yū"* on his worn-out harmonica, however, tears flowed from the eyes of his fellow passengers and, silently, a few coins were dropped into his charity box. This song, thus, had the power to open up people's hearts, albeit slightly, which had been tightly shut since the defeat in the war. I was fifteen years old when I witnessed this scene.

Baltic Fleet

When the Russian troops started withdrawing from Mukden to the north, the Japanese troops had no energy left to chase and destroy them. Nevertheless, the Japanese side won the battle because Japan now controlled the city of Mukden, the center of Russia's Manchurian occupation.

Blamed for the defeat at the Battle of Mukden, Kuropatkin was relieved of his post as commander in chief of the Russian land forces in Manchuria and demoted to the position of commander of the First Manchurian Army. Kuropatkin was succeeded by Nikolay Linevich, who had previously commanded the First Manchurian Army.

Despite this defeat, the will to continue the war never waned in mainland Russia, as reflected in the decision made at a war council attended by the tsar only two days after the defeat. During this council, held on March 12, the navy minister expressed his high hopes for the Baltic Fleet, while the minister of war announced that he was ready to dispatch an additional sixty infantry divisions. As a matter of fact, there was no reason for Russia to surrender at that point. Even if the imminent naval showdown had ended in a draw, the Russian navy would still have been able to disrupt maritime traffic in the Sea of Japan and the Korea Strait as long as some vessels from the Baltic Fleet managed to reach Vladivostok. Most of all, if the additional sixty infantry divisions could be dispatched to the Far East, there would have been nothing, objectively speaking, to prevent Russia from winning the war on the continent. If this reinforcement actually arrived, the Japanese side would have had no choice but to abandon Mukden and Liaoyang and construct a line of defense in the mountainous areas in the southern part of the Liaodong Peninsula to weather massive attacks from the Russians. The only thing the Japanese side could hope for in this case was a deterioration in Russia's political and economic conditions that would make it impossible for it to sustain and supply its massive force of 1 million troops in the Far East indefinitely.

Thus, the Second Pacific Fleet, popularly known as the Baltic Fleet, became the focus of attention. It had long been the tsar's intention to make a naval effort to dispatch a grand fleet to the Far East. Accordingly, the Baltic Fleet was organized on May 2, 1904, and Vice Admiral Zinovy Rozhestvensky was appointed as its commander.

It took half a year, but this fleet finally set sail for the Far East in October 1904. The battleship fitting was behind schedule because Russia had been inactive in sea battles for quite a long time. The fleet also had to wait for the completion of four new vessels that had been constructed in anticipation of the Russo-Japanese War. Moreover, the fleet had to train reserve officers and newly drafted sailors for the imminent battle, another reason for the delay in departure.

Even with an earlier departure, however, the fleet would not have arrived in the Far East in time to affect the outcome of the Battle of Lüshun, and if the fleet opted to go directly to Vladivostok, its port would have been frozen over for the entire month of February. Thus, the fleet was best advised to arrive in Vladivostok no sooner than March—requiring the fleet to depart in October.

The magnificent fleet, composed of seven battleships, four heavy cruisers, nine destroyers, and six special mission vessels, sailed out of the naval port of Libau on October 15, 1904. It would be a great voyage, covering 18,000 nautical miles. Most of the ports on the way were within the sphere of Britain's influence, Japan's partner in the Anglo-Japanese Alliance who controlled the seven seas. To make the situation even worse, the fleet mistook a British fishing boat off Dogger Bank in the North Sea for a Japanese torpedo boat, believing it had come all that way to ambush the fleet, and sunk it, killing three fishermen. The incident invited harsh criticism from the British public.

Although the only ports where the fleet could make a port call were those in French colonies, France remained highly cautious. Because the primary objective of France was to maintain the alliance with Russia in preparation for its imminent revenge on Germany, France would jeopardize its grand strategy of containing Germany if it turned against Britain by servicing the Russian fleet too generously. This was why, each time the British government warned France, it complied with the neutrality requirements.

France had two fine natural harbors on the Baltic Fleet's route to the Far East: Diego Suarez in Madagascar and Cam Ranh Bay in Vietnam. Due to strict warnings from Britain, however, France could not offer the Baltic Fleet anchorage for the sake of obtaining coal supplies or opportunities for personnel to rest. Under a contract with a German coal supplier, the fleet received coal deliveries while sailing. But, because the British government restricted the supply of high-quality Cardiff coal, the Russian fleet had to rely on inferior German coal.

It is not hard to imagine that the seven-month voyage, through the tropical weather without rest and recuperation, gravely affected the morale of the Russian sailors, who were not familiar with such heat. The Russians also had the disadvantage of not having the chance to scrape off barnacles from ship bottoms or to refit and repair hulls; in contrast, the Combined Fleet of the Imperial Japanese Navy had undergone repeated refitting and training since the fall of Lüshun.

Nevertheless, at the time of its departure from Vietnam's offing after a rendezvous with Rear Admiral Nebogatov's Third Pacific Squadron, the Baltic Fleet was a magnificent force, boasting eight battleships against the four of the intercepting fleet under Tōgō. Although a mixed bag of old and new vessels, the First Pacific Squadron's four major battleships were fresh from the dockyard and newer in concept and design than the Japanese flagship *Mikasa*.

In contrast, the Japanese side, even though it was inferior to the Baltic Fleet in terms of the number of battleships, had lined up a greater number of destroyers and torpedo boats with shorter cruising range, taking advantage of its position as the interceptor.

Tsushima Strait or Tsugaru Strait

The greatest issue for both the Japanese and Russian operation commands was to decide which strait the Baltic Fleet would sail through to reach Vladivostok. There are three routes by which to enter the Sea of Japan from the Pacific Ocean: the Korea Strait (comprised of the western channel and the eastern channel, the "Tsushima Strait"), Tsugaru Strait, or La Pérouse Strait. There were also other options, including a refitting stop at Kamchatka, capturing the Bonin Islands, or capturing some German colonies in the South Pacific in hopes of Germany's tacit approval. In retrospect, after the destruction of the Baltic Fleet, it has been argued that any one of these options would have been better than what the fleet actually chose to do.

Meanwhile, the Japanese Combined Fleet was standing by in Chinhae Bay along the Korea Strait. But it was also ready to sail promptly toward Tsugaru Strait when it was judged that the Baltic Fleet was taking the northern route.

In fact, the Japanese fleet was on the verge of deciding to head north on May 25, two days before the Battle of Tsushima, since it had not detected the faintest sign of the enemy's arrival. The Japanese fleet tentatively remained in the bay, discouraged by foul weather, when it received a telegraph a little before 5:00 a.m. on May 27 from the armed merchantman *Shinano Maru,* which had been searching for the enemy. The telegraph said, "I have spotted enemy vessels." A second telegraph followed, with information that the "enemy's course is east-northeast and it appears to be heading for the eastern channel of the Korea Strait [Tsushima Strait]." This was the first occasion in history that telegraphic communication played a role in a sea battle.

Prior to that, the Russian war council had assumed the Japanese navy was divided in three and was ready and waiting along the Korea, Tsugaru, and La Pérouse Straits. Therefore, the Russians were convinced they could beat the Japanese fleet by having the entire Baltic Fleet sail through the Korea Strait, which is the shortest of the three routes. Russian records show that never in their imagination did the Russians expect to confront the entire Japanese fleet at Tsushima Strait.

"You can lose half the vessels to beat the enemy"

Thus, the two fleets met to the west of Okinoshima Island at 1:30 p.m. on May 27. There was only a seven nautical mile difference between the points of encounter independently estimated by Tōgō and Rozhestvensky.

At this point, the Z-flag was hoisted on Tōgō's flagship *Mikasa,* conveying the message: "The empire's fate depends on the result of this battle. Let every man do his utmost duty."

The Battle of Tsushima became well known for the "cross the T" tactic employed by Tōgō. Two fleets, each in a single column, were approaching each other, when the Japanese fleet suddenly made a 90-degree turn first and then another 90-degree turn at the head of the Russian fleet, causing it to sail in the same direction as them. Then, the Japanese fleet made another 90-degree turn at the head of the Russian fleet, blocking its direction.

Since both fleets were approaching one another at combat speed, if the Japanese fleet had sailed straight ahead, the encounter would have been a short one, in which both sides could shoot only a few rounds before they passed each other. From the beginning, the Japanese fleet's only objective had been to destroy the entire enemy fleet. If it allowed a substantial number of Russian vessels to reach Vladivostok, traffic on the Sea of Japan and the Korea Strait would have been obstructed, disturbing Japanese supplies to the Asian continent. Meanwhile, the Russian army in Manchuria would have grown stronger day by day as reinforcements continued to come from European Russia, making the situation unilaterally disadvantageous for Japan.

The Japanese side was prepared to lose all its warships in order to accomplish its objective. Navy Minister Yamamoto Gonbei once explained to Tōgō that two new battleships were about to be completed in a British dockyard and that the construction of a super 10,000-ton warship would start in a Japanese dockyard. Yamamoto encouraged Tōgō by saying, "You can lose half the vessels to beat the enemy."

The Tōgō Turn

With that kind of backup, one can take bold action. When the distance to the enemy narrowed to 8,000 meters, Tōgō ordered his fleet to make a 180-degree turn. Thirty minutes later, all of Tōgō's vessels commenced firing at the enemy when they started sailing in the same direction, parallel to the enemy fleet, at a distance of 6,000 meters.

It was, they say, a long thirty minutes. While this move made *Mikasa* temporarily vulnerable to enemy fire, causing some damage to the flagship, it certainly caused disarray within the enemy's formation. Within two minutes of the start of hostilities at 2:10 p.m., the battleship *Oslabia* at the head of the Russian fleet received some twenty shells, which caused a fire to break out. As a result of about thirty minutes of exchanging fire, the *Oslabia* was sunk, the battleships *Knyaz Suvorov* and *Imperator Alexander III* were incapacitated, dropping out of line, and the battleships *Borodino* and *Orel* were seriously damaged. Rozhestvensky, on board the *Knyaz Suvorov*, lost consciousness when a fragment of a shell, which had smashed the ship's bridge, hit him in the head.

The Russian vessels that survived the initial carnage reorganized the formation and headed for Vladivostok. Although, to its dismay, the Japanese fleet temporarily lost sight of the enemy vessels, it spotted some funnel smoke in the west a little before sunset. Japanese military history describes this sighting as the grace of Heaven. Approaching the smoke, the Japanese fleet resumed its fierce firing at the Russian vessels to block their advance. The catastrophic detonation of their magazines sunk the *Borodino* and the *Imperator Alexander III* within a few minutes, while the remaining four vessels fled in different directions.

Tōgō decided to advance the Combined Japanese Fleet northward during the night so it could intercept enemy vessels heading for Vladivostok at dawn.

In the night, Japanese destroyers and torpedo boats launched death-defying attacks on enemy vessels. Although those small vessels would be easy prey to enemy fire during the daytime, under the cover of darkness they could get close to enemy ships and launch torpedo attacks. In his detailed report on the battle, Tōgō recorded that "According to a Russian prisoner that I interviewed after the battle, the fierceness of the torpedo attacks that night was almost beyond description." Historian Tanaka Hiromi, in his treatise compiled in *Kindai Nippon sensō-shi* (Military history of modern Japan), attributes Tōgō's victory not so much to his famous Tōgō Turn but more to the systematic coordination of roles among different sizes of ships. The night raid by torpedo boats not only sank the battleships *Navarin* and *Sissoi Veliki* and the cruisers *Admiral Nakhimov* and *Vladimir Monomakh* but also seriously damaged most of the remaining vessels, which barely survived and fled to the north.

The next day, when the Japanese fleet was waiting in the morning sun for the enemy to appear near Takeshima Island (竹島), the five remaining vessels of the Baltic Fleet, now under the command of Rear Admiral

Nebogatov, who had replaced the incapacitated Rozhestvensky, appeared on the scene. Surrounded by twenty-six Japanese warships, Nebogatov surrendered after making the following plea to his younger officers:

"Although it would be a heroic act to fight these twenty-six Japanese vessels for the honor of Russia, it is obvious that we will be annihilated if we do so without inflicting any damage on the enemy. I am an old man and I do not hesitate to sacrifice my life, but you are young, and it is you who will one day retrieve the honor and glory of the Russian Navy. The lives of the two thousand four hundred men in these ships are more important than mine. It is me alone that should be blamed for the surrender." It was reported that an indescribable mixture of sorrow and anger filled those five Russian ships.

Unbelievably One-Sided Victory

To sum up the Battle of Tsushima, nineteen out of thirty-eight Russian warships that attempted to sail through Tsushima Strait were sunk, including six battleships. And five ships, including two battleships, were captured. Only a solitary armed merchantman, two destroyers, and a transport ship managed to reach Vladivostok. In contrast, the damage on the Japanese side was limited to three torpedo boats. On the Russian side, 4,524 sailors were killed and 6,168 Russian officers and sailors, including commanders in chief, were taken prisoner. On the Japanese side, 116 sailors died and some 570 were wounded.

This was an unbelievably one-sided victory. It was a perfect victory, unprecedented in the world history of naval battles.

In his battle report, Tōgō analyzed the causes of this one-sided victory as follows: "There was no noticeable difference in force strength between us, and I can testify that enemy officers and sailors also gave their utmost for the honor of Russia. Our miraculous victory is owed to nothing else than the august powers of the Emperor." The notion of "the august powers of the Emperor" had been advocated by Itō Hirobumi as the spiritual pillar of the Japanese constitution when he drafted the Meiji Constitution; it was meant to take the place of references to Christianity in Western constitutions. The reference to "the august powers of the Emperor," therefore, should be interpreted as nothing more than the equivalent to Westerners

Battleship *Asahi*, heading for Sasebo port after capturing the Russian battleships. The Russian battleship *Aryol* is in the back.

attributing their success to the grace of God. It was also an expression of Japanese modesty, stressing the factor of good fortune in one's success.

To be sure, it was fortunate, for instance, that the foul weather and dense fog of preceding days had cleared on the day of the decisive battle. But, if the Baltic Fleet had won the battle instead, the good weather could have been interpreted as good fortune for the Russians.

The strategy the Russian side took was criticized ex post facto from various angles. But it is the Russian defeat that generates this analysis. If the Baltic Fleet had won the battle, its decision to sail through the Tsushima Strait would have been praised as the shortest and most efficient route. In terms of the number of main guns, moreover, the Russian side had twenty-six 12-inch guns, the most powerful weapon on board, against sixteen owned by the Japanese fleet. In terms of 10-inch guns, it was one against fifteen in Russia's favor. Therefore, it would not be surprising at all if the Russian side did not expect to be beaten so thoroughly in a long-range cannonade.

But the fact remains that the Russian fleet was indeed thoroughly defeated in the long-range artillery duel, beaten in the short-range cannonade by the Japanese fleet's 8-inch guns, and finished off by torpedo boats, which the Russian side did not even include in its fleet.

Because the two fleets fired at each other, sailing in parallel in the same direction after the Tōgō Turn, it would have been only natural for both sides to receive a similar extent of damage. The overwhelming gap in the damage incurred between the two sides, therefore, can only be attributed to a difference in marksmanship.

One factor behind this difference in marksmanship was the legendary intensive target practice undertaken in Chinhae Bay while the Japanese were waiting for the arrival of the Baltic Fleet. During this period, Admiral Tōgō changed his meal schedule from breakfast at 8:00 a.m./supper at 5:00 p.m. to breakfast at 5:00 a.m./supper at 8:00 p.m. so as not to miss his men's target practice. As a result of this training, the marksmanship of each vessel in the Combined Fleet of the Imperial Japanese Navy greatly improved.

Established theory in those days held that the on-target rate during a sea battle would not exceed 2–3 percent. A Russian expert who studied the damage on the battleship *Orel* after the war estimated that the Japanese on-target rate had exceeded 12 percent. Accuracy five times greater than average could only have been attained by repeated practice. In any event, one thing that can be said about the Japanese gunnery without any doubt is that it had the ability to fire exceedingly rapidly, perhaps as well as accurately.

Japanese gunners—including those in today's Self-Defense Forces— are renowned as some of the world's finest in terms of both speed and accuracy. This may relate to cultural traditions emphasizing the elimination of any wasted movement, as seen in *chanoyu* (tea ceremony), which has already been elevated to the realm of art. When shopping even today, for instance, the acts of making a purchase, getting the correct change, and having the item properly wrapped in perfect, exacting form would take several times longer in Moscow than in Tokyo. It is easily imagined that the same thing can be said about the execution of the procedure of aiming, loading, and discharging a gun.

The standard of the Japanese people in such actions is arguably the highest in the world. That is why it is still believed that the combination of American generals, German officers, and Japanese noncommissioned officers would make the strongest army in the world.

If you can halve the time to discharge a gun, you can double the number of hits. Moreover, if the enemy becomes tied up with extinguishing fires started by the hits, it would be the same as discharging guns ten times faster than the enemy in terms of impact.

Moreover, the Japanese side had more advantages in the realm of science and technology during the Russo-Japanese War, because Shimose Powder (known overseas as Shimose Melinite) had far greater explosive power than other powders. Also, the shells used by the Japanese navy were equipped with blasting fuses (Ijūin fuses) that were much more sensitive than the mainstream shells of the time, which were manufactured to penetrate armor. When a Japanese shell hit a target, it exploded and blew away everything around it. The Russians called this horrendous shell the "grand sweeper." It is not hard to imagine how these shells, exploding one after another, greatly impaired the capability of Russian vessels to engage in combat.

Seen from these angles, the Japanese victory in the Battle of Tsushima should be attributed more to the high cultural and educational standards of the Japanese people in those days, particularly the tradition of perfectionism that had permeated every social stratum in Japan, than to any particular strategy or tactic.

This national character of the Japanese survived the defeat in World War II and subsequent occupation by the Allied Forces although a number of traditional values were lost. And this character became the engine of miraculous postwar economic reconstruction and growth. This postwar economic success, despite the apparent absence of outstanding leadership or an excellent national strategy, owed a lot to the average capabilities of ordinary Japanese people, which must have towered above the rest of the world.

"Legitimate successor of the Anglo-Saxon"

Japan's victory at the Battle of Tsushima changed the world in many senses. It inspired wonder and admiration throughout the world.

The British were overjoyed by their ally's victory, almost as if it were their own accomplishment. The year 1905 happened to be the one-hundredth anniversary of the great victory at the Battle of Trafalgar, in which the British navy, under the command of Admiral Horatio Nelson, had sunk or captured eighteen ships in the French-Spanish allied fleet without losing any of its own. Annihilating almost half of the enemy's fleet was in itself an amazing accomplishment, and yet it was still no match for Admiral Tōgō's one-sided victory. The British government expressed its jubilation over "the victory of a British ally" that "could even have exceeded the victory at Trafalgar."

Across the Atlantic, the American response was equally enthusiastic, reflecting Americans' natural love of a success story. President Theodore Roosevelt himself admitted that he had been glued to the news of the battle all day long and that "I was too excited to attend to any official duty, as if I had become a Japanese myself, and spent the entire day talking about the sea battle with visitors." When Kaneko Kentarō, Prime Minister Itō's special envoy, entered a restaurant in Washington, DC, other patrons rushed up to him to shake hands and raised their glasses in congratulations for Japan's victory, while the band played *Kimigayo*, Japan's de facto national anthem.

The Washington Times, characterizing Japan's victory as a triumph of civilization, freedom, and progress, editorialized as follows: "It has been predicted by some that the Slav and the Anglo-Saxon will have a decisive clash within the twentieth century, and it appears that this prediction has been at least partially realized today. This is so because the Japanese is a legitimate successor of the Anglo-Saxon."

World Historic Significance of the Battle of Tsushima

It is true that the twentieth century was a period of struggle for world hegemony, between Britain and Russia at the beginning and between the United States and the Soviet Union in the latter half of the century. Except for the tragic twenty-year interval in which Japan antagonized the Anglo-Saxon world, Japan had the fortune of being on the Anglo-Saxon side for twenty years during the Anglo-Japanese Alliance and another fifty years as a partner in the US-Japan Alliance.

And the arrival of that tragic interval, too, had been predicted at an early stage. *The New York Sun* expressed its uneasiness about the rise of Japan only three days after the Battle of Tsushima as follows: "Japan has won a great victory. If Japan continues to grow stronger and more powerful, using this great victory as a springboard, it may not be too far in the future that Britain, which currently boasts the world's strongest naval power, will be pushed away and overtaken by Japan. And when that happens, what will become of the United States?"

It is often after such major incidents that one can glimpse the long-term historical perspective of the world. The above two commentaries seem to have hinted at the future shape of Japan, as well as at the options open to it during the one hundred years of the twentieth century.

At the same time, the Battle of Tsushima became one of the spurs of the Russian Revolution, which profoundly affected world trends throughout the twentieth century.

In Russia, every time the news of a defeat was reported, sorrow and anger spread throughout the country. Illiterate peasants encircled those who could read newspapers, asking for the details of the defeat, which made them all cry.

A Russian newspaper argued, "It was because Russia had rejected progress and westernization that it lost 500,000 soldiers and billions of rubles." Another newspaper editorialized, "Russia has been stupid enough to close its eyes and let the world pass it by. We had been marching toward the depth of devastation, blindfolded, but this defeat had the effect of stripping off the blindfold." As these commentaries hint, the expectation of revolution became all the more rampant.

An antiwar demonstration that erupted in Saint Petersburg spread all over Russia. The June 6 issue of the *New York Times* reported, "The domestic situation in Russia has become increasingly tumultuous and the will to continue the war seems to have waned. There is a danger of revolution in Russia today."

By this time, Poland was in a state of rebellion, with socialists marching on June 19 with the red flag clashing with the Cossack cavalry, resulting in the killing or injury of 2,000 persons. The crew of the Russian battleship *Potemkin* rose up against its officers in the Black Sea port of Odessa; a factor behind the uprising was the alleged financial assistance to insurgents provided by Lieutenant Colonel Akashi Motojirō.

Inspiring Nonwhite People

Perhaps even more significant in terms of world history than the impact of the Battle of Tsushima on the future of the British/Russian strife or on the socialist revolution that shook the entire twentieth century was its impact on the thinking of nonwhite people around the world.

Jawaharlal Nehru wrote in his autobiography:

> Japanese victories stirred up my enthusiasm and I waited eagerly for the papers for fresh news daily . . . Nationalistic ideas filled my mind. I mused of Indian freedom and Asiatic freedom from the thraldom of Europe. I dreamt of brave deeds, of how, sword in hand, I would fight for India and help in freeing her.
>
> In May 1905, when I was fifteen, my family set out to journey to England and arrived in London late in that month. Reaching London by train from Dover, I was elated to read in the newspapers of the victory of Japan, an Asiatic power, over Russia in the naval battle in the Strait of Tsushima.[2]

In letters to his daughter Indira, compiled in *Glimpses of World History* (1934), Nehru wrote of this excitement over Japan's victory; it was shared, he said, by boys, girls, and adults all over Asia. A major European power was beaten. Just as Asia had crushed Europe several times in the past, it could do so again today, Nehru predicted, and noted that there were calls of nationalism from around the entire Asian continent to restore an "Asia for Asians."

Sun Yat-sen (孫文) also remarked that Westerners stopped looking down on Asians after Japan's victory, which not only allowed Japan to enjoy the privilege of a first-class nation but also helped raise the international status of other Asian peoples as well. The Indian nationalist of the early twentieth century, Lajpat Rai, stated, "Japan defended the honor of Asians and proved that Asians, if provided with equal opportunities, were not inferior at all in any aspect."

The psychological impact of Japan's victory in the Russo-Japanese War also contributed to the Persian Constitutional Revolution of 1906, the radicalization of the Indian National Congress in 1907, the Young Turk Revolution in 1908, and the Xinhai Revolution (辛亥革命) in China

---

2   Jawaharlal Nehru, *An Autobiography: With Musings on Recent Events in India* (Bombay: Allied Publishing, 1962), 16–17.

in 1911. Although the victory fell short of shaking up colonial empires, which were at their apex at the time, it powerfully stoked the nationalism of all Asian people, from Vietnam to Egypt.

Japan's victory even gave hope to African Americans in the United States for resisting suppression. Archibald Grimke, American lawyer, intellectual, journalist, diplomat, and community leader in the nineteenth and early twentieth century, contributed the following biblical exhortation to *New York Age*:

> Go . . . ye little brown men, conquering and to conquer.
> Sheath not your terrible sword, lay not aside yet
>   your bloody scourge.
> Ye shall overthrow . . . Ye have thrown Russia down,
>   ye are destined to throw down others than Russia in their pride,
>   in their lust for power,
> To bring down to the dust the mighty of the earth.[3]

It is, however, equally undeniable that Japan's victory had also stirred up wariness of Japan among Western powers. This wariness, the "yellow peril" argument, was behind the discrimination against Japanese residents in the United States, and it later became a controversial issue between Japan and the United States.

Japan's miraculous victory at the Battle of Tsushima could therefore be said to have accelerated historical change throughout the world.

---

3   Quoted in Reginald Kearney, *African American Views of the Japanese: Solidarity or Sedition?* (Albany: State University of New York Press, 1998), 20–21.

12

Treaty of Portsmouth

—No Concession Despite Roosevelt's Persuasion—

"What Good Would Continuing the War Bring to a Poor Country?"

Despite the official victory at the Battle of Mukden, the Japanese army found itself in pitiable condition after the battle. Officers in particular were in short supply, resulting in the reduction of actual combat capability within each division by as much as 30 to 50 percent.

A platoon leader is popularly known as a "shield against bullets." It was the post to which graduates of the Imperial Japanese Army Academy were first appointed. A platoon leader was expected to spearhead a charge at the enemy. As such, graduates of the army academy around the time of a major war have suffered a distinctively high rate of death in battles all over the world. In 1905, the Imperial Japanese Army Academy shortened the officer training of its seventeenth class to only eight months in order to quickly feed platoon leaders to the battlefield. Nevertheless, the academy was able to send only 300 graduates to the field, among whom was Tōjō Hideki, who later became the Japanese prime minister during World War II.

In contrast, the Russian side was able to send 50,000 to 60,000 fresh soldiers every month. They were the cream of the Russian army, both in terms of equipment and personnel, that had been stationed on the German/

Austrian front. According to a calculation by the Imperial General Head-quarters, by mid-September the Russian side would boast thirty-eight divisions against seventeen divisions on the Japanese side (fifteen plus two that had been hastily organized). The Japanese side had less than half the Russian force in terms of numbers, but its combat capability was even more inferior. Postwar Russian official documents revealed the accuracy of the Japanese General Headquarters' estimate.

The Battle of Mukden was concluded on March 20. Only eight days later, on March 28, General Kodama Gentarō, chief of general staff of the Manchurian Army, arrived at Tokyo's Shimbashi Station. The purpose of his visit was kept top secret. However, when Vice-Chief of Staff Nagaoka Gaishi, who came to meet Kodama at the station, quietly asked him in the carriage to share his future battle plans, in a low voice Kodama said, "I did not come back to consult on battle plans. I came back to stop the war." From that point on, Kodama met one top government leader after another to speak his mind, saying, "Those who have started a war have to know when to stop it. What good would continuing the war bring to a poor country like Japan?"

At the Ministry of Foreign Affairs, Kodama met Yamaza Enjirō, direc-tor general of political affairs, who had been obsessed with the hardliner argument under Komura Jutarō's influence. To Yamaza, Kodama warned, "The war situation is such that we require no more reinforcements. What we need instead is peace."

When Foreign Minister Komura stressed the need to "deal a blow to Nikolay Linevich [commander in chief of the Russian land forces in Man-churia] one more time," so as to start peace negotiations on favorable terms, Kodama replied that all the odds were against the Japanese side and it would be extremely risky to fight against a superior enemy at this stage. To Kodama, the big picture of the war was all too obvious.

Russia, for its part, still remained fully confident as far as ground bat-tles were concerned. The most serious stumbling block to Russia continu-ing the war was the domestic situation. In this sense, Japan's victory in the Russo-Japanese War is analogous to North Vietnam in the Vietnam War, during which antiwar movements became rampant within the United States. But the situation in Russia in those days was far more serious than the mood of American society at the time of the Vietnam War. Russian society faced rising doubts about the tsar's autocracy and an upsurge of hope among the Russian people for a revolution, as well as a swelling desire for independence among the many minorities who had been oppressed by the Russians.

Sergei Witte, who was Komura's counterpart during the forthcoming peace negotiations in Portsmouth, described the situation concisely in his memoir. According to Witte, battle by battle the prospects of the Russo-Japanese War were becoming increasingly unfavorable for Russia, which came as an unprecedented shock to Russians in every social stratum. The shock manifested itself in various forms, all of which expressed dissatisfaction with the current political regime.

To begin with, Witte reflected, it was mainly because of its military might that the Russian Empire had been recognized as a world power. Similarly, it was solely due to the power of its troops and bayonets that the tiny, semi-Asian kingdom of Moscow was able to achieve the status of a formidable European power. The world was not awed by Russia's culture or wealth. The world was awed by Russia's military might. The revelation that Russia was actually not that strong—in other words, that it was a house of cards—therefore provoked the rise of enemies both within and outside the country.

After the defeat at the Battle of Mukden, Witte observed, an increasing number of level-headed Russians began to believe the war must not be prolonged any longer.

Mediation Attempt by President Roosevelt

As a result of General Kodama's persuasion, consensus was formed among the Japanese government leaders on the policy to pursue peace with Russia. On May 31, as soon as the Japanese navy achieved its historic one-sided victory at the Battle of Tsushima, Foreign Minister Komura instructed Takahira Kogorō, Japanese minister to the United States, to request that President Theodore Roosevelt mediate peace.

Roosevelt immediately summoned the Russian ambassador to the White House and sounded out Russia's intentions. Although Russia had previously decided to continue the war after the Battle of Tsushima, the tsar's message on June 7 conveyed that Russia would accept President Roosevelt's offer to mediate peace.

Komura and the Japanese minister to the United States, Takahira Kogorō, heading for the peace negotations.

Representing the defeated as chief plenipotentiary at peace negotiations is a thankless and unsavory job, and persuading someone to represent Russia proved so difficult that in the end, Sergei Witte was appointed to the post because nobody else could replace him.

The tsar strictly forbade Witte from conceding even a single kopek in war redemptions or an inch of territory under any condition. Although this instruction was tantamount to the announcement of his downfall, Witte resigned himself to complying with it until the very end. It was due to Roosevelt's private telegram to the tsar that Russia conceded the southern half of Sakhalin Island at the very last minute. Witte did not make the concession.

Although Japan was, officially, on the winning side, everyone in the government knew the country's circumstances were far from victorious. This fact discouraged anyone from volunteering to represent the country at the peace negotiations. Itō Hirobumi adamantly declined the nomination, and in the end, it was decided that Komura had to be the chief plenipotentiary for the peace negotiations. Witte's reluctance found an echo in the remark Komura made at Shimbashi Station on July 8 while on his way to Portsmouth. Being cheered off with a shout of "banzai," he said, "I will be a most unpopular person when I come back from the negotiations."

Prior to Komura's departure, Itō said to Komura, "No matter what others do or don't do, I shall never fail to meet you at the pier when you come back to Japan," a promise Itō indeed kept three months later when he met Komura at Yokohama pier. Everyone in the Japanese government had anticipated the nationwide antipathy toward Komura when he returned from the peace negotiations.

Nevertheless, the predicament of the Japanese forces in Manchuria was top secret, something shared only among top government leaders, which could not be leaked at any cost. Even President Roosevelt in those days was convinced that if the war was prolonged, the Japanese army could drive the Russians out of Manchuria, and doing so would probably claim the lives of a large number of officers and soldiers. It was because this secret was so well kept that Japan was able to conclude the peace negotiations successfully. Had the Russians known of Japan's predicament, the self-assured tsar would never have conceded to Japan's terms.

On July 7, a day before Komura's departure for Portsmouth, the Japanese army captured Korsakov, the central city in southern Sakhalin. Hardliners, including Komura, had long demanded the occupation of Sakhalin, particularly from the viewpoint of obtaining an effective card to play at the peace negotiations with Russia. As a matter of fact, having heard the Russian war council, at a meeting held in the tsar's presence immediately after the Battle of Tsushima, had already decided to continue fighting on the grounds that "not even an inch of Russian territory had been taken away yet," President Roosevelt suggested to the Japanese special envoy Kaneko Kentarō that Japan should occupy Sakhalin. But it appears that this suggestion by Roosevelt was somehow never conveyed to Tokyo. The Japanese government decided on the occupation of Sakhalin on its own, resulting in the subsequent possession of the southern half of the island.

No Intention to Concede on War Redemption or Territory

Prior to Komura's departure for Portsmouth, he was given the following instructions on things that were absolutely nonnegotiable, imperative accomplishments, and desirable outcomes. In sum:

First, it was absolutely nonnegotiable for Japan that Russia accept Japan's discretionary power on the Korean Peninsula, that Russia cede the leasehold of Liaodong Peninsula and the railway between Harbin and Lüshun to Japan, and that both withdraw their forces from Manchuria.

Second, it was imperative that Russia agree to pay war redemptions and cede Sakhalin.

Additionally, if possible, the Japanese side was hoping to disarm Vladivostok and remodel it into a commercial port. Also, it was deemed desirable to restrict Russia's naval power in the Far East.

Comparing the above with the instructions the tsar had given Witte, it is obvious that the things that were absolutely nonnegotiable coincided perfectly for both Japan and Russia, making the outcome of the negotiations easily predictable. But the basic rule of negotiation is to keep one's hand hidden from the other party, and thus, the peace talks turned into two long months of difficult negotiations.

While the eventual outcome of the negotiations between Japan and Russia might have been in retrospect quite predictable from the beginning, there was a wide discrepancy in the views on the future of Manchuria between the mediating United States and Japan—or rather, between the United States and the hawkish element in Japan represented by Komura. This discrepancy remained the source of a fundamental gap in perception between the two countries throughout the Manchurian Incident of 1931–33.

In his tentative proposal for a draft of the peace conditions, which was submitted to Prime Minister Katsura in July 1904, more than a half year before the fall of Lüshun, Komura had already proposed to reject the neutralization of Manchuria. Komura proposed that even Manchuria, not to mention Korea, which had been under Japan's sway from the beginning, had to be brought within the sphere of Japan's influence, replacing Russia to a certain extent. Katsura agreed with this perspective.

This was taking advantage of the earlier announcement by US Secretary of State John Hay that the United States would not oppose Russia's occupation of Manchuria as long as Manchuria was guaranteed equality of opportunity.[1] Now that Japan had defeated Russia, Komura claimed that the tolerance Hay had shown for Russia should also be applied to Japan's occupation of Manchuria.

President Roosevelt, however, had already proposed to Britain, France, and Italy in January 1905 that Manchuria should be returned to Qing and made into a neutral zone guaranteed by the Western powers. Britain had

---

1 For instance, see Tsunoda, *Manshū mondai*, 191.

already agreed. In a nutshell, Roosevelt's proposal was for the Western civilized countries to administer Manchuria in place of Qing, whose administrative capability was at best highly questionable.

Komura officially instructed Minister Takahira to propose that Manchuria should be returned to Qing on the condition that the Qing's sound governance and administrative reform of Manchuria were guaranteed. This proposal was analogous to Japan's demand at the time of the First Sino-Japanese War, when it refused to withdraw its troops from Korea until Korea's domestic reform was accomplished. The proposal aimed to secure Japan's exclusive right to have a say in Manchurian domestic affairs. Moreover, it was intended to enable Japan to justify its occupation of Manchuria for an indefinite period by imposing unrealistic conditions.

In the end, peace negotiations commenced with these two proposals—the US and Japanese proposals—being shelved. Essentially, the difference between the two proposals was whether the administration of Manchuria, which had been de facto in the hands of the Russians, should be undertaken by Japan (Japan's proposal) or Western civilized powers (the United States' proposal). Neither proposal called for a full return of Qing's administration of Manchuria.

Roosevelt's Early Peace Argument

President Roosevelt intended to achieve peace by requesting Japan's self-restraint. When Japan's request for his mediation reached him, he made the following comment, "Japan is showing symptoms of being out of its mind. To be sure, if the United States had accomplished what Japan has had in the past 16 months, we would also be out of our mind."

As soon as Komura arrived in the United States, Roosevelt attempted to convince him of the virtue of concluding a peace treaty at that stage by saying, "While no doubt Japan will win the war if it continues to fight, the damage that Japan would incur will also be enormous. It is high time to negotiate peace."[2] But Komura, who had advocated for a continuation of

---

2   Quoted in Katsura's August 4 telegram No. 15 to Kodama, quoted in Tsunoda, *Manshū mondai*, 255.

Japan-Russia Delegation at the Treaty of Portsmouth, August 14, 1905.
(Photo: Kyodo News)

the war, would not listen.

Despite President Roosevelt's personal persuasion, Komura had no intention of conceding on the issues of territory and war redemption. On August 17, Komura sent a wire to Tokyo, warning that "The likelihood is that we will not be able to accomplish our goals, in which case we have no other choice than to continue the war." Government leaders in Tokyo had been well aware of Komura's hardliner argument. They told Komura beforehand, "If by any chance the negotiations should result in failure, do not abandon them on the spot. You are requested to report to headquarters in advance for advice."

Since Komura refused to follow his advice, President Roosevelt wrote two long letters, on August 22 and 23, to Kaneko Kentarō to appeal directly to Japan's top leaders. Roosevelt stressed, "Now that Japan has achieved the original objectives of the war, it should meet the expectations of the civilized world for peace by not waging a war to obtain greater war redemptions."[3] Hearing about these letters, Komura hardened his convic-

---

3 Morison, *The Letters of Theodore Roosevelt*, 4: 1808–10, 1812–13, quoted in Tsunoda, *Manshū mondai*, 256.

tion that Japan had no other choice than to continue the war and wait for another opportunity to negotiate peace. He advised this to Tokyo.

Around the same time, General Kodama sent an appeal from Manchuria that it would no longer be possible to continue the war, as not a single soldier was in reserve. Both Komura's and Kodama's telegrams were submitted to the cabinet meeting on August 28 for deliberation. Minister of War Terauchi Masatake lamented, "We are so short of officers that we cannot continue to fight." While Minister of Finance Sone Arasuke declared, "It would be impossible to finance the war any longer." In the end, Komura's proposition was rejected, and members of the cabinet decided to pursue the course of negotiating peace with Russia.

Meanwhile, Itō Hirobumi and Saionji Kinmochi, two of the Meiji elders, had strongly insisted on accepting President Roosevelt's advice. Saionji in particular openly expressed his opinion at a Seiyūkai party convention, "Although we in Japan believe that we have won the war, other countries in the world do not necessarily agree with us. We must interpret the US president's proposal as representing the expectations of other countries in the world." This view was a courageous challenge to the clamorous domestic chorus that opposed peace negotiations and demanded the continuation of the war.

When Japan finally agreed to a compromise, President Roosevelt sent a personal letter to the emperor on August 31 saying, "Your Majesty has presented a splendid example to the world on how it is indeed possible for a country which has accomplished a succession of victories to win a war without losing its self-control."[4]

Swaying American Public Opinion

Because Japan succeeded in securing all of its "absolute nonnegotiables" plus the southern half of Sakhalin Island through the negotiations, the Japanese government, objectively speaking, ought to have been content with the outcome.

Nevertheless, it was natural that voices of dissatisfaction were raised

---

4   Ibid., 1328, quoted in Tsunoda, *Manshū mondai*, 261.

among the Japanese public because the people had been unaware Japan was so desperately strained both militarily and financially. Harsh words were hurled at the government, antigovernment meetings were held, and some buildings in Tokyo were even set on fire, resulting in the declaration of martial law. However, being more of a sporadic outburst than an organized rebellion, the riots, which lasted for a couple of days, had mostly subsided by the time martial law was declared. Determined to promptly sign the peace treaty, the government ratified the draft treaty unanimously at the privy council and obtained imperial sanction on October 10 before Komura returned to Japan.

A prevailing myth about Komura is that he was actually a dove who had gone against public opinion and concluded the peace negotiations for the sake of Japan's future, prepared to be the lone target of hardliners' criticism. This was a myth created during the post–World War II era when the doves were lionized. In actuality, Komura was the ultimate hawk, and was bent on ending the negotiations in order to continue the war. He only signed the treaty because he was instructed to do so by the Japanese government. That said, Komura remained true to his character to the end, enduring the accusations of being dovish without making any excuses until he died.

It has been rightly pointed out that, during the two months of the negotiations, the tone of the American press went from being 99 percent pro-Japanese before the negotiations to being more sympathetic toward Russia. This reversal, as Sergei Witte bragged in his memoir, was attributed to "a grave blunder"[5] Komura committed.

During the six-day voyage across the Atlantic, Witte decided on the principles he would base his tactics on while in the United States. In essence, he resolved "not to show that we were in the least anxious to make peace, [because Russia was] undismayed by the fact that the mighty empire had become involved temporarily in a slight difficulty."[6] This was exactly the attitude the tsar maintained, and Witte had no other choice than to assume it.

Additionally, Witte decided, "in view of the tremendous influence of

---

5   *Memoir of Count Witte* (Garden City, NY and Toronto: Doubleday, Page & Company, 1921), 141.

6   Ibid., 139–40.

the press in America, to show it every attention and to be accessible to all its representatives; to behave with democratic simplicity and without a shadow of snobbishness, so as to win the sympathy of the Americans; [and] in view of the considerable influence of the Jews on the press and on other aspects of American life, especially in New York, not to exhibit any hostility toward them."[7]

Witte continued to reminisce that "I took care to treat all the Americans with whom I came into contact with the utmost simplicity of manner. When travelling, whether on special trains, government motor cars or steamers, I thanked everyone, talked with the engineers and shook hands with them. In another words, I treated everybody, of whatever social position, as an equal."[8]

He admitted, "This behavior was a heavy strain on me as all acting is to the unaccustomed, but it surely was worth the trouble." The sympathies of American public opinion and the media began to swing toward Russia. This change of mood was also reflected in the telegram President Roosevelt sent to the Japanese government toward the end of the negotiations, warning that American public opinion had lately become remarkably sympathetic toward Russia and that Japan could no longer expect similar sympathy from Americans as before if the peace negotiations turned out to be unsuccessful.

President Roosevelt's sympathy had originally been with the Japanese side. Bright man as he was and "seeing that American public opinion was becoming favorable toward Russia and fearing that the unsuccessful end of the parley might turn the sympathies of the people away from him and from the Japanese," he knew it was unwise to go against public opinion. This was why, Witte believed, Roosevelt repeatedly advised the Japanese government to accept the conditions offered by Witte.

Witte admitted that another favorable factor for him was the attitude of the Japanese delegates. They were not supercilious, which Americans find intolerable, but their secretive and glum attitude turned off openhearted Americans. "Not supercilious but secretive and glum" is indeed an accurate description of Komura's character.

It has been pointed out that "diplomacy without a face"—diplomacy

---

7   Ibid., 140.
8   Ibid.

devoid of personality or human charm—is a critical flaw of Japanese diplomacy even today, and it seems undeniable in retrospect that this "diplomacy without a face" has worked to Japan's disadvantage on various occasions, particularly those taking place in the United States.

While it may be easy to say that the Japanese could have done the same as Witte, there seem to be obstacles to such conduct in Japanese society, including such negative reactions as denouncing the conduct as being "weird" or calling it "grandstanding." Consequently, it is beyond doubt that even if such conduct yielded successful outcomes, it would never be counted as virtuous in Japanese society. Rather, it would have appeared as against the samurai code of suppressing personal emotion. Also, there might be an element of aversion to exerting one's individuality. If somebody else had been appointed as Japan's representative, he could not have acted like Witte either, and his conduct, like Komura's, would have been totally acceptable to Japanese society, as what was expected of a Japanese, and would never have become a target of criticism.

Change in American Attitudes toward Japan

Some in Japan resented the change in the American attitude toward Japan, which shifted from sympathy before the Russo-Japanese War to apathy after Japan's victory in the war. This interpretation of the American attitude is correct in some senses but wrong in others.

It is a plain fact that during the peace negotiations in Portsmouth, the tone of the American press changed from being pro-Japan to anti-Japan. But the press returned to its pro-Japan stance after the treaty was signed and praised Japan's magnanimity and wisdom, saying that "it takes courage and tolerance on the part of the Japanese to conclude such a treaty." Witte's diplomatic victory and the flip side of the coin, the Japanese diplomatic failure, therefore, was only short-lived—except it occurred at a very critical moment. Overall, the American attitude can be interpreted as one of those fluctuations American public opinion is known for.

From the long-term international perspective, however, it was only natural for the United States to change its policies toward Japan as power in the Far East shifted from Russia to Japan. To risk oversimplification, this transformation was analogous to the sea change in the post–World War II international environment when the Soviet Union and China immediately became the archenemies of the United States in place of the defeated Japan.

No matter how amicable the United States had been toward Japan during the Russo-Japanese War, it was obvious to anyone that the United States would not support the continued expansion of Japan's influence on continental China. It was also only natural for China to regard Japan as its greatest threat and start approaching Western powers to counter Japan.

The long-term American perception of Japan was also affected. While there had been only curiosity about an "exotic" Japan, or contempt of and discrimination against Japanese (and other Asian) immigrants to the United States, a distinctive concern and wariness over Japan and its people emerged, partially fanned by Russia's "yellow peril" argument during the Russo-Japanese War.

Proposed US-Japanese Joint Management of the South Manchuria Railway

Immediately following the signing of the Treaty of Portsmouth, Komura took an important action, which sowed the seeds of the US-Japan conflict that eventually culminated in World War II.

The American railway tycoon Edward Harriman nursed a dream of owning transportation that went around the globe, a grandiose plan in those days. What he envisioned was an around-the-world route: connecting Baltimore on the American East Coast to San Francisco on the West Coast by the Union Pacific Railway; crossing the Pacific to Dalian by the Pacific Mail Steamship; connecting Dalian to Harbin and Moscow by railway, and then from Moscow by railway again to Libau Port along the Baltic Sea; and finally sailing from the Baltic Sea back to Baltimore by steamboat.

Having already arrived in Tokyo amid the public riots in protest of the signing of the Treaty of Portsmouth, Harriman proposed that the Japanese government should form a syndicate with his company to jointly manage the South Manchuria Railway.

Because the syndicate was to buy up the railway and its accessory facilities, it would be de facto cost-free for Japan, except for investment in the form of a railway. Although in principle the venture would be under joint ownership with Harriman, it was proposed that Japan should retain some of its existing say in operations, particularly in the case of war with either Russia or China, in which case the Japanese right to use the railway for military purposes would be fully respected. This was by no means an unfavorable condition for Japan.

Elder statesmen such as Itō and Inoue Kaoru as well as Prime Minister Katsura found this proposal attractive. Inoue in particular went around persuading everyone by saying, "It would be absolutely absurd not to take advantage of this opportunity."

The elderly statesman's thinking was based on two concerns. One was the financial strain caused by the Russo-Japanese War, which made it highly questionable whether the Japanese government could take on the additional financial burden of managing the South Manchuria Railway single-handedly. Much more worrisome, however, was the possibility of Russia's vengeance. Japan was able to win only by taking advantage of Russia's unpreparedness. If and when a fully prepared Russia attempted to gain revenge, Japan would be totally unable to withstand this. Japan was not at all confident that it could protect Manchuria from either Russia's retaliation or diplomatic pressures from Western powers that were engineered behind the scenes by China. In such a scenario, might it not be safer to make Manchuria a sort of internationally managed region, involving, among others, the United States and China?

Although the agreement was scheduled to be signed in Yokohama on October 12 before Harriman departed Japan, the Japanese side proposed the signing be postponed until Komura's return on October 16. Agreeing to this, Harriman left Yokohama and headed home, carrying the draft agreement with him. As soon as Harriman arrived in San Francisco, however, the Japanese consul there visited Harriman onboard his ship and announced the cancellation of the signing.

Behind this reversal was Komura's action. Komura had been convinced from the beginning that Japan's national strategy should be to put Manchuria under Japanese influence. He had no intention of conceding even an inch on this matter. There was a fundamental difference in Komura's and the elderly statesmen's perceptions on this matter. From the viewpoint of the Meiji elders, who had gone through the hardships of subservience since the arrival of Commodore Perry, it was inconceivable that Japan could continue to compete with the Western powers indefinitely. This perspective inclined them toward caution, demarcating them from the younger generation, including Komura, who had been ignited with imperialistic zeal throughout the First Sino-Japanese and Russo-Japanese Wars.

The shortage of finances to manage the railway was a headache for Komura, but a solution to this problem came from an unexpected source. Kaneko Kentarō's record shows that there was an offer from the Morgan financial group, the archrival of Harriman's enterprise, for financial assistance on the condition that Japan would hold onto the South Manchuria Railway and not allow Harriman to monopolize it. Overjoyed by this offer, Komura declared, "Now that we have secured funding for the restoration of the South Manchuria Railway, we can proudly report on the outcome of the peace treaty without hesitation."

Although Komura had been in the United States, recuperating from exhaustion after signing the Treaty of Portsmouth, he decided to return home in haste. When in Yokohama, Komura learned about Harriman's proposal from Yamaza Enjirō, director general of political affairs of the Foreign Ministry who had returned to Japan ahead of Komura, and he immediately started scheming to wreck the proposition. "What a blunder!" he bemoaned. "That's why I had to come back despite my ailment."

The plan Komura came up with was to postpone the signing of the contract until Japan had obtained Qing's approval, which would be necessary even after Russia had formally agreed to hand over the South Manchuria Railway to Japan.

Although this reasoning was somewhat forced given that Qing was at the mercy of Japan at the time and had to do anything Japan told it to, Komura sailed to Beijing in spite of his physical condition, in place of Itō who had been eager to conduct negotiations with Qing himself, and succeeded in inserting a clause in the treaty signed in December that said, "No other country than Japan and Qing is allowed to participate in the management of the South Manchuria Railway," effectively blocking the participation of the United States.

Prior to the negotiations in Beijing, Komura had drafted an outline for the management of Manchuria and Korea that was approved at a cabinet meeting. At the outset, the outline declares, "As the result of the peace negotiations with Russia, a segment of Manchuria is now under the sphere of influence of the Empire of Japan. Japan therefore needs to maintain and consolidate its influence in the region." The outline was even equipped with a contingency plan in case of Qing's resistance: suspend the negotiations and continue the occupation of the Liaodong Peninsula and the South Manchuria Railway.

Although President Roosevelt persuaded Qing to follow Japan's advice without resistance, a commitment he had made at the time of the peace negotiations, he also kept reminding the Japanese government of the importance of keeping the doors to Manchuria open.

Misjudgment that Affected Japan's Fate

Conventional Japanese history books have been mostly favorable to Komura wrecking Harriman's scheme.

Komura gaikō-shi (小村外交史; History of Komura diplomacy), compiled by the Ministry of Foreign Affairs, praised it as, "hidden efforts by Komura to resolutely quash the scheme," while *Nichibei gaikō no keifu* (日米外交の系譜; Genealogy of Japan's diplomacy vis-à-vis the United States) by Kuroha Shigeru expressed admiration for Komura's "keen insight and decisiveness."

To be sure, the argument that Japan should not give up Manchuria after sacrificing 100,000 soldiers to acquire it was very convincing, even if a little sentimental. And it is a historical fact that the Empire of Japan succeeded in protecting its special interests in Manchuria for the next forty years, including the years during the Manchurian Incident (1931–33).

In 1906, one year after his proposal was turned down, Harriman met Takahashi Korekiyo (高橋是清), who became governor of the Bank of Japan in 1911, minister of finance in 1913, and prime minister in 1921, and predicted that "Within ten years, Japan will regret having lost the opportunity to jointly manage the South Manchuria Railway with the United States." As it turned out, Harriman's prophesy did not come true in ten years and, in this sense, it may be said that Komura's judgment was sounder than Harriman's.

In retrospect, though, it is undeniable that luck played an important role in Japan's good fortune. After the Russo-Japanese War, the focus of world politics shifted to Europe, where war erupted only ten years later. Russia was consequently forced to stake its fate on a war with Germany, depriving it of any energy to take revenge on Japan. No other countries could afford to pay attention to the Far East. Also, fifteen-year-long power vacuums emerged on the Asian continent: fifteen years between the Xinhai Revolution of 1911 and the 1926 launching of the Kuomintang's Northern Expedition for one and fifteen years between the Russian Revolution in 1917 and the completion of the First Five-Year Plan under Premier Joseph Stalin in 1932 for another, during which Japan's monopoly of Manchuria faced no threats. However, if war had not erupted in Europe, allowing Russia to recuperate from defeat in the Russo-Japanese War and in time advance into the Far East again, or if China had managed to evade disintegration and schemed to retrieve concessions in Manchuria in cooperation with Russia and the United States, the world might have experienced what Harriman had predicted in more or less than ten years. All of the above suppositions could have easily come to mind at the time immediately after the Russo-Japanese War. In other words, Komura's decision put Japan at the risk of these developments.

International relations are, after all, power relations. If any one of the above suppositions had become reality, the sentimental argument of defending the land that was obtained in exchange for Japanese blood would have become nonsensical, and Japan would have been cornered into either accepting the consequences that reflected Japan's relative power or waging a hopeless war. What happened was the fulfillment of Harriman's prophesy in thirty years, instead of ten, in the form of the Pacific War after all of Japan's luck had run out. In retrospect, therefore, it would have been wiser for Japan to accept Harriman's proposition. In this sense, it should be admitted that Komura made the wrong choice for the future of Japan.

Intellectual Energy of Itō Hirobumi

During the Russo-Japanese War, as Japanese troops captured one city after another that had been occupied by the Russians, the Japanese military did not return those cities to Chinese authorities but instead put them under its own military administration with the purpose of "keeping them as they had been under the Russian occupation in order to establish Japan's rule in the future." Fukushima Yasumasa was put in charge of the military administration of Manchurian cities, and he aggressively pursued the establishment of Japan's rule there.

This was not how Komura had envisioned things. In the cabinet meeting on October 27, after the peace treaty was signed, Komura remarked that everything under the treaty, except Japan's acquisitions from Russia, should be returned to Qing. Komura thought Japan would lose credibility in the international community if it held onto Manchuria, which it had occupied as a result of a military victory in the Russo-Japanese War. While this argument may appear to contradict his own ideal of putting Manchuria under Japan's sphere of influence, this was the mainstream view at Japan's Foreign Ministry. This view was shared by the later diplomacy of Shidehara Kijūrō in the 1920s: an aversion to the coercive seizure of a territory that diplomacy fails to obtain, while resolutely defending what was acquired through a treaty.

During the Russo-Japanese War, Manchuria had been under the military administration of the General Headquarters of the Imperial Japanese Army's Manchurian Army, and the Japanese military administration continued even after the signing of the peace treaty. But Japanese consulates were stationed in major cities of Manchuria because, legally speaking, it was a foreign country.

Because this military administration had aimed to establish Japan's rule in Manchuria, resisting, openly and covertly, American and British demands for an open door as well as Qing's request for the restoration of sovereignty, it was only natural that it caused friction with these countries. Each country filed complaints with the Japanese consuls. And this was the starting point of the differences in views between the Japanese military and foreign ministry that culminated in World War II. Hagiwara Moriichi, who was appointed to consul general at Mukden, sent the following wire, which accurately depicted the discontent on Qing's side: "If our military administration should misrule the occupied areas and invite further criticism from the international community, it would tarnish our glorious victory and negatively affect our relations with Qing and other friendly nations." Wary of the situation, Itō requested four elder statesmen (Yamagata Aritomo, Ōyama Iwao, Matsukata Masayoshi, and Inoue Kaoru), two semi-elders (Katsura Tarō and Yamamoto Gonbei), as well as major cabinet members (starting with Prime Minister Saionji) and Kodama Gentarō, chief of the Imperial Japanese Army's general staff, to participate in the historic "Consultative Meeting on the Manchurian Issue" that convened on May 22, 1906 at the office of the prime minister.

At the meeting, Itō made the opening remarks based on a proposal he handwrote, a lengthy (the equivalent of some thirty 400-character pages) and substantial document written in classical Chinese style. Itō's intellectual energy, which produced such a rich work single-handedly, was incomparable among all the modern statesmen in Japan.

In the document, Ito first analyzed Japan's situation as follows:

If Japan continued with the current military administration, Britain and the United States would end up with the impression that Japan, despite many years of announcements and accumulated statements, aspired to monopolize interests in Manchuria and close its doors. Sir Claude MacDonald, the new British ambassador to Japan who was famous for his sympathy for Japan, unofficially sent a warning; the continuation of the military administration of Manchuria would be a suicidal act that would make countries sympathetic to Japan turn their backs, which would be a critical handicap when Japan had to fight Russia again in the future.

If Japan persisted with the current military administration of Manchuria, it would only benefit Russia's militaristic faction, who could use it as an excuse to expand war preparations in the Far East, degrading the Portsmouth Treaty to merely a temporary armistice.

The goodwill that Japan had shown to Qing, paying a dear price in doing so, would be wasted, making Japan a target of Qing resentment. If the military administration was left untouched, public sentiment, not only in Manchuria but also in all twenty-one provinces of China, would turn against Japan.

On the basis of these considerations, Itō proposed a detailed action plan to abolish the military administration. Participants at the consultative meeting deliberated on the plan.

Itō was basically a statesman with a flexible mind. While advocating the suprapartisan constitution, he became the party president of Seiyūkai. Similarly, Itō approved the Anglo-Japanese Alliance in the end, although he had persisted in advocating the possibility of an entente with Russia until the last minute. In this meeting, however, Itō was determined to be adamant, and the firmness of his conviction was simply commendable. Having sensed the direction of public opinion and the intention of the military, Itō might have determined that there was nobody else who could restrain the flow of events.

As Kodama, who became the chief target of Itō's questioning, tried to defend the military administration in all sorts of ways, Itō went on to ruthlessly argue him down. Kodama stated that not all of what the Japanese military was doing was, given the examples of foreign countries, unlawful, but Itō counterargued: "What I am worried about is the immense influence of American public opinion. No matter how sympathetic the United States government might be to Japan, once public opinion changes, it will have to adopt policies that are acceptable to the public." This reasoning was exactly what all leaders in the twentieth century had to seriously address. Itō refuted the argument for military action by stressing that it was the impression of the American public, not logical explanations, that mattered most.

Minister of War Terauchi tried to wrap up the argument, saying that although time would not allow participants to discuss each of Itō's proposals individually, he was in favor of the spirit of the proposals as a whole. In response, Itō retorted, "it is lukewarm to say 'no objection to the overall spirit.' If you have no objection, I urge you to deliberate on concrete measures to implement my proposals."

In the end, Prime Minister Saionji, who had shared Itō's concern, led the meeting to adopt Itō's proposals unanimously, with no modification. It was decided that every proposal would be carried out.

"Elder statesman" was not a legal status, nor was it an official position. If it had to be defined, it was an advisor to the emperor who was personally appointed by the emperor. Itō was an elder statesman both in name and reality, and in this consultative meeting, he played the role of the nation's helmsman superbly.

Not all elder statesmen were like Itō though. Yamagata, who could be comparable to Itō in terms of his status and influence, represented the interests of the military and the *han* clique all along, impeding the development of democracy in Japan. Saionji, "the last elder statesman," may have made correct judgments in each situation, but he was not endowed with the personal will and power to resist the flow of public opinion.

In the end, the most critical element in politics is human resources. Japan was able to hold onto parliamentary democracy, the main course of the world's political thought, and maintain cooperation with Britain and the United States, the mainstream of world politics, thanks to the wisdom of Itō.

CHAPTER

13

Annexation of Korea

—Did Japan Have Any Other Alternative?—

The Korea-Japan Protocol

Until 1897, Korea was called Joseon (朝鮮). While many in contemporary Korea seem to dislike their country being called by that name, it does not really deserve such aversion. At the start of the Yi dynasty in 1393, its founding King (Taejo of Joseon) Yi Seong-gye (李成桂) asked Ming if the new kingdom's name should be Joseon, which the legendary Chinese sage Jizi (Gija in Korean; 箕子) was believed to have ruled, or Hwaryong (和寧), where Yi Seong-gye was originally from. Ming's emperor chose the former name for its beauty as well as its ancient origin.

But because the very act of asking Ming to choose the kingdom's name implied Yi Seong-gye's acceptance of subjugation to the Chinese kingdom, the name Joseon was changed to Daehan-jeguk (大韓帝国; Greater Korean Empire, or Han) in 1897 when Qing's suzerainty was denied as the result of the First Sino-Japanese War. Thus, the name "Han" carries special nationalist meaning for its people—freeing themselves from the control of Qing—and it is correct and proper to refer to the country after this period as Han.

As is obvious from the events leading up to the war, the greatest objective for Japan in waging the Russo-Japanese War was to put Korea under its control. Also, because the battle ground at the initial stage of the war was on the Korean Peninsula, it was imperative for the Japanese military to secure freedom of movement on the peninsula.

Thus, immediately after the eruption of the war in February 1904, the Japanese minister to Korea negotiated with the Korean government to sign the Korea-Japan Protocol (日韓議定書). This protocol enabled Japan to take necessary actions to defend Korea and, at the same time, barred the Korean government from providing similar arrangements to a third country (i.e., Russia). With this protocol, the Japanese side obtained free use of the Korean territory for military purposes while also restricting Korea's foreign policy. This was Japan's first step toward converting the country to a protectorate.

Because the Japanese troops landed on Incheon and captured Seoul immediately following the start of the war, there was nothing the Korean court could have done to resist the situation. It should be noted, however, that in those days Koreans did not have a strong will to resist restrictions on their own sovereignty.

Resistance came exclusively from the pro-Russian faction in the Korean court. There had been a division between the pro-Japanese and the pro-Russian factions within the Korean court prior to the eruption of the Russo-Japanese War. Each faction was connected to their respective legations in Seoul to receive various kinds of support, including, allegedly, financial assistance. The pro-Russian faction's stance, however, was not necessarily based on blind trust in Russia. It was more of a realistic precaution against Russia, which could use Korea's agreement with Japan as a pretext to annex Korea if and when it defeated Japan.

Ordinary people in Korea harbored little hostility toward Japan in the beginning. In his *The Tragedy of Korea*, Frederick McKenzie, who roundly denounced Japan's occupation of Korea, wrote: "I traveled largely throughout the northern regions in the early days of the war, and everywhere I heard from the people during the first few weeks nothing but expressions of friendship toward the Japanese. The coolies and farmers were friendly because they hoped that Japan would rectify the oppression of the native magistrates. A large section of better-class people, especially those who had received some foreign training, were sympathetic because they believed Japan's promises and had been convinced by long experience that no far-reaching reforms could come to their land without foreign aid."[1] What McKenzie saw was the Korean expectation that pressure from Japan would promote political reform within Korea. His book is about the process through which the Korean people's expectations that Japan would assist Korea's independence were betrayed in no time and how the people's discontentment became rampant as abuses by the Japanese became more frequent.

The Korea-Japan Protocol was easily concluded without much commotion while key members of the pro-Russian faction were sent to Japan for a tour by order of the king, a maneuver engineered by the pro-Japanese faction. From this point forward, throughout the duration of the Russo-Japanese War, Japan consistently pursued the expansion of its discretionary power on the Korean Peninsula through behind-the-scenes diplomacy while on the surface pretending to promote Korea's independence.

Theodore Roosevelt: Man of Power Politics

The number one priority among the "absolute nonnegotiables" that Komura had been instructed on when he departed for Portsmouth was to "make the Russians accept Japan's discretion on the entire Korean affair."

President Theodore Roosevelt supported Japan's Korea policy from the beginning to the end. He was an exceptional statesman within American diplomatic history; he understood the power politics at work in international relations and was a staunch opponent of the Wilsonianism that became one of the guiding principles of American diplomacy throughout the twentieth century. Roosevelt attacked Woodrow Wilson and his followers with such relentless criticism as: "I am of the view that trust in a visionary peace treaty or a piece of paper that is not endorsed by power, an attitude manifested by the likes of Woodrow Wilson, is detestable. As far as foreign policies are concerned, I am convinced that the tradition of Friedrich the Great and Bismarck is far better for the well-being of a state as well as the world than the Wilsonian attitude. To become elated by justice without endorsement of power is much more harmful than power that

---

1   Frederick Arthur McKenzie, *The Tragedy of Korea* (New York: E. P. Dutton & Co., 1908), 110.

ignores the pretext of justice." As for the annexation of Korea by Japan, Roosevelt continued by stating: "Korea is absolutely Japan's. To be sure, by treaty, it was solemnly covenanted that Korea should remain independent. But Korea was itself helpless to enforce the treaty, and it was out of the question to suppose that any other nation . . . would attempt to do for the Koreans what they were utterly unable to do for themselves."[2] In other words, Roosevelt reiterated his conviction on the uselessness of a piece of paper (i.e., a treaty) that is not endorsed by power and declared that the United States would not seek to enforce the stipulations of the treaty.

Before Wilsonianism thinking became the mainstream in the United States, this line of argument was not uncommon. The US minister to Korea Horace Allen was a typical, well-meaning American who arrived in the country as a Presbyterian missionary and later joined the diplomatic corps. He remained so pro-Korean, defending Korea vis-à-vis the American government and persuading the Korean court to rely more on the United States, that Roosevelt found it necessary to replace him with the more pro-Japanese Edwin Morgan in 1905.

Even Allen eventually grew disillusioned with the corruption and intrigue within the Yi court and concluded that the Korean people were incapable of self-rule. While not avowing himself to be a Japanese sympathizer, he nonetheless regarded Korea as being better off under Japanese control and wrote to Washington that Japanese annexation would be in the best interests of the Korean people and would also further the cause of peace in the Far East.[3]

The Taft-Katsura Agreement

On July 29, 1905, an agreement was exchanged between Japanese Prime Minister Katsura Tarō (桂太郎) and the visiting US Secretary of War William Taft that reciprocally recognized the Philippines as a possession of the United States and Korea as Japan's protectorate.

---

2   John Morton Blum, *The Republican Roosevelt* (Cambridge: Harvard University Press, 1954), 131.
3   Tsunoda, *Manshū mondai,* 136.

A protectorate was a form of colonial government during the age of imperialism—while a protectorate's autonomy was in principle respected, its foreign relations and military affairs were controlled by its suzerain. In terms of international politics, forming a protectorate was an act of putting a country within the suzerain's sphere of influence.

In a consultation with Taft, Katsura emphasized the need to make Korea Japan's protectorate. Katsura contended that if Korea was left to conduct its own diplomacy, it would return to the tradition of "improvidently" making promises to foreign countries, thus stirring up international issues as it used to before the Russo-Japanese War. Taft concurred with this view.

This view was an expression of Japan's genuine concern. The government policy toward Korea that received imperial sanction on June 11 stated a dangerous and highly unpredictable situation might occur if Koreans were entrusted with their own diplomacy. Nobody in the Korean government, so the policy stated, would sacrifice himself for the cause of the state. Officials made empty promises left and right for their own financial and/or personal gains, and the Korean court was full of conspiracies.

It should be recalled that during the First Sino-Japanese War the then foreign minister Inoue Kaoru visited Korea in order to promote domestic reforms there, placing high hopes on cooperation with the pro-Japanese reformist elements in Korea. Inoue, however, had to abandon his mission because "justice is neither within the conservatives nor the reformists, both of whom are just having a power struggle" and "either side would run to the Russian minister for help if we interfere and take sides with one or the other." This observation found an echo in Horace Allen's disillusionment with the corruption and intrigue within the Yi court twenty years later. It appeared that American diplomats must have gone through similar experiences as Inoue with the Koreans.

In the current world of national self-determination and sovereign equality, what Inoue and Allen deplored does not in any way constitute a reason to violate the sovereignty of a nation. Moreover, it is absurd to aspire to conquer such a cumbersome country. But at the apex of imperialism, the argument that any Western power could at any time advance on such an unstable country as Korea—posing a serious threat to Japan—was quite an acceptable notion.

Thus, both Britain and Russia recognized Korea as Japan's protectorate through the Second Anglo-Japanese Alliance, revised on August 12, and the Treaty of Portsmouth, signed on September 5, 1905. In both cases, the signing parties went over Korea's head, but those were the days when a lesser latecomer to international relations, particularly a country of nonwhite, non-Christian people, was not treated as an equal actor in international law. Subsequently, Japan began nullifying Article 3 of the Korea-Japan Protocol, which guaranteed the independence and territorial integrity of the Greater Korean Empire, by restricting Korea's sovereignty little by little, thus paving the way for the eventual annexation of Korea.

This was, of course, a process that had completely ignored the will of the Korean court and its people. The Japanese government resorted to both threats and placation to counter and eliminate resistance from the Koreans.

Koreans Did Show Resistance

Quite a number of history books in the pre–World War II era attributed Korea's ruin to the lethargic attitude of the Korean people, on the grounds that they had yielded to Japan's pressure without any resistance.

But, as recorded in various historical documents, including Itō Hirobumi's correspondences with the Korean side, Korean monarchs and court officials were far from being acquiescent. They tried to defend their nation and the court both overtly and covertly. Many took up arms to save Korea from foreign domination, including the Confucian scholar Choi Ik-hyun (崔益鉉) and An Jung-geun (安重根), who later assassinated Itō. These insurgents became quite a nuisance for the Japanese military.

We should be aware, though, that to characterize this resistance as anti-imperialistic, as was fashionable among post–World War II Leninist-Wilsonian historical views, would hinder our understanding of the truth. Considering the educational background of these Koreans, their conduct should be attributed to genuine feelings of self-sacrificing patriotism. Such sentiment had run throughout Asian thought from ancient times and found manifestation in historic figures. Yue Fei (岳飛), a twelfth-century Northern Song military general, fought to rescue the kingdom from the Jin (金) dynasty's invasion, only to be betrayed by corrupt officials headed by Qin Hui (秦檜); he died while imprisoned, leaving the inscription "Heaven knows everything" on the wall of his cell. Wen Tianxiang (文天祥), a thirteenth-century Southern Song scholar-general, followed Southern Song to the grave, leaving behind the famous classic "Song of Righteousness" (天地正気の歌) as his refusal of Kublai Khan's offer of a post in the Yuan (元) dynasty.

But at the dawn of the twentieth century, imperialism was at its apex. The Korean partisan resistance was buried in total oblivion, along with contemporary independence movements in Vietnam and Burma, and it failed to make any impact on the main flow of international relations at this point in time.

The despair and desperation of these patriots as well as the hardship and humiliation of the Koreans, who later lost their own country, deserve our deep sympathy. And these emotions led the Korean people to harbor a grudge against the Japanese, which is still deep and strong even today.

Subsequent developments can be summarized as follows: By May 1904, the Japanese government had decided on a policy to make Korea its protectorate, and the Korean government agreed during the Japan-Korea Agreement in August 1904 to consult with the Japanese government on every aspect of their finances and foreign relations.

After the signing of the Treaty of Portsmouth in 1905, the Japanese government concluded the Eulsa Treaty (or Japan-Korea Protectorate Treaty) with the Korean government in November in order to materialize its gains from the victory in the Russo-Japanese War. Through this, the Japanese government took over Korea's diplomacy. Itō Hirobumi was appointed the first resident-general of Korea.

In a desperate effort to use foreign leverage to restrict Japan's oppression, the Korean court dispatched an emissary to The Hague Peace Conference in 1907. The emissary was ignored by countries participating in the conference, and the exposure of his scheme forced the Korean emperor to resign. Under the Japan-Korea Treaty of 1907 (also known as the Japan-Korea Annexation Treaty), the jurisdiction of the resident-general of Korea was expanded to include not only diplomacy but also all Korean domestic affairs.

After the conclusion of the Russo-Japanese War, Komura had been stationed in London, but he was appointed once again to the post of foreign minister in the second Katsura cabinet in 1908. As foreign minister, in March 1909 Komura drafted a policy to annex Korea at an appropriate time, and the policy received imperial sanction.

Itō was transferred to the post of the president of the privy council in June 1909, and Deputy Resident-General Sone Arasuke took over Itō's post in Korea. On October 26, Itō was traveling in Manchuria when he was assassinated by An Jung-geun, a Korean nationalist and independence activist, at Harbin Railway Station. Using this incident, the Japanese government further advanced its preparation for the full annexation of Korea, encouraged by the benign responses of the Western powers. The government replaced Sone, who was skeptical about the annexation, with Terauchi Masatake. Korea was officially annexed by Japan in August 1910.

Protectorate or Annexation?

Itō remained fairly circumspect about the annexation of Korea until the very last minute.

We can trace Itō's thinking through his remarks. Prior to his departure to Seoul in January 1906 to become Japan's resident-general, Itō told newspaper reporters that he wished to accomplish his mission in cooperation with the Korean officials and people. It is particularly noteworthy that Itō spent half of the interview criticizing Japanese conduct in Korea as follows:

> There is much to be denounced about the conduct of some of our people in Korea so far. They have been insulting the Korean people with the worst kind of affronts imaginable. Korean people are forced to swallow their tears and endure the humiliation. . . . These cruelties are the very conduct that the Japanese residing in Korea must refrain from most of all. . . . It would be highly regrettable if such conduct has made the Korean people obedient on the surface but caused them to harbor a grudge against the Japanese underneath, thus adversely affecting Japan-Korean relations. . . . As Japan's Resident-General of Korea, I intend to exercise strict control over such undesirable conduct.

These remarks by Itō reveal the fundamental problem of Japan's rule in Korea. While ruling India, the British government allowed only well-educated and well-respected British citizens to immigrate to India. When petty merchants arrived in India, thirsty for money, they were deported by the order of the British viceroy and governor-general of India as "undesirable British." Those who were only interested in land and money had the choice to head for Australia or other colonies.

Unfortunately for Japan, overseas destinations were limited for Japanese settlers because all the fertile frontier lands, such as Australia, had already been taken by Western powers. Also, because President Roosevelt wished to accept only educated Japanese immigrants, people from the lower strata of Japanese society were rejected by the United States on the basis of the Japan-US Gentlemen's Agreement of 1908. These people flocked to Korea to seek opportunities.

Nevertheless, it is undeniable that there was some imperialistic intention on the Japanese side, particularly on the part of Komura. In the March 1909 memorandum, written at the time of the official decision to annex Korea, Komura suggested that Japan should send as many Japanese emigrants as possible to Korea to establish a solid foundation for Japan's power.

Needless to say, Komura was not the only one guilty of thinking this way; the majority of Japanese in those days were thinking along the same lines. A high-ranking Japanese official who McKenzie met had the following to say: "There are only two ways of colonial administration. One is to rule over the people as aliens. This you English have done in India, and, therefore, your Indian Empire cannot endure. India must pass out of your rule. The second way is to absorb the people. This is what we will do. We will teach them our language, establish our institutions, and make them one with us." In those days it was predominant among the Western powers to refer to underdeveloped regions as "the white man's burden" and regard their colonial rule as "protection and guidance provided by the rulers." In order to make a foreign land its own permanent territory, however, a colonial power could only resort to a policy of assimilation, which is basically the same as the Sinicization policy China has been pursuing more recently in Tibet and the Xinjiang Uygur Autonomous Regions.

As McKenzie observed, once Korea became a protectorate of Japan, thousands of ambitious Japanese rushed to the Korean Peninsula to try their luck. Uninhibited by Japan's domestic regulations, these Japanese audaciously abused the Korean people and exploited their lands and other rights while enjoying the protection of the Japanese authorities. At this point, the only person in Japan who was endowed with the integrity and authority to fearlessly remonstrate against these developments was Itō.

Even with the authority of Itō, however, the overall trend was unstoppable, especially when all of Itō's subordinates thought and acted like Komura. While McKenzie respected the arrest and deportation of undesirable Japanese as genuine accomplishments by Resident-Governor Itō, which earned him the trust of the local people, McKenzie observed that, judging from the overall behavior of the Japanese, "It has become obvious that Japan's true aim is nothing but the full annexation of Korea and the complete obliteration of Korean racial characteristics."

Itō made several remarks opposing the annexation of Korea. In a July 1907 speech in Seoul, he proclaimed that Japan was satisfied with seeing the Japanese and Korean flags flying side by side and there was no need for Japan to toil for Korea's destruction. He continued to say, admitting it would be extremely cumbersome for Japan to annex a country, that Korea must become self-governing, although it would not be able to accomplish sound self-government without Japan's guidance. In another speech in 1908, in front of *yangban* (Korea's traditional ruling class or nobles) Confucian scholars, Itō said, "In the olden days, it was deemed to be the goal for heroes to invade another land and conquer it. But that is not so today. . . . Weak countries are burdens for strong countries. Therefore, strong countries today must assist weaker countries to become prosperous and strong so that they can defend themselves together hand in hand." It is hard to imagine that, given Itō's frame of mind in those days, he was saying something that he did not mean. In fact, Itō made Evelyn Baring, first Earl of Cromer, his role model. Baring had put all of Egypt under his de facto control for thirty years, between 1877 and 1907, during which time he reconstructed Egypt's broken finances and made tremendous contributions to the country's modernization, including education and public health. Thus, it is not hard to conjecture that Itō's true intention was to promote the protectorate administration. His intention was followed by Sone, who succeeded Itō as the resident-general and was skeptical about Japan's annexation of Korea until the last minute.

Itō's Sudden Change in Stance

Itō was also well-trusted in Korea. According to McKenzie: "It is noteworthy that, although the Marquis [Itō] has been the main representative of the Mikado in wresting its independence from Korea, he is yet regarded by the responsible men there with a friendliness such as few other Japanese inspire. Everyone who comes in contact with him feels that, whatever the nature of the measures he is driven to adopt because of Imperial policy, he yet sincerely means well by the Korean people. The faults of his administration may be the necessary accompaniments of Japanese Imperial expansion, but his virtues are his own."[4] Thus, when Katsura and Komura decided on the annexation of Korea, they started to persuade Itō, who, they thought, would most certainly oppose the decision. To their surprise, however, Itō readily admitted that annexation would be inevitable sooner or later.

This unexpected response by Itō has been interpreted in many ways. To those hoping for Korea's independence, it was a reversal from his usual words and promises and a betrayal of the Korean people's trust. From the perspective that Japan should aspire to increase its national prestige and that imperialistic expansion was a means to do so, which was a historical view prevalent in pre–World War II Japan, Itō's response was interpreted as an indication that after all, he had not been so weak-kneed.

In my view, this need not be such a complex issue. The bewilderment and confusion stem from approaching history with the post–World War II values that posit the annexation of a foreign land as evil and preserving a foreign country's self-rule as good—or vice versa. From this approach, the change in Itō's stance could be seen as a contradiction within a man or as a 180-degree turn from good to evil, or vice versa.

In Itō's mind, perhaps, annexation and the continuation of protectorate status were both realistic options on equal footing. He might have thought that although continuation of the protectorate was still preferable, it might be too lukewarm to pursue a Japanese protectorate over Korea now that Koreans' distrust of Japan had become so deep, which left only the annexation option open to Japan. His perplexity, perhaps, was in facing these two options.

Itō had once converted himself from an advocate of suprapartian government to a supporter of party politics and, in the realm of foreign policy, from a proponent of entente with Russia to an upholder of the Anglo-Jap-

---

4   McKenzie, *The Tragedy of Korea*, 142.

anese Alliance. Similarly, from Itō's viewpoint, the options of annexation and a protectorate each had their own advantages and disadvantages, but either could be a realistic choice if its disadvantages were attended to and its advantages were further promoted.

Itō, however, remained very adamant in the Manchurian dispute. From his viewpoint, the Korean issue was totally different from the Manchurian issue. Since Japan's discretionary rights in Korea had been recognized by Qing as the result of the First Sino-Japanese War, by Russia due to the Russo-Japanese War, by Britain through the Anglo-Japanese Alliance, and by the United States as the result of the Taft-Katsura Agreement, Japan's security was in no danger whichever option Japan decided to take regarding Korea (i.e., protectorate or annexation). Japan's security would be, so to speak, protected by diplomatic relations.

However, because Japan was planning to advance to Manchuria against the wishes of the United States, China, and Russia, that action was liable to isolate Japan within the international community and, worse, corner Japan sooner or later into fighting all three of them, as exemplified by the Manchurian Incident in later years. History shows that Japan did in the end have to fight a war against all three of these countries, and this led to the ruin of the Empire of Japan.

In the historical views prevalent in post–World War II Japan, the annexation of Korea and the founding of Manchu State (満州国; Manchu-kuo) are treated equally as evils of imperialism. If one thus approaches history solely from an ethical viewpoint, one will not be able to evaluate the skill or lack thereof in diplomacy, or the soundness of the strategy.

Simply put, the annexation of Korea and the maintenance of its protectorate status were both within the latitude of the flexibility of Itō's state policy.

Was There Any Option Other Than Annexation?

Looking back, was there really no other option than annexation? If the Korean side had put up fiercer resistance, there was always a possibility it would have been conquered by Japan simply by force. That was why the Korean leaders swallowed their tears and made concessions one after another. When the dispatch of the Korean emissary to The Hague Peace

Conference in 1907 was disclosed, Itō claimed the action to be a violation of the spirit of the Korea-Japan Protocol and threatened the Korean side with a possible declaration of war. At the Korean cabinet meeting attended by its emperor, pro-Japanese members, fully aware of the futility of doing so, declared, short of an official apology, Korea would have no other choice than to dauntlessly fight against Japan. If Korea had refused to yield to the threat, it would probably have been annexed by coercion, instead of by agreement, like many other colonies of the Western powers, most typically those of Central Asia. And no Western powers would have objected to Japan's conduct.

Observers of the international situation in those days unanimously agree that had Japan not fought Russia, Korea would have become a territory of the latter. While the truth of this is almost beyond doubt, the most difficult historical hypothesis to verify is whether, after eliminating Russia's territorial ambitions, Japan would have had the option of recognizing Korea's independence and consolidating long-term relations with Korea based on mutual trust. Looking back from the viewpoint of the post–World War II world of decolonization and sovereign equality, obviously this would have been the ideal choice, but the real issue is whether it was actually a realistic scenario in those days.

To state the conclusion first, there was hardly any possibility this could have materialized. To begin with, Japan in those days was far from having successfully eliminated Russia's ambition to conquer Korea. The threat of retaliation from Russia hovered over Japan until the ruin of the Russian Empire, or until Japan was defeated in World War II —which, as Joseph Stalin declared later, completed Russia's revenge for the humiliation of the Russo-Japanese War.

Nor were the prospects for building long-lasting relations of mutual trust with Korea realistic either. Koreans had harbored fear and suspicion toward Japan since the assassination of Empress Myeongseong, or even since the days of the Japanese invasions of Korea from 1592–98, by Toyotomi Hideyoshi (豊臣秀吉). The Korean court was so obsessed with fear and suspicion over Japan's next move, given its past record, that it even considered actively collaborating with Russia. Viewed another way, there was absolutely no need for Koreans to give Russia an easy reason to annex their country by officially siding with Japan in the next war, which was likely to be won by Russia.

Korea would have refused to have any kind of special relationship with Japan—even under the name of friendship. The more demanding Japan became in regard to its special position in Korea, the more the latter would have relied on Russia or China to keep the balance, which would have been a natural course for a smaller sovereign nation to pursue diplomatically. If Korea had approached Russia, there was no knowing when and how Russia would come back to intervene with smooth talk and threats. Judging from the Japanese documents that have been introduced in this volume, the Japanese side had well anticipated this possibility. It was, therefore, unthinkable for Japan at that time to easily give up the fruits of the Russo-Japanese War—Korea.

In other words, the situation could be likened to a vicious cycle between Korea's obscure resistance, driven by a suspicion of Japan that was based on history, and the Japanese response in the form of increasing threats and coercion—which, in turn, made Koreans more suspicious of Japan. And this vicious cycle became the powerful driving force for Japan's tragic annexation of Korea. It was impossible at this stage to change the course of history.

No Safe Haven for Weaker Countries in the Age of Imperialism

The sad fact is that there was no safe haven for countries without power until the age of imperialism—a dog-eat-dog world in which the law of the jungle, in the name of "social Darwinism," dominated international relations—ended and was followed by the age of decolonization and, eventually, the dissolution of the Soviet Union. Japan might have lost its ability to survive as a sovereign state had it not won the Russo-Japanese War.

Siam and Persia, two Asian countries that barely maintained their independence during the age of imperialism, were able to do so as buffer zones between Britain and France and between Britain and Russia respectively, allowing themselves to be divided up into spheres of influence for these powers. As we have seen earlier, however, Russia had no intention of turning Korea into a buffer zone, except as a temporary measure to prepare for eventual annexation, because its ultimate concern had always been the southern coast of the Korean Peninsula. This being the case, Korea had been destined to be conquered either by Japan or Russia, just like Egypt, which suffered from the power struggle between Britain and France when they contested control of the Suez Canal that runs through Egypt.

The least that Japan could have done would have been to strictly refrain from taking the assimilation measures, block the inflow of undesirable Japanese, as Britain did in India, and respect the Korean people's lands and rights. Whether these measures, if taken, could have completely broken the vicious cycle of grudges and suppression is uncertain. Nevertheless, judging from the descriptions left by Frederick McKenzie, there was a good possibility that Japan could have secured the support of the ordinary people and some of the intellectuals in Korea. If that had happened, Korea could have remained as a protectorate, as Itō had originally envisioned, allowing it to wait for the arrival of the age of decolonization, along with countries such as Egypt and Morocco, without losing its right to self-government.

Seen from this perspective, Itō's approach was ahead of its time in the age of imperialism and was also in agreement with the direction that experts in Britain and the United States in those days believed to be best for the welfare of the Korean people. But Itō died in 1909, his life ironically taken by a Korean nationalist. His death symbolized the end of the Meiji era, where liberal and open-minded spirits, liberated by the Meiji Restoration, thrived, co-existing with the then prevalent imperialism.

EPILOGUE

The End of Meiji

Revision of the Anglo-Japanese Alliance

The Russo-Japanese War brought about tectonic changes, not only to the balance of power in the Far East but also to the power balance among the Western powers. One of the reasons behind these changes was the revision and bolstering of the Anglo-Japanese Alliance.

Before the war, the intelligence division of the British army had predicted that the best Japan could do, even if it won the war with Russia, was to defend southern Manchuria. The intelligence division predicted that should Russia be victorious, it would not only occupy the entire Korean peninsula but possibly threaten Japan.

This was why Britain designed the alliance to allow it to remain strictly neutral when Japan alone fought Russia. Britain could not afford to risk sharing the fate of a country that was likely to lose.

After the fall of Lüshun and the Battle of Mukden, however, the British attitude toward Japan showed a marked change. Japan was no longer a burden for Britain because it was recognized as a trustworthy partner who was powerful enough to fight alongside Britain.

From the British point of view, the Japanese victory temporarily eliminated the fear of Russia's advance to Manchuria, northern China, the

Korean Peninsula, and the Japanese archipelago. But now Britain had to worry about what Russia's next move would be.

Britain faced two worries at the time. One was the possibility that Russia would acknowledge the toughness of the Japanese resistance and shift the direction of its expansion toward India, which would directly threaten Britain's sphere of influence. If this situation had actually come about, Britain would have wanted Japan to pressure Russia from the east and, moreover, to support its defense of India.

The other worry was over the possible weakening of Russia due to its internal problems. A weakened Russia would disturb the balance of power in Europe, giving Germany freedom of movement. In this case, Britain would wish to leave the Far East to Japan's discretion so it could concentrate its naval forces in Europe to counter Germany.

Thus, Britain wished to revise the Anglo-Japanese Alliance into an offensive and defensive alliance by which Japan would be obliged to come to Britain's rescue when Britain was attacked by a third party and vice versa, setting aside wars in which the two countries were already engaged. In other words, if and when Russia restarted the war against Japan, Britain would be obliged to participate in the war, and Japan would be obliged to assist Britain if Russia made an advance toward India and Afghanistan.

Needless to say, the Japanese side more than welcomed the strengthening of the alliance as a way of preparing for future retaliation from Russia, but there was some hesitation to expand the scope of the treaty to areas other than Manchuria and Korea.

Nevertheless, Japan at that time was under tremendous strain, waiting for the imminent arrival of Russia's Baltic Fleet, which had just departed Cam Ranh Bay, and it was not in the frame of mind to turn down the offer from Britain, its precious ally. On May 24, three days before the Battle of Tsushima, the Japanese cabinet decided to accept the British proposal and instructed Minister Hayashi Tadasu in London to commence negotiations with the British government.

Britain's decision to propose the revision of the Anglo-Japanese Alliance paid off, even when it was still too early to predict the outcome of the Battle of Tsushima. The biggest worry for Britain at the time of signing the original Anglo-Japanese Alliance was that Japan would reach an agreement with Russia before it did with Britain. If that had happened, the supremacy of British naval power in the Far East would have been completely lost. Thus, even during the original negotiations for the alliance, the British side repeatedly demanded that Japan must not reach an agreement with Russia ahead of Britain.

As a matter of fact, Itō Hirobumi did attempt to strike an agreement with Russia by bartering influence in Manchuria (Russia) for special rights in Korea (Japan), although his attempts proved futile because Russia would not give up the Korean Peninsula.

After Japan's great victory, however, the possibility emerged for Japan to build a stable peace with Russia because the latter was now confined to the north of the demarcation line in Manchuria. History shows that subsequent developments in the Far East did move in that direction for a while.

Britain was worried about the possibility of a Russo-Japanese entente based on mutual understanding as a result of the peace negotiations. Therefore, by revising the Anglo-Japanese Alliance, Britain was able to forestall this possibility.

Japan's major concern during the negotiations toward the revision of the alliance was to secure Britain's approval of Japan's predominant position in Korea—or, to put it more bluntly, Japan's right to make Korea its protectorate.

On this issue, the British minister to Korea John Jordan said: "To become a protectorate . . . seems to be the only viable solution for the interest of the Korean people. Korean people, with the exception of government officials, would prefer the status of protectorate to the mere nominal independence they've had in the past decade." In the end, the British government decided to approve Japan's wish on the condition that it would respect equality of opportunities. Thus, the Anglo-Japanese Alliance was revised with the full agreement of both sides.

In retrospect, the period during which the revised Second Anglo-Japanese Alliance was in effect was a time when the Japanese felt the safest. If and when Japan's security was threatened, Britain was prepared to immediately jump in to assist it. In the era before the advent of air forces, the security of the Japanese archipelago was 100 percent guaranteed by the combined naval powers of Japan and Britain, which had by far the largest navy in the world. As an equal partner of the British Empire, Japan, too, was capable of defending British interests and was determined to do so if need be. Consequently, Japan was able to benefit from the British Empire's resources and markets, which were spread all over the world, as

Komura, the advocate of the alliance with Britain, had pointed out. Peace and prosperity would naturally make people aspire for freedom as their next goal, and this was how the flow toward Taishō Democracy in the next generation began in Japan.

During this period, many people in Japan turned into Anglophiles. They found that the virile and patriotic temperament of the British gentleman and the traditional spirit of the samurai had something in common. The Japanese even began to call themselves "Britain in the Far East."

Reshuffling of World Politics

The Russo-Japanese War further promoted the rapprochement between Britain, France, and Russia that had already been the undercurrent of international politics since the turn of the century.

Russia's defeat in the Far East had the effect of relieving the tension between Britain and Russia in the region that had been the theater of their struggle over global hegemony. Russia's new foreign minister, Alexandr Izvolskii, held the view that it should be Russia's national strategy to concentrate its attention and military forces in the Balkans while also reconciling with Japan by giving up on the Far East and settling the dispute with Britain over the Indian border.

France, on the other hand, was apprehensive of the Asian nationalism stoked by the Russo-Japanese War, fearing that it could threaten the French colonial rule of Vietnam.

Phan Boi Chau, a pioneer of Vietnamese twentieth-century nationalism, wrote in his *History of the Loss of Vietnam* (越南亡国史; 1905) that in reference to the Russo-Japanese War, "news of an incident had been carried on the wind from the east, with the roar of gunfire in Lüshun and Liaodong, which invigorated the activists who wanted to restore independence of Vietnam." He admitted that the "transformation of the world and changes in world trends were beyond Vietnamese imagination in those days, and their long-standing struggle had only been driven by great indignation and the instinct of retaliation, unfounded on concrete plans for independence." Phan underwent a complete change in his thinking while in Japan after fleeing Vietnam, a change that Phan believed was brought about by the Russo-Japanese War.

Thus, when Phan arrived in Japan in 1905, he made contact with Meiji dignitaries such as Inukai Tsuyoshi and Ōkuma Shigenobu to plot a scheme for the independence of Vietnam.

It was, therefore, only natural for France to wish for Japan's cooperation in restricting the Vietnamese independence movement. France had been waiting for the opportunity to form a coalition with Russia and Britain as part of its national strategy to take revenge on Germany for its defeat in the Franco-Prussian War (1870–71). In 1904, France succeeded in concluding the long-sought-after Entente Cordiale (between France and Britain). This was followed by the conclusion of the Franco-Japanese Entente in June 1907, which took advantage of Japan's desire to float its foreign bonds on the French market in light of the rising interest rates in the British market. France then assisted in the successful conclusion of the Russo-Japanese Agreement of 1907 in July, and, finally, the signing of the Anglo-Russian Entente in August, thereby achieving the goal of its grand strategy in one sweep.

This completed the European line of battle to enclose Germany and Austria, which eventually led to the eruption of World War I.

The first Russo-Japanese Agreement was necessary for Japan to take care of the aftermath of the Russo-Japanese War. Even after the signing of the Treaty of Portsmouth, negotiations on the details for the transfer of the management of the Manchurian railway or fisheries in the northern sea had made little progress. Russia was wary about when Japan would decide to advance north to invade northern Manchuria, while Japan was obsessed with the fear that Russia would someday resume its meddling in Korean affairs, degrading the Treaty of Portsmouth to something akin to a temporary armistice.

The Russo-Japanese Agreement of 1907 took care of all these problems. Pending issues such as changing the management of the Manchurian railway had been settled one after another before the signing of the Russo-Japanese Agreement. The document also included secret agreements that left no room for Russia to interfere in Korean affairs, with a demarcation line that ran from east to west in the middle of Manchuria, assigning the north of the line to Russia's sphere of interest and the south of the line to Japan's sphere of interest.

Subsequently, as his last service to the country before he passed away, Komura successfully led negotiations toward the renewal of the Russo-Japanese Agreement in 1910 and the revision of the Anglo-Japanese Alliance in 1911.

The Second Russo-Japanese Agreement

The second Russo-Japanese Agreement was different in nature from the first Russo-Japanese Agreement of 1907. The first agreement was concluded in order to deal with the aftermath of the Russo-Japanese War and eliminate issues that could provide an excuse to restart the war. Two particularly important points were the blocking of Russia's interference in the Korean Peninsula during the agreement's term of validity and preventing Japan and Russia from invading each other's spheres of interest by dividing Manchuria from east to west.

The purpose of the second agreement was to jointly protect what Japan and Russia had agreed to be their respective spheres of influence from external forces. Japan and Russia were mainly guarding against one external force in particular—the United States.

Earlier, the United States had proposed to Japan that the two countries jointly manage the Southern Manchurian Railway, but Komura's maneuvering had crippled that proposal. Sometime later, when William Taft succeeded Theodore Roosevelt as president of the United States in 1909, his Secretary of State Philander Knox proposed the internationalization of the management of the Southern Manchurian Railway—allowing Qing to buy back the railway, which had been divided between Japan and Russia, with funds provided by the Western powers and to put the railway under the joint management of the Western powers.

Agitated by this American proposal, Russia consulted with Japan and the two countries agreed to cooperate to protect their respective interests in Manchuria. This was the genesis of the Russo-Japanese Agreement of 1910. Both Britain and France reacted negatively to the American proposal because both had developed good relations with Japan and Russia, anticipating a possible confrontation with Germany. Consequently, the proposal was buried.

Meanwhile, Japan and Russia continued to consult with each other, and they agreed on a secret clause, which stipulated that should the mutually agreed special interests of the two countries be threatened, both countries must cooperate with and assist one another to defend their interests. This was the essence of the second Russo-Japanese Agreement of 1910. Russia, instead of Britain or the United States, remained Japan's partner in its Manchurian policy until the breakdown of Imperial Russia during World War I.

Komura also made a critical decision during the course of the revision of the Anglo-Japanese Alliance that, in later days, affected Japan's policies toward the United States and Britain.

Around 1910, an argument emerged that Britain and the United States should conclude a treaty on comprehensive arbitration—in other words, that any future disputes between the two countries would be referred to arbitration. Simply put, this meant that Britain and the United States would no longer go to war against one another. This proposal marked the beginning of the Anglo-American cooperation that won two world wars in the twentieth century and allowed the two nations to boast of Anglo-Saxon world hegemony.

Britain sounded out Japan's preferences on the matter. Would it prefer to revise the Anglo-Japanese Alliance, to exempt the United States from application of the treaty, or would it prefer to join the proposed treaty on comprehensive arbitration?

Komura judged that matters that could determine the fate of a state should not be left to arbitration and, furthermore, that Japan could be put at a disadvantage in an arbitration tribunal because of its culture, which is different from the West, and because of racial and religious prejudice against the Japanese. For these reasons, Komura chose the former option.

If Japan had signed the treaty on comprehensive arbitration, that would have been the de facto formation of an Anglo-US-Japanese alliance. Because the United States Senate did not pass the bill, the proposed treaty on comprehensive arbitration did not materialize in the end. The mere signing of the treaty, however, would have sent out a strong message that Japan would not antagonize the United States. If the treaty had been concluded between Japan and Britain alone, it would have powerfully reinforced the Anglo-Japanese Alliance.

Now that we have experienced the disaster caused by Japan's autonomous diplomacy, it is beyond doubt that Japan's future would have been much more peaceful if it had abandoned its maverick diplomacy and, instead, relied on the Anglo-Saxon world in one way or another. What Komura did was to nip in the bud one of the means that would have made that possible.

Completing Revision of the Unequal Treaties

One of the last contributions Komura made before his death was to complete the revisions of the unequal treaties on tariffs with the Western powers. The twelve-year transitional period of the old unequal treaties, which were set by Mutsu Munemitsu with most of the Western powers, expired in 1911 (forty-fourth year of Meiji).

Revision of the unequal treaties was a major enterprise that took Japan the entire forty-five years of the Meiji era to accomplish.

The unequal treaty issue revolved around two discriminatory policies that had to be remedied. One was consular jurisdiction—the jurisdiction of alien criminals was in the hands of the consul of the offenders' country. This practice had been established on the grounds that Japan was underdeveloped in terms of Western-style legal and court systems. Within five years of the signing of the treaties in 1894, this practice had already been eliminated.

The other discriminatory policy was a restriction on import tariffs to a maximum of 5 percent. This restriction had been imposed on Japan by the Western powers amid the confusion at the end of the Tokugawa shogunate. Tariff autonomy, therefore, had to be achieved.

Although the Western powers had little reason to justify the continuation of this tariff restriction, they instituted a transition period of twelve years before the implementation of full tariff autonomy for two reasons. First, they wanted to avoid setting a precedent: If tariff autonomy had been given immediately to Japan, it would have been the first case of a non-white nation being treated equally. And, second, substantial profits were at stake.

Toward the last one-third of the nineteenth century, Britain no longer enjoyed a monopoly over industrial products, and competition among nations had already become fierce. Each nation imposed high tariffs on imports to protect their own industries. Against this background, it is actually quite amazing that despite the low tariff rate it had been forced to accept, Japan developed its industry to the extent that it was able to defeat both Qing and Russia in two wars. Compared with the special treatment that developing countries in the post–World War II era have enjoyed—high tariff barriers on their own products and the privilege of low tariffs on their exports—the labor of our Meiji ancestors, who pulled themselves up by their own bootstraps, must be highly admired.

In later years, China attempted to repeal its own unequal treaties. Instead of improving its own legal system or using diplomatic persuasion, as Japan had done, China relied on such unruly measures as antiforeigner movements, and thus rode the tide of the time's nationalism. These attempts occurred while domestic conditions in China were still in a state of utter confusion and there was absolutely no way to guarantee the safety of foreigners. The Japanese had reason to act like a Dutch uncle toward China at that time.

Country-by-country negotiations for agreements to replace the existing tariff restrictions naturally turned into highly cumbersome economic bargaining for Japan, but all of the negotiations were eventually concluded.

In 1905–6, after the conclusion of the Russo-Japanese War, Japan reached an agreement with Britain, the United States, Germany, and France to mutually upgrade their legations stationed in each other's countries to embassies. The first Russo-Japanese Agreement of 1907 stipulated that each respective legation be promoted to embassy status. In those days, there was a strict demarcation in the world between major powers and lesser countries, and the status of ambassador was reserved for diplomatic missions exchanged between major powers only; the missions major powers sent to lesser countries and vice versa were ranked ministers.

Thus, at this point, Japan became a fully independent, sovereign nation and was accepted as a first-tier country both in name and substance.

The Passing of Nogi and Komura

When Prime Minister Katsura stepped down in August 1911, Komura resigned as foreign minister. Komura passed away toward the end of November of the same year.

Komura's death heralded the end of the Meiji period. Emperor Meiji passed away on July 30, 1912. He was followed to the grave by General

Nogi Maresuke, who disemboweled himself on the evening of the Imperial funeral. Tōyama Mitsuru (頭山満), a leading figure in Pan-Asianism in Japan from the Meiji to early Shōwa periods, commented that "His Majesty must have been pleased to be accompanied by Komura as vanguard and Nogi as rear guard."

Nogi's disembowelment manifested the samurai spirit and deeply moved the entire nation. It was this honorable disembowelment that immortalized Nogi in the minds of the Japanese until Japan's defeat in the World War II. Nogi's death poem reads:

Now that the living God has departed from this world
I shall follow after Him.

This is a serene poem, free from any pretentiousness or effusion. It was not that Nogi had not been endowed with poetic genius, but perhaps to Nogi, it was conduct per se that mattered.

Meiji was over.

It was also a great turning point for Japan. In 1912 (forty-fifth year of Meiji/first year of Taishō), even before the mourning period for Emperor Meiji had expired, the Taishō Political Crisis (大正政変) began. This led to a nationwide movement in early 1913 (second year of Taishō) which called for the protection of the constitution, that is, a parliamentary democracy. This movement heralded the imminent arrival of Taishō Democracy.

The Chinese continent also entered a totally new era with the eruption of the Xinhai Revolution in 1911.

With the rise of democracy within Japan and the rise of nationalism overseas, the world had entered an era when straightforward advocates of national interest, like Komura, were no longer wanted.

Looking back on this period, what were the merits and demerits of Komura's diplomacy?

Komura accurately judged that Japan had no other option than war with Russia, given Russia's intentions, and this allowed the Empire of Japan to stay on the right track. This merit belongs to Komura alone.

All the other merits and demerits of Komura's diplomacy are directly connected to the merits and demerits of the steps taken by the Empire of Japan that eventually led to defeat in World War II. Komura's diplomacy, therefore, automatically calls into question Japan's national strategy itself: consistently pursuing independent diplomacy instead of entrusting the country's fate to international cooperation or, put more specifically, to collaboration with the Anglo-American world and, in Asia, expanding Japan's exclusive sphere of influence beyond the Korean Peninsula deep into the Asian continent.

Now that we know this national strategy met a disastrous end, it is easy for us to blame Komura for it. If one singles out one generation—about twenty to thirty years—after Komura's death, however, there were times when Komura's strategy was clearly successful. At least, most of the Japanese people in those days believed so.

In any event, it would not do Komura justice to say that he had been swept along by the tide of statism. Komura was merely functioning as its spearhead at the time. Even if someone else had been in the position of Komura, the tide was so powerful that he could not have changed or halted its course.

The only person who could possibly have halted the trend of the time was Itō Hirobumi. The passing of Itō two years prior to Komura's death was, therefore, the end of the Meiji era in another sense.

REFERENCES

Bemis, Samuel Flagg. *A Diplomatic History of the United States.* New York: Henry Holt & Company, 1938.

Blum, John Morton. *The Republican Roosevelt.* Cambridge: Harvard University Press, 1954.

Dōdai Keizai Konwa-kai, ed. *Kindai Nihon sensō-shi* [Military history of modern Japan]. Tokyo: Dōdai Keizai Konwa-kai, 1995.

Hamilton, Ian. *A Staff Officer's Scrap-book During the Russo-Japanese War.* London: Edward Arnold, 1906.

Hasegawa, Masamichi. *Keikō Nogi Shōgun* [Revering General Nogi]. Tokyo: Shitori-sha, 1937.

Itō, Masanori. *Gunbatsu kōbō-shi* [Rise and fall of warlords]. Tokyo: Bungei-Shunjū, 1958.

——. *Dai Kaigun o omou* [Remembering the great navy]. Tokyo: Kōjin-sha, 1981.

Jones, Robert L. *History of the Foreign Policy of the United States.* New York: G. P. Putnam's Sons, 1933.

Kaigun Rekishi Hozon-kai, ed. *Nihon Kaigun-shi* [History of the Japanese navy]. Tokyo: Kaigun Rekishi Hozon-kai, 1995.

Kajima, Morinosuke. *Nihon gaikō-shi 7* [Diplomatic history of Japan 7]. Tokyo: Kajima Kenkyū-jo, 1970.

Kan, Jeon. *Chōsen kindai-shi* [Modern history of Korea]. Tokyo: Heibon-sha, 1986.

Kearney, Reginald. *African American Views of the Japanese: Solidarity or Sedition?* Albany: State University of New York Press, 1998.

Kissinger, Henry A. *Diplomacy.* New York: Simon & Schuster, 1994.

Kojima, Noboru. *Nichi-Ro sensō* [Russo-Japanese War]. Tokyo: Bungei Shunjū, 1990.

Kurihara, Ken. *Tai Manmō seisaku-shi no ichimen* [An aspect of Japanese policies toward Manchuria and inner Mongolia]. Tokyo: Hara Shobō, 1966.

Kuroha, Shigeru. *Nichi-Ei dōmei no kiseki* [The history of the Anglo-Japanese Alliance]. Tokyo: Bunka Shōbō Hakubun-sha, 1987.

Memoir of Count Witte. Garden City, NY and Toronto: Doubleday, Page & Company, 1921.

Ministry of Foreign Affairs, ed. *Komura gaikō-shi* [History of Komura's diplomacy]. Tokyo: Hara Shobō, 1966.

Mizuki, Yō. *Dōran wa waga shōchū ni ari* [Riot is in my power]. Tokyo: Shinchō-sha, 1991.

McKenzie, Frederick Arthur. *The Tragedy of Korea.* New York: E. P. Dutton & Co., 1908.

——. *Chosen no higeki* [The tragedy of Korea]. Translated by Watabe Manabu. Tokyo: Heibon-sha, 1972.

Murakami, Hyōe. *Shujō no hito* [Man who defends the castle]. Tokyo: Kōjin-sha, 1994.

Nehru, Jawaharlal. *An Autobiography: With Musings on Recent Events in India.* Bombay: Allied Publishing, 1962.

Nish, Ian H. *The Anglo-Japanese Alliance: The Diplomacy of Two Island Empires, 1894–1907.* London: Athlone Press, 1966.

Nozawa, Keiichiro. *Hoshi Tōru to sono jidai* [Hoshi Tōru and his time]. Tokyo: Heibon-sha, 1984.

Okazaki, Hisahiko. *Mutsu Munemitsu to sono jidai.* Tokyo: PHP Kenkyū-jo, 1990.

Ōtake, Hirokichi, editorial supervisor. *Witte-haku kaisō-ki* [Memoir of Count Witte]. Tokyo: Hara Shobō, 1972.

Sakurai, Tadayoshi. *Shōgun Nogi* [General Nogi]. Tokyo: Jitsugyō no Nihon-sha, 1928.

Shimanuki, Shigeyoshi. *Senryaku Nichi-Ro sensō* [Strategic Russo-Japanese War]. Tokyo: Hara Shobō, 1980.

Shinobu, Seizaburō. *Nihon gaikō-shi* [Diplomatic history of Japan]. Tokyo: Mainichi Shimbun-sha, 1974.

Tabohashi, Kiyoshi. *Kindai Nippon gaikoku kankeishi* [History of modern Japan's foreign relations]. Tokyo: Hara Shobō, 1976.

Tōgō Heihachirō no subete [All about Tōgō Heihachirō]. Tokyo: Shin-Jinbutsu Ōrai-sha, 1986.

Tsunoda, Jun. *Manshū mondai to kokubō hōshin* [Manchurian issue and national defense policy]. Tokyo: Hara Shobō, 1967.

Wang, Yunsheng. *Nisshi gaikō 60-nen shi* [60 Years of Sino-Japanese diplomacy]. Tokyo: Kensetsu-sha, 1936.

Warner, Denis and Peggy Warner. *Nichi-Ro sensō zenshi* [Entire history of the Russo-Japanese War]. Translated by Senō Sakutarō and Mitani Yasuo. Tokyo: Jiji Tsūshin-sha, 1978.

Woodhouse Eiko. *Nichi-Ro sensō o enshutu shita otoko Morrison* [Morrison: The man who staged the Russo-Japanese War]. Tokyo: Tōyō Keizai Shimpō-sha, 1988.

——. *The Chinese Hsinhai Revolution: G. E. Morrison and Anglo-Japanese Relations, 1897–1920.* London: Routledge, 2013.

Yamabe Kentarō. *Nihon no Kankoku heigō* [Japan's annexation of Korea]. Tokyo: Taihei Shuppan-sha, 1970.

Appendix
Chronogical Table of Komura Jutarō's Life and Accomplishments

Year	Japanese Era	Age	Life Events	Domestic/Overseas Incidents
1853	Kaei 6			US Commodore Matthew Perry's East India Squadron arrives in Uraga
				Russian Admiral Yevfimy Putyatin's squadron arrives in Nagasaki
				Crimean War (until 1856)
1854	Ansei 1			(US-Japan) Convention of Kanagawa concluded
				Anglo-Japanese Friendship Treaty/(Russo-Japanese) Treaty of Shimoda concluded
1855	Ansei 2	1	Komura born as the eldest son of Komura Kanpei, a low-ranking samurai of Obi-*han*, and Umeko	Nagasaki Naval Training Center established
1858	Ansei 5	4		Ii Naosuke appointed to *tairō* (senior-most minister)
				Treaty of Amity and Commerce (US-Japan) concluded
				Japan concludes treaties of amity and commerce with the Netherlands, Russia, Britain, and France
				Fall of the Mughal Empire and British annexation of India
				Qing concludes the Treaty of Aigun with Russia
				Ansei Purge
1860	Man-en 1	6		Sakuradamon Incident (Tairō Ii Naosuke assassinated by ronin samurai of the Mito and Satsuma-*han*)
				Russian occupation of Primorsky Krai
1867	Keio 3	13		Tokugawa Yoshinobu steps down as shogun and returns governing power to the Emperor (Taisei Hōkan)

Year	Japanese Era	Age	Life Events	Domestic/Overseas Incidents
1868	Meiji 1	14		Declaration of Restoration of Imperial Rule
				Meiji Restoration
				Fall of Edo
				The Charter Oath promulgated
				Russian annexation of Khanate of Bukhara
1869	Meiji 2	15	Ogura Shohei sends Komura to an English cram school in Nagasaki	Satsuma/Chōshū/Tosa/Higo-han return the *han* registers to the Meiji Emperor
				Emperor Meiji allows domain lords to return their *han* registers and appoints them govenors of their respecive *han*
1870	Meiji 3	16	Komura chosen from the Obi-*han* to enter Daigaku Nankō School on the recommendation of Ogura	Kaisei Gakkō renamed Daigaku Nankō and Igakkō renamed Daigaku Tōkō
				Kōshin-sei (貢進生) system adopted to recruit brilliant students to Daigaku Nankō from 300 domains all over Japan according to the rank of each domain.
1871	Meiji 4	17		Abolition of the *han* system and Establishment of the prefecture system
				Japan-Qing Treaty of Friendship concluded
				Iwakura Mission departs for the United States and Europe
1873	Meiji 6	19	Komura writes a lengthy autobiography in English	Iwakura Mission returns
				Indefinite postponement of dispatch of Saigō Takamori to Korea
				Saigō resigns from all of his government positions in protest
				(In Korea) Heungseon Daewongun forced to retire by the Ming clan, which took over the government

Year	Japanese Era	Age	Life Events	Domestic/Overseas Incidents
1874	Meiji 7	20		Japanese troops dispatched to Taiwan under the pretext of the murder of Ryūkyū residents
1875	Meiji 8	21	Komura dispatched to Harvard University as the first Ministry of Education scholarship student	(In Qing) Tongzhi Emperor passes away and Empress Dowager Cixi takes over the reigns of government
				Treaty of Saint Petersburg concluded between Japan and Russia
				Ganghwa Island incident
1877	Meiji 10	23		British India Empire founded
				Satsuma Rebellion
1878	Meiji 11	24	Komura graduates from Harvard Law School	
			Komura trained in lawsuit practice in New York City	
1880	Meiji 13	26	Komura returns home from study in the United States	
			Komura enters Ministry of Justice's Criminal Affairs Bureau	
1881	Meiji 14	27	Komura married to 17-year-old Asahina Machiko in September	Imperial edict on the establishment of parliament in 23rd year of Meiji
			Komura appointed to judge and stationed in Osaka Appellate Court in October	Ōkuma Shigenobu dismissed as the result of Political Upheaval of 1881
				Jiyūtō established (Itagaki Taisuke, President)
1882	Meiji 15	28	Komura appointed to judge of the Supreme Court in charge of criminal cases	Rikken-Kaishintō established (Ōkuma Shigenobu, President)
				(In Korea) Imo Incident (riot of Korean soldiers in Seoul; raid on the Japanese legation; Minister Hanabusa arrives in Seoul with two companies of the Japanese Army; Treaty of Jemulpo concluded between Japan and Korea)
1883	Meiji 16	29	Kin'ichi, eldest son of Komura, born in May	

Year	Japanese Era	Age	Life Events	Domestic/Overseas Incidents
1884	Meiji 17	30	Komura transferred from Ministry of Justice to Ministry of Foreign Affairs and assigned to communication bureau	Sino-French War (until 1885); Kapsin Coup (Kim Ok-gyun and Japanese minister to Korea Takezawa Shin'ichiro lead Japanese troops to occupy Korean royal court); Japanese troops defeated by Qing Army
1885	Meiji 18	31	Komura transferred to foreign ministry's translation bureau in April as the communication bureau is abolished	Treaty of Hanseong concluded between Japan and Korea to attend to the aftermath of unsuccessful Kapsin Coup
			Komura starts teaching British law as a lecturer at English Law School (presently Chuo University)	Convention of Tientsin concluded between Japan and Qing, stipulating simultaneous withdrawal of respective troops from Korea and mutual prior notification when dispatching troops in the future
1886	Meiji 19	32	Komura promoted to deputy director-general of the translation bureau in March	Fierce debate on Foreign Minister Inoue Kaoru's Westernization policy
			Fumiko, Komura's eldest daughter, born in July	First conference on revision of unequal treaties
1888	Meiji 21	34	Komura lectures on English criminal law at University of Tokyo's law school between April and July	Japan-Mexico Treaty of Amity, Commerce, and Navigation (Japan's first equal treaty with a Western country) concluded
			Komura promoted to director-general of the translation bureau in October	(In Qing) Establishment of the Beiyang Fleet
1890	Meiji 23	36		The first session of the Imperial Diet
1893	Meiji 26	39	Komura appointed to counselor at the Japanese legation in Qing	House of Concillors rejects the budget for building naval ships. The budget passes by an imperial order.
			Komura appointed to chargé d'affaires at the Japanese legation and stationed in Beijing as its acting minister in November	
1894	Meiji 27	40	Komura returns home in August as Japan severs diplomatic relations with Qing and closes the legation in Beijing	Kim Ok-gyun assassinated in Shanghai/Donghak Peasant Revolution in Korea
			Komura appointed to the civilian administrator for territories Japan's First Army had captured in Manchuria (October)	Both Japan and Qing announce the dispatch of respective troops to Korea

Year	Japanese Era	Age	Life Events	Domestic/Overseas Incidents
1894	Meiji 27	40	Komura promoted to minister resident and returned home to be appointed to director-general of policy affairs of the foreign ministry	Japanese fleet attacks Qing's fleet off Pungdo (Battle of Pungdo); Japanese army occupies Seonghwan and Asan (Battle of Seonghwan & Battle of Asan); Japan declares war against Qing (First Sino-Japanese War)
				The Combined Fleet of the Japanese Navy destroys Qing's Beiyang Fleet (Battle of Yalu River)
				Battle of Lüshunkou (Japan's Second Army conquered Lüshunkou)
1895	Meiji 28	41	After contributing to the signing of the Treaty of Shimonseki, Komura develops typhoid fever and is hospitalized for a month. While he is recuperating in Ōiso, his second son, Shūji, is born.	Itō Hirobumi and Mutsu Munemitsu, representing the Emperor of Japan, and Li Hongzhang, on behalf of the Emperor of Qing, start the peace negotiations that lead to the signing of the Treaty of Shimonoseki (approval of Korea's independence; cession of Liaodong Peninsula, Taiwan, and Penghu Islands; and Qing to pay as a war indemnity the sum of 200 million taels)
				Triple Intervention by Germany, France, and Russia, leading to return of the Liaodong Peninsula to Qing
				Revolt of Taiwanese people, leading to Japanese army's occupation of Taipei
				Empress Myeongseong killed by Japanese assassins in Seoul
1896	Meiji 29	42	Komura appointed to envoy extraordinary and minister plenipotentiary to Korea in April	Korean court evacuated to the Russian embassy in Seoul, leading to establishment of a pro-Russian Korean government and execution of pro-Japanese cabinet members
			Komura returns home after signing the Komura-Waeber Memorandum	The Komura-Waeber Memorandum on Korean affairs signed

Year	Japanese Era	Age	Life Events	Domestic/Overseas Incidents
1896	Meiji 29	42	Komura appointed to Vice Minister for Foreign Affairs in June	Sino-Russian Secret Treaty signed
				The Yamagata-Lobanov Agreement on Korean affairs signed
1897	Meiji 30	43		The office of Japanese Governor-Genereal of Taiwan established
				Joseon (Korea) renamed the Korean Empire. King Gojong becomes Emperor Gojong.
1898	Meiji 31	44	Komura appointed to Japanese minister to the United States in September and stationed in Washington, DC, in November	Germany obtains lease of Jiaozhou Bay from Qing
				Russia obtains lease of Lüshun and Dalian from Qing
				Spanish-American War erupts
				Japan secures a promise from China not to sell any part of Fujian (Japan's sphere of influence)
				Britain obtains lease of Weihaiwei and Kowloon Peninsula
				United States' annexation of Hawaii
				Empress Dowager Cixi engineers a coup d'état, forcing reform-minded Guangxu into seclusion
				United States' annexation of the Philippines and Guam (as a consequence of the Spanish-American War)
1899	Meiji 32	45		Boxer Rebellion (until 1901)
				United States declares its Open Door Policy toward China in September
				France obtains lease of Kwangchowan from Qing
				Boer War (unitl 1902)
1900	Meiji 33	46	Komura appointed Japanese minister to Russia	Qing declares war against all Western powers

266

Year	Japanese Era	Age	Life Events	Domestic/Overseas Incidents
1900	Meiji 33	46	Komura's father, Kanpei, dies at the age of 71	Britain requests Japan to dispatch troops. Japanese cabinet meeting agrees to dispatch reinforcement force of a mixed brigade
			Komura returns home, and is immediately appointed to Japanese minister to Qing	Eight-Nation Alliance forces advance to Beijing
1901	Meiji 34	47	Komura arrives in Beijing in January and participates in peace negotiations between Qing and the foreign powers, representing Japan	Qing court compelled to sign the "Boxer Protocol" (Peace Agreement between the Eight-Nation Alliance and China)
			Komura returns home in September and is appointed to foreign minister of the Katsura cabinet	Li Hongzhang dies
				Yuan Shikai appointed to Viceroy of Zhili and Minister of Beiyang
1902	Meiji 35	48		The Anglo-Japanese Alliance signed
				Trans-Siberian Railway completed
				Russia completes the first withdrawal of its troops from Manchuria
1903	Meiji 36	49	Komura starts negotiating with the Russian minister to Japan Roman Rosen on troop withdrawal from Manchuria	Russia fails to comply with the commitment for the second troop withdrawal from Manchuria and, instead, occupies Yongauipho, Korea
1904	Meiji 37	50		Japan purchases two cruisers (*Nisshin* and *Kasuga*)
				Russo-Japanese War (until 1905)
				Protocol signed between Korea and Japan on February 23, 1904
				Blockading of Lüshunkou
				As the result of the Battle of Yalu River and the Battle of Nanshan, Japanese troops conquer the area around Dalian Bay

Year	Japanese Era	Age	Life Events	Domestic/Overseas Incidents
1904	Meiji 37	50		First full-scale offensive at Lüshun Port
				Japan-Korea Treaty of 1904 signed
				Battle of Liaoyang (occupation of Liaoyang)
				Battle of Shaho
				Second and third full-scale offensives at Lüshun Port
1905	Meiji 38	51	Komura appointed to chief plenipotentiary for peace negotiations in Portsmouth (July)	Fall of Lüshun
			Komura appointed to ambassador plenipotentiary on special mission to Qing in November	Bloody Sunday in St. Petersburg
				Battle of Mukden
				Battle of Tsushima
				The Anglo-Japanese Alliance renewed
				Treaty of Portsmouth signed between Japan and Russia (Japan secures recognition of Korea as Japan's protectorate, southern Sakhalin, and lease of the Liaodong Peninsula)
				Eulsa Treaty (or Japan-Korea Protectorate Treaty) signed allowing Japan to control Korea's diplomacy
				Itō Hirobumi appointed to first Resident-General of Korea
1906	Meiji 39	52	Komura steps down as foreign minister in January because the Katsura cabinet resigns	The South Manchuria Railway Co. Ltd. established
			Komura appointed to Japanese ambassador extraordinary and plenipotentiary to Britain	
1907	Meiji 40	53	Komura bestowed the title of count for his distinguished services	French-Japanese agreement on Vietnam signed
				Korean court dispatches an emissary to the Second Hague Peace Conference of 1907 to appeal the invalidity of the Eulsa Treaty

Year	Japanese Era	Age	Life Events	Domestic/Overseas Incidents
1907	Meiji 40	53		Resident-General of Korea Itō Hirobumi claims Korean court's action to be a violation of the spirit of the Korea-Japan Protocol and threatens the Korean side with the possibility of the declaration of war, forcing the Korean emperor to resign
				Japan-Korea Treaty of 1907 (also known as the Japan-Korea Annexation Treaty) concluded, with which the jurisdiction of the resident-general of Korea is expanded to include not only diplomacy but the entire expanse of domestic politics
				The Russo-Japanese Agreement of 1907 signed
				The Triple Entente (among Britain, France, and Russia) formed
				Radicalization of the Indian National Congress and its anti-British movements
1908	Meiji 41	54	Komura returns home from London and is appointed to foreign minister of the second Katsura cabinet	The Young Turk Revolution
				Qing announces constitutional program, pronouncing the establishment of a parliament in nine years
				Qing's Guangxu Emperor and Empress Dowager Cixi die
1909	Meiji 42	55	Komura infected by pleuropneumonia in May	Itō Hirobumi resigns as resident-general of Korea
			Komura appointed to chairman of the preparatory committee on revision of unequal treaties in November	Japanese cabinet meeting decides to annex Korea
				Itō Hirobumi, president of the privy council, assassinated by Korean nationalist/independence activist An Jung-geun at the Harbin Railway Station

Year	Japanese Era	Age	Life Events	Domestic/Overseas Incidents
1910	Meiji 43	56		Terauchi Masaki, minister of war, appointed to resident-general of Korea
				The Second Russo-Japanese Agreement signed, dividing Manchuria into two spheres of interest (Japanese and Russian)
				Japan-Korea Treaty of 1910 (on Japan's annexation of Korea) signed announcement on renaming Korea "Chosen" and establishment of the office of Governor-General
				Third Resident-General of Korea Terauchi appointed to the first governor-general of Chosen (concurrently minister of war)
1911	Meiji 44	57	Komura bestowed the title of marquis for his distinguished services in April	Japan signs treaties of commerce and navigation with the United States, Britain, and Germany, achieving tariff autonomy
			Komura resigns as foreign minister in August	Second renewal of the Anglo-Japanese Alliance
			Komura moves to his villa in Hayama in September	(in Qing) Xinhai Revolution
			Komura's condition deteriorates; he dies in November	
1912	Meiji 45			Formation of the Republic of China
				Emperor Meiji passes away at the age of 61
				Crown Prince Yoshihito succeeds the throne
				Japanese era name changed to Taishō

INDEX

（英文版）小村寿太郎とその時代
Komura Jutaro and His Time

2020年3月27日　第1刷発行

著　者　　岡崎久彦
訳　者　　野田牧人
発行所　　一般財団法人出版文化産業振興財団
　　　　　〒101-0051 東京都千代田区神田神保町2-2-30
　　　　　電話　03-5211-7283
　　　　　ホームページ　https://www.jpic.or.jp/

印刷・製本所　　大日本印刷株式会社

© 2003 Okazaki Hisahiko, Okazaki Akiko
Printed in Japan
ISBN978-4-86658-072-2